THE FOOD OF
ASIA

THE FOOD OF
ASIA

**Authentic Recipes
from China, India,
Indonesia, Japan
Singapore, Malaysia,
Thailand and Vietnam**

**Introduction and essays
by Kong Foong Ling**

PERIPLUS

Published by Periplus Editions (HK) Ltd.,
with editorial offices at
5 Little Road #08-01
Singapore 536983 and
153 Milk Street, Boston MA 02109.

ISBN: 962-593-452-9
LCC Number: 98-86219

Publisher: Eric Oey
Production: Mary Chia, T.C. Su, Jeffrey Ang

Printed in Singapore.

Photo credits: Doan Duc Minh (page 140); Michael
Freeman/ Photobank (page 83); Jill Gocher (pages
2–3, 11 [fishing boys] 60, 62, 103); Tim Hall (pages
141, 143); Heinz Holzen (pages 11 [Balinese proces-
sion],63, 84, 85, 87, 144); Catherine Karnow (page
142); Leong Ka Tai (page 28); Shin Kimura (page 20);
Karl Mulder (page 61); Eric Oey (page 82); Photobank
(pages 8, 10 [Japanese girl], 26, 86 [tea ceremony],
123, 124); Luca Invernizzi Tettoni (pages 4, 10 [tea
house], 11 [banana leaf restaurant],24, 25, 27, 42,
43, 44, 45, 46, 47, 102, 104, 106, 122, 125, 126).

Distributor
USA   Charles E. Tuttle Co.,Inc.
                   RRI Box 231-5, North Clarendon,
                   VT 05759-9700
                   Tel.: (802) 773-8930
                   Fax.: (802) 773-6993

Pages 2-3, photograph of paddy field in Malaysia.
Page 4, a selection of Thai dips and vegetables.

Cont

ents

Left, main picture: Friends and family enjoying a traditional steamboat dinner. The steamboat, a meal which is not only eaten but cooked by all those at the table, demonstrates one of the fundamental roles that food plays in Asia: that of bringing people together.

The flavors of Asia

From the roadside hawker stall in the large cities to the food court to five-star restaurants to home cooking, food is an all-consuming interest.

There is so much good food in Asia that the first-time traveler cannot help but be enchanted. It frequently comes as a surprise to people unfamiliar with Asian cultures how much the joy of living of the Asian peoples centers around the preparation, sharing and discussion of food. As a chef once said, food in Asia is an exercise in tradition, in aesthetics, mutual caring and moral lessons.

Even out of Asia, it is hard to find a place on earth with cuisine that has not been touched by some aspect or other of Asia, be it in the form of ingredient, cooking method or presentation. From elegant New York brasseries to stylish Sydney restaurants, Asian food has come a long way since the American take on Chinese food, *chop suey*, or soupy, flavorless curries made with lots of curry powder and nothing else. These days, modern cooks around the world use coriander with the same confidence as rosemary (though not in the same dish!); add lemongrass and kaffir limes to their tomato broths; and, with their family and friends, want to eat their food spicier and spicier.

Chopsticks are placed alongside the trinity of spoon–fork–knife in Western-style restaurants—if indeed such a category still holds—that now serve roast lamb and tandoori chicken on the same menu. And just as kids in some Asian countries are demanding cornflakes and milk for breakfast, some people in the West are trading in their breakfast cereals for steaming bowls of noodles or plain rice with *miso* soup and pickles. The popularity and pervasiveness of Asian food, particularly in the West, have never been higher.

But in order to cook Asian food—any food— properly, you need to understand the origins of the particular cuisine. You also need to know the best way of getting the most out of your ingredients. As many good cooks will tell you, if you do the basics properly, the rest will follow. Once you understand why a certain ingredient is tempered with another or used in conjunction with something else, you can then play and let your imagination (and taste-buds) take you to new taste sensations.

Let *The Food of Asia* be your guide through a diverse selection of cuisine from China, India,

Japan, Indonesia, Malaysia, Singapore, Thailand and Vietnam. Because the countries covered here encompass a diverse geography and climate, from the temperate to the tropical, all the cuisines are quite distinct, despite the similarity in cooking techniques and some ingredients. All, however, emphasize freshness and flavor; in Asia, they believe that good eating is essential to good living.

Many of the popular favorites from each country are represented here: the gorgeous red and green curries of Thailand, invigorating Vietnamese *pho*, fluffy Indian breads, refreshing *sushi* and *sashimi* from Japan, and incendiary *laksas* and noodle soups from Malaysia and Singapore. There are simple dishes that require just a little cooking and no complicated techniques, making them ideal for day-to-day use in the home. For the confident cook, there are more complex dishes that are guaranteed to impress family and friends at your next dinner party or Sunday lunch, and taste delicious, too! Most of the dishes are readily adapted to a Western-style table, and hints and tips have been included as to how best to serve them.

Common to the tables of all these countries is grain, which holds pride of place during a meal, as distinct from the Western table where the meat component or main course is the height of the meal. In most tropical countries located on or near the equator, such as Malaysia, Singapore and Indonesia, plain steamed rice is the staple. However, be warned: there is rice and there is rice, and they are not always interchangeable. The Chinese prefer the fragrant long-grain jasmine rice; the Japanese, a starchier short-grain variety. The Thais and Indonesians often serve glutinous rice to mop up their curries. The Indians favour the basmati. As you venture above the equator, preference is frequently given to wheat, which may be served in the form of noodles, buns or pancakes.

Another characteristic of Asian food is its dependence on the humble soybean and its by-products. Bean curd (tofu), soy sauce, bean curd wrappers and bean paste sauces are used in dishes from China to Indonesia, with a little tweaking to local tastes.

And then there is the noodle . . . whether it be flat, round, dried, fresh, or is made of egg, buckwheat, mung bean, potato starch, wheat or ground rice, the Chinese love affair with noodles has left its mark on other Asian cuisines. The machines and factories have taken over from the hand-pulled noodles that the Chinese were particularly famous for, but there is no denying the versatility of the end product. In Asia they are stir-fried or pan-fried, or used in soups, salads and spring rolls, or eaten with a sauce. They can be eaten as part of a meal or be a meal in a bowl, eaten at all times of the day, from breakfast to supper.

Asian cooks demand—and receive—the very best there is to be offered from their local markets and suppliers, a hangover from their agricultural heritage perhaps, or because supermarkets were few and far between until recently. The ingredients have to be of the freshest quality: the vegetables just picked, the fish just out of the water, the chicken just caught. This ingredient is then quickly cooked, usually in a simple manner that would allow the essence of the produce to shine through.

Please do not be wary of the foreignness of some of the ingredients used in this book; remember that the now-ubiquitous ginger and cilantro had to start somewhere, too! Most of the ingredients called for in *The Food of Asia* are readily available from your local Asian grocery store, and it is worth your while searching out a good

one and befriending the people who run it—they will be a rich source of advice and hints on how best to prepare your purchases. Many Asian food stores these days have an extensive range of fresh greens and vegetables, and they do not have to be used only in the Asian way.

Try to use the best of what's in season and don't be afraid to experiment. For instance, there is no reason why you can't serve Chinese broccoli in place of conventional broccoli with your next leg of lamb, or use coconut milk instead of milk to make a crème caramel, or serve steamed baby *bok choy* instead of green beans with a traditional roast chicken. You may also like to try smearing tandoori paste over a rack of lamb for a change of pace, or baste the next chicken you roast with green curry paste, and serve it with roast potatoes and a crisp green salad. The recipes are meant to be a guide and not a constraint! Frequently, ingredients may be substituted for each other without compromising on authenticity—just make sure you do try the recipe as it is set out at least once though. If you are attempting a recipe for the first time, it is very important that you read the recipe all the way through to the end to make sure you have the right equipment and ingredients to hand. With much Asian cooking, the time-consuming work is in the preparation. After the ingredients have been cleaned, chopped and sliced, the cooking process itself is usually fairly simple and straightforward.

Below: The men in this Chinese tea-house have gathered to gossip as much as to drink tea. *Right:* Like modern Japanese culture, Japanese food is a striking blend of the old and the new.

A comprehensive illustrated glossary (see pages 12–19) has been included to help you demystify and use some of the knobby tubers and jars of brown stuff you may find in food stores. There is also a chapter on cooking implements and a few simple techniques to help you prepare Asian food. Despite the advent of modern methods and gadgets in Asian kitchens, some traditional implements are still regarded as irreplaceable. Not all kitchens, for instance, have stoves complete with an oven, as most cooking is done over the burners. Many Asian kitchens are functional rather than aesthetic, with meals cooked over an open fire. In urban areas, gas rings fueled by LPG are increasingly used.

Measurements in this book are given in volume as far as possible. A conversion guide has been included on page 158 for your convenience. Unless otherwise stated, these recipes will serve four to six

Top, main picture: **This Balinese ritual should help ensure a plentiful crop of rice.** *Above:* **In Indonesia, you're never too young to contribute to the family dinner table.** *Right:* **An array of succulent offerings at a Singaporean banana-leaf restaurant.**

opposed to all at once). The recipes in this book have been structured with this in mind, into categories such as appetizers, soups, salads, main courses and desserts for ease of use. You may need to increase the quantities of the main dishes slightly if you are not planning to serve rice or bread with the meal. A number of suggested menus— for family meals, dinner parties etc.— are included in each chapter to help you plan your meals.

Most diners in Asian countries drink tea throughout a meal. Spirits are also popular, especially at formal dinners and banquets. But there's no reason why you can't drink your favorite red or white wine if you are eating Asian food—with some judicious tasting you will soon find out which goes best with what.

people as part of a shared meal of two to three dishes with rice.

The Asian table is a communal table. All dishes, with the exception of dessert, are usually presented at once and served with rice. Diners help themselves to whatever they want and to as much as they desire. There will usually be a soup, followed by or accompanied with one or two meat dishes and a vegetable dish. Dessert, especially in a domestic situation, is almost always sliced fresh seasonal fruit.

Of course you may like to serve a series of Asian dishes for a Western-style dinner, where the dishes come out sequentially (as

We hope *The Food of Asia* will inspire you, with its pictures, words and delicious recipes, to prepare these luscious dishes at home. It will also let you gain a better understanding of the wonderful cuisines of the region and give you many years of happy eating. And don't forget to have fun in the kitchen!

Asafoetida   Bamboo Shoots   Banana Blossom   Horapa Basil

Ingredients

Most of the ingredients called for in this book are readily found at Chinese or Asian grocery stores or some supermarkets.

Benitade   Bonito   Box Thorn Berries   Candlenuts

AGAR-AGAR A setting agent derived from seaweed, which hardens without refrigeration, used for cakes and desserts. It comes in long strands or in powder form; 1 teaspoon of powder sets 1–1¹/₂ cups liquid. To use, sprinkle powdered agar-agar over liquid and bring it gently to a boil, stirring until dissolved.

ANCHOVIES, DRIED Most are usually less than 1 inch long, and used to season many Malaysian and Indonesian dishes. Discard the heads and any black intestinal tract before using. Sometimes sold as "silver fish."

ANNATTO SEEDS The dark reddish-brown seed of the "lipstick plant," commonly used as a colouring agent. The seeds are fried in oil to extract an orange colour and discarded. The oil is used for cooking.

ASAFOETIDA A strong-smelling gum derived from a Persian plant believed to aid digestion. Use sparingly.

ASAM GELUGUR, DRIED Slices of a sour fruit (*Garcinia atnoviridis*) used in place of tamarind pulp in some Malay and Nonya dishes; the latter can be used as a substitute.

BAMBOO SHOOTS Used fresh, vinegared or dried in Asian cookery. Fresh shoots are sweet and crunchy. Peel, slice and boil for about 30 minutes before adding to dishes. Soak and boil dried shoots before use. If using canned bamboo shoots, drain and boil in fresh water for 5 minutes to remove the metallic taste.

BANANA BLOSSOM The flower bud of the banana plant. Slice finely and use as garnish for noodle soups or in salads.

BANANA LEAVES Used primarily for wrapping sweetmeats,

sausages and pâtés before cooking. The leaves preserve moisture and impart a mild fragrance to the food.

BASIL Three varieties are used in Thailand. The most common variety, *horapa*, is fairly similar to European and American sweet basil, and used liberally as a seasoning. "Lemon basil" or *manglak* is added to soups and salads. *Kaprow*, sometimes known as "holy basil," is stronger in flavor and has purplish markings. Basil is known as d*aun selasih* or *kemangi* in Indonesia.

BEAN CURD Widely used in Thai, Chinese, Malaysian and Japanese cuisines. The most common variety is sometimes called **"cotton"** or *momen* tofu. Use this unless otherwise specified. "Regular" bean curd is generally sold packed in water in containers and is firmer and easier to handle than fine-textured **"silken" bean curd**, which is often available in plastic trays or rolls (cut with a sharp knife while still in the plastic so it keeps its shape).

    Deep-fried bean curd or *aburage* is available in plastic bags and should be rinsed in boiling water to remove excess oil before using. A **grilled bean curd** (*yakidofu*), which has a speckled brown surface, is also sold in plastic bags. Small cubes of dried deep-fried bean curd are added to slow-cooked dishes and some soups. Fermented bean curd (*nam yee*), sold in jars and either red or white in color, is used in small amounts as a seasoning in Chinese dishes.

BEAN CURD SKIN The skin that forms on top of soy milk when it is brought to a simmer, skimmed off and dried. Reconstitute the sheets in warm water before using as a wrapper or in braises. The

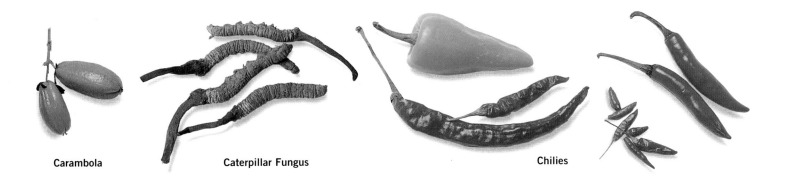

Carambola   Caterpillar Fungus   Chilies

stuffed skins can be deep-fried, simmered or sautéed.

BEAN SPROUTS Sprouted green mung beans are eaten blanched in some salads and soups, or quickly stir-fried as a vegetable. Pinch off the straggly tails just before use if desired.

BELIMBING See CARAMBOLA

BENITADE Decorative maroon-colored sprouts with a slight peppery taste. A popular Japanese garnish. Substitute alfalfa sprouts or very finely shredded red cabbage.

BESAN Flour made from Bengal gram or *channa dal*, sometimes referred to as gram flour or chickpea flour. Used to make a batter for vegetables or fish and to thicken and add flavor to Indian dishes.

BITTER GOURD A firm gourd that looks like a fat, knobby, green cucumber. It has a crisp texture and a strong, bitter flavor. Remove the seeds and inner membrane before cooking. Slice thinly if using in salads, or cut into thick chunks for stuffing.

BLACK BEANS, SALTED Fermented salted black soybeans, a common seasoning for fish and beef. Sold in packets or cans, they can be kept for several months if stored in a covered jar in the fridge. Rinse before use to remove excess salt.

BLACK MOSS FUNGUS A fine, hair-like fungus valued in Chinese cooking. Soak in warm water until pliable before using.

BLACK SAUCE, SWEET A thick, molasses-like sauce used in fresh spring rolls (*popiah*).

BONITO, DRIED With dried kelp, an essential component of Japanese stock or *dashi*. Shaved *bonito* flakes (*katsuo-bushi*) are now available in plastic packs.

BOX THORN BERRIES Oval red berries sometimes known as wolf berries, prized by the Chinese for their medicinal properties. Used in soups.

BURDOCK The root of the burdock plant, popular in Japanese cuisine. Scrape off the skin and place into water to stop it discoloring until ready to slice or shred. Fresh and canned burdock are available from Japanese stores.

CANDLENUT A waxy, cream-colored nut similar in size and shape to a macadamia, which can be used as a substitute (although less expensive almonds or cashews will also do). It is ground and used to add texture and a faint flavor to Malay and Nonya dishes. Do not eat raw. Store in the fridge.

CARAMBOLA A pale-green acidic fruit about 2–3 inches long that grows in clusters. A relative of the starfruit, carambola is used whole or sliced to give a sour tang to soups, curries, fish dishes and *sambals*. Sour grapefruit juice or tamarind juice are good substitutes.

CARDAMOM About 15–20 intensely fragrant brown-black seeds are enclosed in a straw-colored pod. Try to buy the whole pod rather than seeds or powder for maximum flavor. Bruise lightly with the back of a cleaver to break the pod. More common are small, greenish or straw-colored pods containing a dozen or so tiny, intensely aromatic black seeds. Large black cardamom pods, which are at least six times the size of the green, are used in some northern Indian dishes.

CAROM *Carum ajowan* comes from the same family as cumin and parsley. Known as carom or bishop's weed in the West, it is called *ajwain* in India. The flavor is similar to caraway with overtones of thyme.

CATERPILLAR FUNGUS Neither a caterpillar nor a fungus, these dried pods (*Cordyceps sinensis*) are used in Chinese dishes for their medicinal value.

CELERY The celery used in Asia is much smaller than the Western variety, with slender stems and particularly pungent leaves. Often known as "Chinese celery" and used as a herb rather than vegetable, it is added to soups, rice dishes and stir-fries. Substitute regular celery leaves.

CENTURY EGGS Duck eggs coated with a mixture of powdered lime, rice husks and salt and left to cure for several months. To use, peel off the shell and quarter or chop the eggs, which have a translucent black albumen and greenish-grey yolk.

CHAYOTE An oval-shaped squash that looks like a light green cucumber, with a small white seed inside. Peel before using as a vegetable. Zucchini is a substitute.

CHILLI Many different varieties of chilies are used in Asia. The flavor of fresh and dried chillies is different, so be sure to use the type specified in the recipes. Large, finger-length **green** (unripe) and **red** (ripe) **chilies** are usually moderately hot.

In India chilies are used fresh only in their unripe green state. The majority of ripe red chilies are dried and a large percentage ground. Cut or break dried chilies into pieces and soak in hot water for about 10 minutes to soften before grinding or blending. If you want to reduce the heat without losing flavor, discard some or all of the seeds.

The main types of chili used in Thailand, Malaysia and Indonesia include the normal finger-length **red** or **green chili**; tiny but fiery-hot **bird's-eye chilies** (which may be red, green or yellowy-orange) and **dried red chilies**. Be careful to wash your hands thoroughly after handling chilies—use rubber gloves if possible.

CHILI OIL Dried chilies or ground chilies steeped in oil, used to enliven some Sichuan dishes.

CHILI PASTE Pounded chilies, sometimes mixed with vinegar, sold in jars. The heat varies from brand to brand. Sichuan chili paste is made from dried chilies, soaked and ground with a touch of oil.

CHILI POWDER Made from finely ground dried chilies, such as cayenne. Do not confuse with American chili powder, which is a blend of a variety of seasonings.

CHILI SAUCE Chilies mixed with water and seasoned with salt, garlic, sugar and vinegar, sold in bottles and jars. Some sauces are sweeter than others, and others may have added flavorings like garlic or ginger.

CHINESE CABBAGE The three most common types are bok choy, which has white stems and bright green leaves and is often sold in immature form; Napa or "**celery**" **cabbage**, which has long pale green leaves and white celery-like stems; and **green cabbage**.

CHINESE RICE WINE Wine made from fermented rice used in cooking. Wine from Shaoxing, generally considered the best, is available from Chinese food stores. Dry sherry is a substitute.

CHINESE SAUSAGES Thin, sweet Chinese pork sausages that are delicately perfumed with rice wine. Used as a seasoning rather than eaten on their own. They will keep almost indefinitely without refrigeration.

CHIRONJI NUTS Small brownish nuts that look a little like large sunflower seeds, sometimes ground with other nuts, such as cashews or almonds, or with white poppy seeds to enrich some dishes. The flavor is similar to that of hazelnuts. Substitute a mixture of hazelnuts and almonds.

CHIVES "Chinese," "coarse" or "garlic" chives have dark green flat leaves about 12 inches long. They are used as a vegetable and as a herb. The flavor is stronger than normal chives.

CHRYSANTHEMUM LEAVES Enjoyed as a vegetable for their distinctive flavor and bright green color. Spinach leaves can be used as a substitute.

CINNAMON True cinnamon comes from the fragrant bark of a tree native to Sri Lanka, and is lighter in color, thinner and more expensive than cassia bark, which is often sold as cinnamon. Powdered cinnamon is not a substitute.

CLOUD EAR FUNGUS Sometimes known as wood fungus, this crinkly greyish-brown dried fungus swells to many times its original size after soaking in warm water for a few minutes. They have little flavor but are prized for their texture.

CLOVES A small, brown, nail-shaped spice that emits a floral, spicy fragrance. Used in spice blends.

COCONUT Widely used in Malaysia, Singapore and Indonesia, not just for cooking but also for palm sugar, alcohol, housing, utensils and charcoal. The grated flesh is often added to food; it is also squeezed with water to make coconut milk. To make fresh coconut milk, put the flesh of a grated coconut into a bowl and add 1/2 cup lukewarm water. Squeeze and knead for 1 minute, then squeeze handful by handful, straining into a bowl to obtain thick milk. Repeat the process with another 2 1/2 cups of water to obtain thin milk. Combine both batches of milk for the coconut milk called for in this book, unless thick milk is specified. Coconut milk can be frozen; thaw and stir thoroughly before use.

High quality canned coconut milk is readily available and can be used in place of fresh coconut milk. Use canned coconut cream in desserts and drinks.

CORIANDER (CILANTRO) Widely used in Asian cooking. Thais use the whole coriander plant: leaves, seeds and roots. The roots are pounded together with garlic and black pepper to make a common basic seasoning. The seeds are roasted and ground for spice blends, and the leaves, sometimes known as cilantro or Chinese parsley, are eaten as a vegetable or used as a herb.

CORNSTARCH This fine white powder is widely used to thicken sauces. Mix cornstarch with water, stir and add to the pan. Cook, stirring constantly for a few seconds, until the sauce thickens.

CUCUMBER Japanese cucumbers are short, roughly 1 inch in diameter, and have a sweeter flavor and better texture than large slicing cucumbers. English cucumbers are an ideal substitute.

CUMIN Pale brown to black fragrant seeds that look similar to caraway. Frequently partnered with coriander in spice mixtures and curry pastes.

CURRY LEAF Sprigs of these small, dark green leaves with a distinctive fragrance are often used in Indian curries. A sprig is about 8–12 individual leaves. Dried curry leaves are milder, but a more satisfactory substitute than *daun salam* or bay leaves.

CURRY POWDER Various spices are ground together to form curry powders. Certain spice combinations are appropriate to different basic foods, and curry powders labeled "fish," "chicken" and other more specific dishes such as "*korma*" or "*rendang*" should be used for that particular purpose only. Curry powders are often blended with water to a stiff paste before being fried. For maximum freshness, store in a jar in the freezer.

DAIKON: see RADISH, GIANT WHITE

DAL Also "*dhal.*" Refers to dried legumes, usually husked and split. Varieties include ***channa dal*** or Bengal gram, which resembles a small yellow pea and is often sold split; ***moong dal***, a small green pea; ***urad dal*** or ***blackgram dal***, which is sold either with its black skin still on or husked; ***masoor dal*** (salmon-pink lentils); ***toor***, ***tuvar*** or ***arhar dal***, a pale yellow lentil which is smaller than the Bengal gram; and ***kabuli channa*** or chickpeas, also known as *garbanzos*.

DASHI A stock made from dried kelp and dried *bonito* flakes, the basis of Japanese soups and sauces. Instant *dashi* granules (*dashi-no-moto*) are sold in glass jars in Japanese stores.

DAUN KESUM This pungent herb (*Polygonum hydropiper*) has long, pointed green leaves tinged with purple. Used in Vietnamese table salads and other Asian dishes.

DEVIL'S TONGUE A greyish-brown mass made from a starchy root known as devil's tongue (*konnyaku*). It is sold in plastic packets and used in Japanese soups and one-pot dishes and to make noodles called *shirataki konnyaku*. Keep refrigerated.

DRIED MANGO POWDER Dried and ground unripe mangoes, used to give a sour tang to some Indian dishes. If unavailable, use a squeeze of lemon juice.

DRIED SHRIMP See PRAWNS, DRIED

EGGPLANT Known also as aubergine or brinjal, this vegetable is much smaller and thinner throughout Asia than its Western counterpart. Japanese eggplants are often no more than about 4–8 inches long. The Thais also use a rather bitter pea-sized egg-

Chinese Sausages   Cloud Ear Fungus   Garlic Chives   Cilantro

plant and the apple variety. Use slender Asian or Japanese egg-plants for most recipes in this book—they are less bitter and have a better texture. They do not need salting before use.

FENNEL Only the seeds are used in Asian cooking. The spice smells of aniseed, and looks like a larger, paler version of cumin. Used to add a sweet fragrance to Malay and Indian dishes.

FENUGREEK These almost square, hard yellowish-brown seeds are strongly flavored and generally used whole in southern Indian dishes and frequently in pickles and fish curries. Fenugreek leaves are eaten as a vegetable and because of their rather bitter taste, are combined with other greens or potatoes. Substitute spinach if fenugreek leaves are not available. The dried leaves (*methi*) are sometimes used as a seasoning.

FISH SAUCE The distinctive *nam pla*, made from salted, fermented fish or shrimp, is used in Thai and Vietnamese marinades, dressings and dipping sauces. Good quality *nam pla* is golden-brown in color and has a salty, pungent flavor.

FIVE-SPICE POWDER A Chinese spice combination of star anise, Sichuan peppercorns, fennel, cloves and cinnamon. A very strong seasoning, so use in small amounts.

GALANGAL A member of the ginger family, used in Thai, Malay and Nonya dishes. Peel off the tough skin before pounding or slicing. The young, pinkish galangal is the most tender and imparts the best flavor. Slices of dried galangal (sometimes sold under the Indonesian name, *laos*) must be soaked in boiling water for about 30 minutes until soft before use. Jars of tender, sliced galangal packed in water from Thailand make an adequate substitute for the fresh root. As a last resort, use the powdered form (1 teaspoon = 1 inch).

GALANGAL, LESSER A white, ginger-like rhizome believed to have medicinal properties. Do not confuse with the fragrant greater galangal used in Southeast Asia. Omit if unavailable.

GARAM MASALA An Indian blend of several strongly aromatic spices designed to add flavor and fragrance to meat dishes. Powdered *garam masala* can be bought from stores specializing in spices. Store in a jar in the freezer.

GARLIC Widely used as a flavouring and for its medicinal qualities. It is often pounded or puréed before use in curries. Garlic cloves are often much smaller in Southeast Asia than in Western countries, so adjust to taste.

GINGELLY OIL A light oil made from unroasted sesame seeds, quite different in flavor from Chinese sesame oil. It adds a distinctive touch to Indian pickles.

GINGER This pale, creamy yellow root is widely used not just to season food but for its medicinal properties. Always scrape the skin off fresh ginger before using, and do not substitute the powdered. Store in a cool, dark place. To make ginger juice, finely grate about 3 inches fresh ginger. Squeeze it little by little in a garlic press, or wrap in cheesecloth and squeeze to extract the juice. Depending on the age of the ginger (young ginger is far more juicy), you will obtain 1–2 tablespoons of juice. **Pickled ginger**

(*benishoga* or *gari*), sometimes dyed red, is sold in jars and widely used as a garnish. Slender pink young ginger shoots are also pickled and sold in jars.

GINSENG A highly prized medicinal root, sometimes used in cooking. Available from Chinese medicine shops.

GREEN PEPPER, JAPANESE Tiny slender green peppers which have none of the spiciness of green chilies. Eight Japanese peppers are the equivalent of a green bell pepper. The latter is closer in taste to Japanese peppers and makes a better substitute than seeded green chilies.

HOISIN SAUCE A sweet sauce made of soy beans, with spicy and garlicky overtones. Used to season meat and served as a dipping sauce. Refrigerate the jar after opening.

HORSERADISH See WASABI

IKAN BILIS See ANCHOVIES, DRIED

JACKFRUIT A large, green fruit with a tough, knobby skin. The segmented flesh is sweet and perfumed when ripe. In Vietnam, young jackfruit, which is whitish in color, is used as a vegetable.

JAGGERY A crude sugar most commonly made from cane sugar and the sap of coconut or palmyrah palms. Southeast Asian palm sugar makes an acceptable substitute, or use soft brown sugar.

JASMINE ESSENCE The heady perfume of fresh jasmine flowers, soaked overnight in water, adds a unique fragrance to many Thai desserts and cakes. Substitute bottled jasmine extract.

JICAMA This crunchy, mild tuber has a crisp white interior and beige skin, which peels off easily. Its taste is sometimes described as a cross between a potato and an apple. Excellent raw with a spicy dip, and can be cooked. Also known as yam bean.

KAFFIR LIME Also known as fragrant lime, this citrus fruit has intensely fragrant skin but virtually no juice. The grated skin or rind is added to food, while the fragrant leaves are used whole in soups and curries, or shredded finely and added to salads. Round yellow-skinned limes slightly larger than a golf ball (*jeruk nipis*) and small, dark green limes (*jeruk limau*) are used in Indonesia and Malaysia for their juice. Use lemons if limes are unavailable.

KALE Known also as *gai lan*, this vegetable is enjoyed for its firm texture and emphatic flavor. Only the leaves and tender portions of the stems are eaten. Peel and halve lengthwise if they are thick. Broccoli stems are a good substitute.

KELP See SEAWEED

KENARI A soft, oily nut found in Maluku; the almond is the closest substitute.

KENCUR *Kaemferia galanga* is sometimes incorrectly known as lesser galangal; the correct English name is zedoary. *Kencur* has a unique, camphor-like flavor, so use sparingly. Wash and scrape off the skin before using. Dried sliced *kencur* (sometimes spelled *kentjoer*) or *kencur* powder are substitutes. Soak dried slices in boiling water for 30 minutes; use $1/2$–1 teaspoon of powder for 1 inch fresh root.

KINOME Their refreshing, minty taste makes the leaves of the prickly ash a popular garnish. Available in Japanese stores, they

Curry Leaf

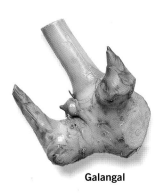

Galangal

Kaffir Lime

Kinome

Lime

Shiitake Mushrooms

Golden (enokitaki) Mushrooms

Dried Mushrooms

will keep refrigerated for about 1 week, or use watercress.

KRACHAI This rhizome, sometimes referred to as "lesser ginger," looks like a bunch of yellowish-brown fingers. Enjoyed for its mild flavor and crunchy texture. Dried *kracha*i is a poor substitute; omit if the fresh is unavailable.

KRUPUK Also known as shrimp crackers, these dried wafers made from tapioca starch, shrimp or fish are a popular snack and garnish. Dry thoroughly and deep-fry in oil until they puff up and become crisp.

LAKSA LEAF See DAUN KESUM

LEMONGRASS A lemon-scented plant that grows in clumps. Use only the bottom 2–4 inch portion. If it is to be pounded or blended to a paste, discard the outer leaves and use only the pale, tender part. Or bruise the stem before adding to stews. Also available in fresh, frozen, dried and powdered form. About 1 teaspoon powdered equals one stalk.

LILY BUDS, DRIED The Chinese call these "golden needles" because they are thin and golden in color. They are usually knotted for a neater appearance and added to soups or vegetable dishes. No substitute.

LIME Various types are used. Large limes are about the size of a small egg with a greenish-yellow skin, and have a tart flavor similar to lemons. Small green limes, frequently known as *kalamansi*, are about the size of a walnut and have a less acidic, more fragrant juice. These are preferred for squeezing over noodle dishes and into *sambals*. See also KAFFIR LIME.

LOOFAH A gourd with an earthy flavor, often used in Vietnamese soups. Any type of gourd can be substituted.

LOTUS The tumescent root has a delicious crunchy texture and decorative appearance when sliced, making it a popular vegetable and garnish in Japanese and Chinese cooking. Its seeds are used fresh for sweets or dried in stews. Soak dried lotus nuts in boiling water for 1 hour, peel, and poke out the central core with a thin skewer or toothpick. (Canned lotus nuts normally have this core already removed.)

MACE The lacy orange-red covering or aril of the nutmeg seed. Used in spice mixes and *garam masala* for flavoring sweet and savory dishes. For maximum flavour, grind as you need.

MINT Peppermint and spearmint are often used in salads and as flavor accents. See also DAUN KESUM.

MIOGA BUD This pretty pale pink bud with green tips, a member of the ginger family, is used for its spicy flavor and appearance in some Japanese dishes. No substitute.

MIRIN A bottled sweet rice wine used in Japanese cooking. If mirin is not available, use 1 teaspoon sugar as a substitute for 1 tablespoon mirin.

MISO A protein-rich salty paste of fermented soy beans, the mainstay of Japanese soups. Many different types are available, varying in taste, texture, color and fragrance. The most common are **red *miso***, which has a reddish-brown color and an emphatic flavor, and **white *miso***, which is actually golden-yellow in color,

has a lighter flavor and is less salty than the red variety, making it ideal for soups and dressings. Plastic bags or tubs of *miso* are generally sold in Japanese or health-food stores.

MITSUBA Both the stems and leaves of this decorative herb, a member of the parsley family, are used in Japanese cuisine. Parsley makes an acceptable substitute, although the flavor of *mitsuba* is more like celery.

MONOSODIUM GLUTAMATE (MSG) Some cooks in Asia make use of this taste enhancer. If you use only top-quality ingredients, there should be no need for MSG.

MORNING GLORY: See WATER SPINACH

MUNG BEANS Husked, dried green mung beans are known as yellow mung beans. Sprouted beans have a subtle flavor and a slight crunchiness. In Vietnam, yellow beans are used to make yellow bean sauce or other sauces. The starch from the beans is processed into cellophane noodles.

MUSHROOMS DRIED Black (*shiitake*) mushrooms are prized in Japanese and Chinese cooking for their flavor and texture. Soak in warm water for 15–20 minutes before use and discard the fibrous stems. Do not substitute with European dried mushrooms. Fresh *shiitake* are increasingly available outside Asia.

Fresh and delicate sheathed **straw mushrooms** are excellent in soups and vegetable dishes. **Button mushrooms** and the large, bland **oyster** variety are good for stir-frying. **Golden mushrooms** (*enokitaki*), clusters of slender cream-colored stalks with tiny caps, are available fresh and canned – discard the tough ends before use.

Reddish-brown **nameko mushrooms** have a slippery texture and attractive reddish-brown cap; they are more commonly found in jars or cans. See also CLOUD EAR FUNGUS.

MUSTARD OIL Oil made from ground mustard seeds is used as a cooking medium in some parts of India, particularly in Bengal. The oil gives a distinctive flavor to the food and is worth looking for in Indian grocery stores. Substitute any refined, flavourless vegetable oil.

MUSTARD SEEDS Both yellow and brownish-black mustard seeds are used in Indian cuisine. They are not interchangeable.

NIGELLA These small, black seeds are known as *kalonji* in India. Omit if not available. If specified for Indian breads, substitute with black sesame seeds.

NOODLES Both fresh and dried noodles made from either wheat flour, rice flour or mung bean flour are used in Asian cooking. The most popular types are **fresh yellow** or "Hokkien" noodles, spaghetti-like noodles made from flour and egg; **dried wheat-flour noodles**, plunged into boiling water to soften; fresh flat **rice-flour noodles**, ribbon-like noodles about 1/2 inch wide, used in soups or fried; fresh **laksa noodles**, which look like white spaghetti; dried rice-flour **vermicelli**, sometimes known as rice-stick noodles; and **dried mung bean noodles**, generally used in soups and usually referred to as "cellophane" or "transparent" noodles.

Palm Sugar   Pandan Leaf   *Sato-imo* Potato   Giant White Radish

In Japan the wheat noodle, **udon**, comes in various widths and is either flat or round. Packets of dried *udon*, whitish-beige in color, are readily available in Japanese stores. **Somen** are also made from wheat, but are very fine and white in color. **Soba** are made from buckwheat, and are sometimes flavored with green tea. Devil's tongue is used to make *shirataki konnyaku*—soak in hot water until they swell and become transparent.

NORI See SEAWEED

NUTMEG A native of the Moluccan islands, the nutmeg is actually the seed of a fleshy fruit. Try to purchase whole if possible and grate as required.

OIL, COOKING Blended vegetable oils (never olive oil) are used by Chinese cooks for frying. Peanut oil is sometimes specified for its distinctive flavor.

OKRA A green, ridged vegetable about 2^1/2–8 inches long, favored by Indians and Southeast Asians as a vegetable. Has a mucilaginous quality. Also known as lady's finger.

ORANGE PEEL, DRIED Dried orange peel is added to slow-cooked dishes for flavor. Although usually available in Chinese stores, fresh peel can be used as a substitute.

OYSTER SAUCE A thick sauce made from ground oysters, water, salt, cornstarch and caramel coloring, used primarily to flavor stir-fried vegetables and meat. It is commonly used in Chinese cooking. Refrigerate after opening. Look for MSG-free brands.

PALM SUGAR Made by boiling down the sap of various palm trees, usually sold in solid cakes or cylinders and varies in color from gold to light brown. If unavailable, substitute soft brown sugar or a mixture of brown sugar and maple syrup. To make palm sugar syrup, combine equal amounts of chopped palm sugar and water (add a pandan leaf if it is available). Bring to a boil, simmer for 10 minutes, strain and refrigerate.

PANDAN LEAF A fragrant member of the *pandanus* or screwpine family, pandan leaf is used to wrap seasoned morsels of chicken or pork, and added to various cakes and desserts. Bottled pandan essence can be used as a substitute in sweets.

PAPADS Also known as *poppadum*, these wafer-thin disks of seasoned wheat and lentil flour crisp up when fried in hot oil. Dry thoroughly before frying.

PEPPERCORNS Thought to be native to the Malabar coast of India, peppercorns are generally sold black (with their skins intact) and are frequently added whole to dishes. If crushing or grinding, do so just before use for maximum flavor and freshness.

PLUM SAUCE Sold in cans or jars, this piquant reddish-brown condiment is made from salted plums, chilies, vinegar and sugar. Refrigerate after opening. Available from Chinese stores.

POMELO A citrus somewhat similar to grapefruit, the pomelo is drier, sweeter and has a much thicker and tougher peel. It is eaten as a fruit or broken up for salads.

POPPY SEEDS Tiny white poppy seeds are prized for their delicate nutty flavor and used as a thickening agent. Soak in warm water for 10–15 minutes and grind before use. Substitute cashews or almonds.

POTATO *Yamato-imo*, often referred to as a potato in Japan, is actually a type of mountain yam which is grated and used raw for its gluey texture and bright white color. **Sato-imo** is a type of yam with a much finer texture and slightly different flavor from Western potatoes. New potatoes make an acceptable substitute.

RADISH, GIANT WHITE A vegetable about 6–10 inches long, widely used in Japanese cooking. *Daikon* is shredded and used raw as a garnish, sliced for stews and stir-fries, and pickled. Preserved salted radish keeps almost indefinitely on the shelf, and is often added to rice porridge (*congee*) and other dishes.

RED BEANS Dried red azuki beans are used in Chinese and Japanese sweets, or cooked with sugar to make red-bean paste, a popular filling for buns and pancakes. The paste is also sold in cans.

RED DATES Valued for their medicinal properties as well as their prune-like flavor, these are added to soups. Soak in boiling water for 1 hour to soften before use.

RICE Many types of rice are eaten throughout Asia, the most popular for daily meals being fragrant long-grain **jasmine** rice. Some Indian recipes call for the nutty-flavored **basmati** rice. White and brownish-black **glutinous** rice are used in sweet and savory dishes. The absorbency of rice is affected by its age—young rice absorbs less water than older rice. When you use a new packet of rice, be conservative when adding water until you find out its degree of absorbency.

Wash rice thoroughly in several changes of water before using. To make plain rice, measure a minimum of ^{1}/2 cup of rice per person and wash thoroughly. Put into a heavy-bottomed pan with enough water to cover the rice and come up to the level of the first joint on your forefinger (about ^{3}/4 inch). Cover the pan and bring to a boil over high heat. Set the lid slightly to one side, lower heat slightly and simmer until all the water is absorbed and dimples or "craters" appear in the top of the rice. Reduce heat to the absolute minimum, cover the pan and leave the rice to cook for at least another 10 minutes. Remove the lid, fluff up the rice with a fork (do not stir before this), wipe any condensation off the lid and cover the pan. Set aside until required. The rice should keep warm for at least another 15–20 minutes.

Short-grained rice with a somewhat sticky texture is used in Japan. Do not serve fragrant Thai or basmati rice with Japanese food.

RICE PAPER Made from a batter of rice flour, water and salt, then steamed and dried in the sun on bamboo racks. Moisten with a little tepid water before using to make Vietnamese rolls.

RICE WINE See CHINESE RICE WINE

ROCK SUGAR Crystallized cane sugar, sold in chunks in boxes. Added to Chinese red-braised dishes, desserts and drinks.

ROSE WATER A heady fragrance from the Middle East, used in Malay desserts, drinks and some Indian rice dishes.

SAFFRON The world's most expensive spice, actually the dried stigma of a type of crocus. Infuse saffron strands in warm milk before adding to rice and dessert dishes. Store saffron in the freezer as it loses its fragrance quickly.

SAGO PEARLS The pith of the sago palm that has been ground to a paste and pressed through a sieve. It is very glutinous, with little taste, and used in Asia for desserts.

SAKE Popular as a drink, *sake* or Japanese rice wine is available in many different qualities and is an important cooking ingredient. It is almost always heated to get rid of the alcohol for Japanese cuisine. A bottle of *sake* will keep for about a month after opening. If red *sake* is not available, use regular *sake*.

SALAM LEAF A subtly flavored leaf of a member of the cassia family, infused in curries. If you cannot obtain fresh or dried leaf, omit altogether.

SALTED FISH Salted and sun-dried freshwater fish that do not require soaking before using. Grill whole or cut into fine slices and fry to a crisp, and serve as a condiment. Salted fish is also sometimes pickled.

SALTED CABBAGE Various types of heavily salted cabbage are used in some Chinese and Nonya dishes; the most common is made from mustard cabbage. Soak in fresh water for at least 15 minutes to remove excess salt, repeating if necessary.

SALTED DUCK EGG A popular accompaniment to rice and savory Malay dishes. Wash off the black coating (often added to protect the egg), boil for 10 minutes, then cut egg in half while still in the shell.

SALTED SOY BEANS Salty and with a distinctive tang, these are often lightly pounded before being used to season fish, noodle or vegetable dishes. Varieties packed in China are sometimes labeled "Yellow Bean Sauce." Mash slightly before using. Sichuan brands contain additional chili. Keeps indefinitely on the shelf.

SANSHO A peppery powder made from the seeds of the prickly ash, available in small glass bottles in Japanese stores. The dried Sichuan (Szechuan) pepper is an exact substitute.

SCALLION Sometimes known as spring onion, this popular herb is often used as a garnish and to add flavor to many dishes. It has slender white stalks with dark green strap-like leaves.

SEAWEED Used extensively in Japan. Dark green **dried kelp** or *kombu* is an essential ingredient in basic stock or *dashi*. It is sold in packets. Wipe clean with a damp cloth but do not soak before using. Other varieties include a fine **golden kelp** (*shiraita konbu*), **mozuku**, which are hair-like shreds, small squares of **salted dried kelp** (*shio-kobu*), and **laver** (*nori*), which is dried and sold in very thin, dark green sheets. **Wakame** is sold either dried or in salted form in plastic bags. Reconstitute by soaking in water.

SESAME Both black and white sesame seeds, the latter more common, are used in Japanese cooking. White sesame seeds are toasted and crushed to make a paste; if you don't want to do this yourself, you can buy either a Chinese or Japanese brand of sesame paste. Middle-Eastern *tahina* has a slightly different flavor as the sesame seeds are not toasted.

SESAME OIL Added to some Chinese dishes—usually at the last minute—for its fragrance and flavor, but never used on its own as a frying medium.

SESAME RICE CRACKERS Thin crackers made from rice flour sprinkled with sesame seeds. Grill or lightly bake before serving, and use like a cracker for dipping. Shrimp crackers or puffed rice crackers may be used as a substitute.

SEVEN-SPICE POWDER A mixture of different spices and flavors, *shichimi* contains *sansho*, ground chilies, hemp seeds, dried orange peel, *nori* flakes, white sesame seeds and white poppy seeds. *Shichimi togarashi* contains chili. Both are available in bottles in Japanese stores.

SHALLOTS Small, round and pinkish-purple, shallots add a sweet onion flavor to *sambals* and curries. Packets of deep-fried shallots are generally available in Asian supply stores. If they lose their crispness, scatter in a large baking dish and put in a very low oven for a few moments to dry thoroughly. Cool before storing. Indonesian shallots are smaller and milder than those found in many Western countries.

SHARK'S FIN Transparent threads of dried shark's fin (generally sold in packets) are highly valued for their gelatinous texture and added to soups or sometimes cooked with egg. Soak in boiling water for about 30 minutes to soften before use. Shark's fin is also available canned.

SHISO The tangy, attractive green leaves of the *Perilla frutescens* or beefsteak plant, related to the mint family, are a common garnish in Japan. There is no substitute for the flavor of *shiso* leaf. The flower is often used as a garnish, and the tiny seeds for cooking. If the seeds are not available, omit as there is no good substitute.

SHRIMP PASTE Known variously as *kapi*, *trasi* and *belacan*. A dense mixture of fermented, ground shrimp used extensively in Southeast Asian cooking. There are many different types, ranging in color from pink to blackish-brown. The former is good for curry pastes, the latter for making dipping sauces. Shrimp paste should be cooked before eating; if the recipe you are using does not call for it to be fried together with other ingredients, either broil or dry-fry the shrimp paste before pounding. To broil, wrap a piece of the paste in a piece of foil and toast under a broiler or dry-fry in a pan for about 2 minutes on each side.

SHRIMP SAUCE, BLACK A very thick syrupy paste, usually sold in jars or plastic tubs, with a strong shrimp flavor. It is commonly added to *rojak*, a fruit and vegetable salad, and Penang *laksa*.

SHRIMPS, DRIED Small dried shrimp are a popular seasoning in many Asian dishes, particularly in sauces, condiments (*sambals*) and vegetable dishes. Choose dried shrimp that are bright pink in color, and soak in warm water for about 5 minutes to soften before use.

SICHUAN PEPPER A round, reddish-brown berry with a pronounced fragrance and flavor, used primarily in Sichuan cuisine and as an ingredient in five-spice powder. It is also known as prickly ash or fagara, and often sold powdered under the Japanese name *sansho*.

Seaweed—Kelp (left) and Wakame (right)   **Shallots**   **Shrimp Paste**   **Star Anise**

SOY SAUCE Three types are used in Chinese cooking. **Light soy sauce** is thinner, lighter in color and saltier than **black soy sauce**, which is often added to give a dark coloring to a dish. Delicately flavored **red soy sauce** is seldom used and can be substituted with light soy sauce.

For Japanese food, use the Kikkoman brand. **Tamari** is very strong, thick and black and available from Japanese stores; dark soy sauce is a reasonable substitute.

In Indonesia, **thick sweet soy sauce** (*kecap manis*) is most frequently used as a condiment, followed by the thinner, saltier **light soy sauce** (*kecap asin*). If you cannot obtain *kecap manis*, use thick black Chinese soy sauce and sweeten with brown sugar.

STAR ANISE A sweet-smelling star-shaped, eight-pointed pod with a pungent flavor of aniseed or licorice. Frequently used in soups.

STARFRUIT A star-shaped fruit, eaten raw and finely sliced. Young starfruit has a tart taste and is often served on the Vietnamese vegetable platter as a complement to grilled or fried foods.

SUGAR CANE Fresh sugar cane juice—extracted from the stalks by a crushing machine—is a very popular drink in Vietnam. In addition to the familiar uses of sugar cane, the peeled stalks are also used as skewers in cooking.

TAMARIND A large, brown pod with several seeds, tamarind has a tangy, acidic taste, and is a popular sour flavoring. It can be bought fresh, dried or in pulp form, and is most commonly sold in compressed blocks, with the seeds removed. The paste is used in hot and sour soups, and fresh crab dishes. To make tamarind juice, add 1 part pulp to 3 parts hot water for 5 minutes before squeezing to extract the juice. Discard the seeds and fibrous matter before using.

TAPIOCA The root of this plant (also known as cassava) and the tender green leaves are both eaten, though the leaves have to be cooked for at least an hour to remove the mild toxins. The root is grated and mixed with coconut and sugar to make candies. Fermented tapioca root is added to some desserts, while the dried root is made into small balls and used in the same way as pearl sago. Substitute spinach for tapioca leaves.

TAPIOCA STARCH Used as a thickening agent, and sometimes in the making of fresh rice papers. Combined with rice flour, it adds a translucent sheen and chewiness to pastries. Available in many Asian food markets.

TARO A barrel-shaped oval root, with hairy, brown skin and white flesh with purple-brown fibers, which can be used like a potato in soups. The tubers are best eaten when the fibres are small and barely noticeable.

TEMPEH Cakes of compressed, lightly fermented soybeans with a nutty flavor. Often available in health food stores. No substitute.

TURMERIC A bright yellow-orange tuber from the ginger family, turmeric is often used in curries and as a coloring agent. It is also used for medicinal purposes. Peel before using. Substitute 1/2 teaspoon powder for 1/2 inch fresh.

UMEBOSHI Salty pickled plums are very popular with plain rice for breakfast in Japan, as they are believed to aid digestion. These dull-red plums are available in jars, and should be refrigerated after opening.

VIETNAMESE MINT: see DAUN KESUM

VINEGAR Black, red and white Chinese vinegars are all made from rice, and as the flavor differs, be sure to use the type specified. **Red vinegar** has a distinctive tang, while full-bodied **black vinegar**, sometimes known as Tientsin vinegar, has a faint flavor similar to balsamic vinegar. Use sparingly as a seasoning or dip. **Japanese rice vinegar** makes an acceptable substitute for the white. There are no good substitutes for red and black vinegar. Slightly diluted cider vinegar can be used in place of rice vinegar.

WAKAME See SEAWEED

WASABI Indispensable in Japanese cuisine, and widely available in tubes. *Wasabi* powder (available in tiny cans), mixed with a little water 10 minutes before required, gives a much closer approximation of the freshly grated root.

WATER CHESTNUT Although it is troublesome to peel away the dark brown skin of this crunchy tuber, it's well worth using fresh water chestnuts if you can find them. Their crisp texture and sweet flavor make them ideal in salads, stir-fried vegetable dishes and desserts. Fresh jicama is a better substitute for fresh water chestnuts than the canned variety.

WATER SPINACH This aquatic plant, a member of the convolvulus or morning glory family, is sometimes known as swamp cabbage or water convolvulus. The arrowhead-shaped leaves and tender tips are usually stir-fried. Discard the tough, hollow stems. Young shoots are often served as part of a mixed platter of raw vegetables for dipping into hot sauces.

WHITE FUNGUS A crinkly golden-colored dried fungus that turns transparent after soaking. Prized for its chewy texture, and used in Chinese soups and desserts.

WILD GINGER BUD The pink waxy flower from a ginger plant, sometimes known as torch ginger (*Etlingera elatior*). Used in some Malay and Nonya dishes. No substitute.

YUNNAN HAM A smoked salted ham used mainly as a seasoning. It is sold in cans, although smoked Italian, French or Spanish ham could be substituted.

YUZU ORANGE An orange-colored citrus fruit used for its fragrant rind. Lemon or lime rind could be used as a substitute, or else kaffir lime.

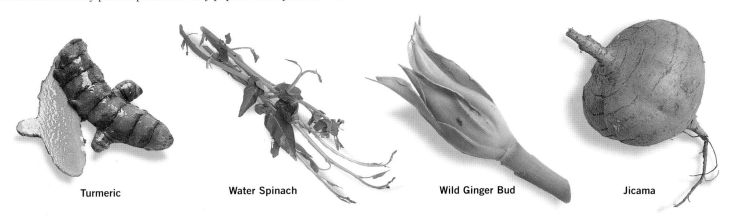

Turmeric   Water Spinach   Wild Ginger Bud   Jicama

The traditional open hearth or *irori* is virtually a museum piece in Japan today

Spoons made of coconut shells or wood are put to countless uses in the Indonesian kitchen.

A bamboo rolling mat is indispensable in a Japanese kitchen.

Granite mortar and pestle.

The Asian Kitchen

You do not need a range of exotic implements to cook Asian food. Perhaps that is the most surprising aspect of Asian cooking—that often sophisticated food is prepared with so few utensils! Most of the implements found in the average Western kitchen can be adapted for use in Asian cooking, although several items, such as a wok or rice cooker, will make the preparation and cooking of certain dishes much easier. Far more time is usually spent on the preparation of the ingredients, which have to be peeled, chopped, grated, ground and blended before the cooking begins.

You should be able to obtain most of the implements mentioned here from Asian grocery stores.

Cooking Implements

Perhaps the most essential ingredient in the Asian kitchen is the **wok**—known as a *kuali* in Malaysia and Indonesia—a deep, curved pan traditionally made of cast iron and used for just about everything except cooking rice: stir-frying, deep-frying, braising, making sauces, steaming and so on. The shape of the wok distributes the heat evenly, while its sloping sides ensure that food falls back into the pan and not over the edge during stir-frying. It's also practical for deep-frying, requiring less oil than a conventional saucepan or frying pan. It allows just the right amount of evaporation for many dishes which begin with a large amount of liquid and finish with a thick sauce. When choosing a wok, avoid aluminum or Teflon-coated types; a heavy cast-iron wok that won't tip over easily is preferable, or best of all, a nonstick alloy that will

not scratch when metal scoops are used.

A wok should be "seasoned" before its first use so that food will not stick. Wash the inside of the wok with warm soapy water but do not use a scouring pad. Rinse with fresh water and dry thoroughly. Put some oil on a paper towel and wipe the inside of the wok. Repeat until the paper towel comes away clean. Chinese cooks always heat the wok before adding oil to be sure that it is dry and the oil will not splatter. After cooking, never clean your wok with detergent or harsh abrasives; just rinse it with warm water and wipe dry. Remember to buy a lid for your wok—invaluable for when you want to steam food and for finishing off dishes.

In India, the **kadai**, a large wok-like utensil, is used for frying and sautéing. The *kadai* is made of iron, brass or aluminum, and is slightly deeper than a wok, but the latter makes an excellent substitute. For rice and curries, a flat-lidded, straight-sided pan known as a **degchi** is used, but a good heavy-bottomed pot will do.

To partner your wok, a **frying spatula**, as well as a **perforated ladle** for lifting out deep-fried food, are useful. Chinese cooks use a round-edged spatula for tossing stir-fried ingredients in the wok. Indonesian cooks use an assortment of wooden or coconut husk spoons for stirring.

Other useful utensils include a **wire mesh basket** on a long handle, good for scooping out deep-fried food or boiled noodles. Chinese cooks also use a pair of long wooden **chopsticks** for turning over food during deep-frying, although this requires a certain dexterity, only acquired with practice. You may be happier with tongs.

The multi-purpose wok.

Traditional Indian grinding slab.

Chinese claypot for slow cooking.

Extremely high heat is needed when stir-frying food in a wok, and many electric stoves cannot achieve the ideal heat. Malaysian cooks—especially Chinese—insist on at least one gas burner, often with a double ring of gas jets. If you are using an old-style electric stove that cannot reach a very high heat nor be reduced in temperature quickly, you should consider investing in a gas-fired ring to be used with your wok.

Almost any **saucepan** can be used for cooking Asian dishes, but take care to choose one that has a nonreactive lining, since many dishes contain acid, such as tamarind or lime juice. Nonstick saucepans are ideal for Asian food as they avoid the problem of spices sticking on the bottom and allow you to use less oil when frying. **Claypots** of various shapes and sizes, with a sandy outside and a glazed interior, are used for slow cooking and for making soups and stocks. These are attractive and inexpensive, but any type of saucepan can be used.

Rice is usually cooked in an aluminum or a stainless steel saucepan, although many affluent homes in the cities boast an electric **rice cooker**—a great boon if you eat rice fairly often. It's foolproof, produces dry fluffy rice every time, and also keeps rice warm for latecomers. Alternatively, use a heavy saucepan with a tight-fitting lid.

Steaming is a healthy method of cooking in Asia, and a multi-tiered **bamboo steamer** with a woven cover to absorb any moisture (unlike a metal cover where moisture condenses and falls on the food) is invaluable. If you are using a multi-tiered metal steamer, put a tea towel under the lid to prevent moisture from dripping back onto the food. The steaming basket is placed inside a wok on a trivet above boiling water. Chinese stores also sell perforated metal disks that sit inside a wok above the water level; these are useful for steaming a single plate of food. Cover the wok with a lid and keep the water level topped up and at a gentle simmer during steaming.

Just as indispensable as a wok is the **cleaver**, which comes with either a heavy rectangular blade about 3–4 inches deep, ideal for cutting through bones, or a lighter weight blade for chopping, slicing, mincing, bruising garlic cloves and scooping up food on the flat edge to carry to the pan. A cleaver does the work of a whole battery of knives in a Western kitchen. You will also need a strong chopping board.

In addition to the usual knives found in any kitchen, a useful implement used by traditional Asian cooks is a narrow, double-bladed knife for carving vegetables into decorative shapes, and slicing fruit and vegetables thinly for the various rolls and wraps.

If the thump-thump of the stone, granite or porcelain **mortar** and **pestle** is not for you, blenders, food processors and coffee grinders make light work of the pounding, grinding and blending of spices and seeds. It's essential that all the ingredients to be made into a paste be finely chopped before blending. Whether using a mortar and pestle, blender or food processor, the principle is to grind or blend the toughest ingredients first, adding softer and wetter ingredients towards the end. First grind any dried spices or nuts until fine, then add hard ingredients such as chopped-up lemongrass and galangal. Pound or process until fine, then add softer rhizomes such as fresh turmeric and ginger, soaked dried chilies and sliced fresh chilies. When these are minced, add the ingredients that are full of moisture, such as chopped shallots and garlic, and soft shrimp paste.

If you are using a food processor or blender, you will probably need to add just a little liquid to keep the blades turning. If the spice blend is to be fried, add a little of the specified amount of cooking oil. If it is to be cooked in coconut milk, add some of this. While processing, you will probably need to stop the machine frequently to scrape down the sides. Continue until you have a fine paste.

Some cooks add water rather than the cooking medium to the blender; this means that the spice mixture will need to be cooked for a longer period of time before adding the other ingredients, to allow the water to evaporate and the mixture to fry rather than stew.

The multi-purpose **banana leaf** is often used in Southeast Asia to wrap food in for grilling, steaming, or placing directly onto hot coals. If you are able to obtain banana leaf, wipe it clean and cut to the required size. Hold it directly over a gas flame or plunge in boiling water until it softens before wrapping the food. Aluminum foil is generally recommended as a substitute, but for a texture that is closer to that obtained by using the leaf, wrap food in parchment paper first, then in the foil.

In Japan, **bamboo baskets** are used for draining noodles (a colander or sieve makes an adequate substitute). **Bamboo mats**, available in specialty Asian stores, are useful for rolling rice inside wrappers of seaweed, rolling up Japanese omelets and for squeezing

Old stove with a griddle or *tawa* for cooking *chapati*.

Traditional pottery is still used in Indonesian kitchens.

Wooden mortar and pestle.

Bamboo steamer.

A lined copper *kadai* for frying and sautéing.

Traditional coconut scrapers.

the liquid out of cooked vegetables.

The **Japanese grater**, usually made of porcelain or bamboo, is perfect for grating ginger or horseradish, since it breaks down the fibers beautifully.

Indian breads are rolled out with a wooden rolling pin on a flat circular stone slab or wooden board, and cooked on a heavy iron griddle or **tawa**. A heavy cast-iron frying pan or griddle makes a good substitute.

Coconut graters are essential in Asian countries. They are sometimes available in Western countries.

Cooking Techniques

The general cooking techniques used in Asian cooking are not too different from those used in the West.

The most common cooking method is probably **stir-frying**, which is fast cooking over a high heat in oil, usually in a wok. Evenly sliced ingredients are tossed about constantly; contact with the heat from the sides as well as the bottom of the wok means that food cooks very rapidly, sealing in the juices and flavor. Timing is absolutely crucial to the success of stir-frying, so chop all ingredients, measure all the seasonings, and have the garnishes and serving dishes on hand before starting.

Deep-frying involves cooking food by immersing it totally in heated oil. For best results, cook the food in small amounts so that the temperature of the oil does not drop too much. The optimum temperature for deep-frying is 375–400°F. Properly deep-fried food is not greasy at all—usually the result is a crisp exterior and a moist, succulent interior. Drain well on paper towels before serving.

Steaming is a cooking technique much prized by the Chinese and Japanese. The gentle cooking is an excellent method for showcasing the freshness of the produce, since all the natural flavors are retained. Make sure the water level in your steamer or wok is always topped up when you're steaming.

Grilling is another popular cooking technique, and it is hard to imagine Indonesia, Malaysia and Singapore without their variations on the satay, or Vietnam without its sugar-cane shrimp. The meat to be grilled is marinated and placed on skewers (remember to soak them in water for 1 hour before using so they do not burn). Most of

the dishes in this book can be cooked under a domestic broiler or over a grill. Baste with some of the marinade as you cook.

Braising involves cooking food over a low heat in flavored liquid for a long time, and is ideal for tougher cuts of meat and some vegetables. To **red braise** meat is to cook it in dark and light soy sauces, star anise or five-spice powder, Chinese cooking wine and sugar.

Poaching is carried out in water or stock that is barely simmering. The liquid should only just cover the meat which must be fished out as soon as it is ready.

To **blanch**, bring a pot of water to a rolling boil and immerse the food—usually vegetables—in small batches. Cook until they are tender but still crisp.

Many Indian, Indonesian, Malaysian and Thai dishes involve the use of spices, and as each spice takes a different amount of time to release its flavor and aroma, it is important to follow the correct order given when adding spices to the pan. Many spices need to be **dry-roasted** before use. It is best to do this in a heavy cast-iron pan without oil. Watch the heat carefully, shaking frequently so that the spices do not stick. To be sure of maximum flavour and aroma, buy whole spices and grind them just before cooking.

When cooking with coconut milk, it is important to prevent it from curdling or breaking apart. Stir the milk frequently, lifting it up with a large spoon or ladle and pouring it back into the saucepan or wok while it is coming to a boil. Once the coconut milk is simmering, be sure never to cover the pan. Thick coconut milk is sometimes added at the final stages of cooking to thicken and enrich the flavor of the dish. Stir constantly while heating but do not allow to boil.

Cooking rice is a subject that often arouses controversy, and if you have a reliable method, stick with it. Whatever method is used, first wash the rice thoroughly to remove any impurities and excess starch until the water runs clear. The absorbency of rice depends on the variety of rice and its age, with older rice absorbing more liquid. Cooking times depend on the type and weight of your saucepan, and the heat of your stove. See page 17 for a recipe for plain rice.

Thai woven storage baskets are as attractive as they are practical.

Traditional Indonesian rice steamer.

Long-handled scoops.

"An ancient Chinese proverb says, 'To the ruler, people are heaven; to the people, food is heaven.' "

CHINA

An ancient and inventive cuisine, known and loved all over the world.

Left: Three generations sit down to a meal in the courtyard of an old house in Fujian province, in Southern China.

Right: Steamed dumplings are popular in most regions of China and connoisseurs can recognize their provincial origin by their stuffing and accompanying sauces.

From a country whose usual greeting is "*Chi fan le mei you*?"—Have you eaten?—you can expect nothing less than a passionate devotion to food. Chinese food is known the world over, thanks to the peripatetic nature of its people, but the success of its food hinges on much the same things: fresh ingredients and the balance of flavors. The next time you go to an Asian market, observe: The Chinese shoppers are likely to be the ones who prod the fish, inspect entire bunches of vegetables, and accept and reject a batch of shrimp based on the kick in their legs.

While the array of seasonings and sauces used by Chinese cooks is not vast, every dish must meet three major criteria: appearance, fragrance and flavor. The Chinese also prize texture and the health-giving properties of food.

An old Chinese proverb says, "To the ruler, people are heaven; to the people, food is heaven." This is no truer than in China, where gastronomy is a part of everyday life.

The Making of a Cuisine

So large is China, and the geographic and climatic variations so diverse, that you can travel through the country and never have the same dish served in exactly the same way twice. The paradox of Chinese food is that it is one borne of hardship and frequent poverty: this is, after all, a country that houses 22 percent of the world's population and has only seven percent of the world's arable land.

There is much debate and confusion about how many regional cuisines there are, but most gourmets agree that at least four major Chinese regional styles exist: Cantonese, centered on southern Guangdong province and Hong Kong; Sichuan, based on the cooking of this western province's two largest cities, Chengdu and Chongqing; Hunan, the cooking of eastern China—Jiangsu, Zhejiang and Shanghai; and Beijing or 'Northern' food, with its major inspiration from the coastal province of Shandong. Some would add a fifth cuisine from the southeastern coastal province of Fujian.

All regions use various forms of ginger, garlic, scallions, soy sauce, vinegar, sugar, sesame oil and bean paste, but combine them in highly distinctive ways. What distinguishes these regional styles is not only their cooking methods but also the particular types and combinations of basic ingredients.

The southern school of cooking was the cuisine taken to the West by Chinese migrants—egg rolls, *dim sum*, *chow mein*, sweet and sour pork, *chop suey* and fortune cookies. With the exception of the last two, which were American inventions, the other dishes are orthodox Cantonese creations.

Cantonese food is characterized by its extraordinary range and the freshness of its ingredients, a light touch with sauces, and the readiness of its cooks to incorporate "exotic" imported flavorings

Smiling Shanghai children enjoying a snack. Each region has its own special array of morsels for when the next meal is just too far away.

Strong spices provide a pick-me-up in cold and humid weather, and make a useful preservative. The most popular spices are chilies and Sichuan peppercorns (fagara or prickly ash), tempered with sugar, salt and vinegar. Despite the province's incendiary reputation, many of the famous dishes are not spicy at all, for example, the famous camphor- and tea-smoked duck, made by smoking a steamed duck over a mixture of tea and camphor leaves. But it is the mouth burners that have made Sichuan's name known all over the world, dishes like *ma po dou fu*—stewed bean curd and ground meat in a hot sauce; *hui guo rou*—twice-cooked (boiled and stir-fried) pork with cabbage in a piquant bean sauce; *yu xiang qiezi*, eggplant in "fish flavour" sauce; and *dou ban yu*—fish in hot bean sauce.

When the Grand Canal was built in the Sui dynasty (581–618 a.d.), it gave rise to several great commercial cities at its southern terminus, including Huaian and Yangzhou, after which this regional cuisine (Hunan) is named. Its location on the lower reaches of the Yangtze River in China's "land of fish and rice" gave it an advantage in terms of agricultural products, and it was renowned for seafood such as fish, shrimp, eel and crab, which were shipped up the canal to the imperial court in Beijing. Hunan cuisine is not well known outside of China, perhaps because it rejects all extremes and strives for the "Middle Way". Freshness (*xian*) is a very important concept in the food of this region, but *xian* means more than just fresh. For a dish of steamed fish to be described as *xian*, the fish must have been swimming in the tank one hour ago, it must exude its own natural flavour, and must be tender yet slightly chewy. *Xian* also implies that the natural flavour of the original ingredients should always take precedence over the sauce. Some of the best known dishes from this region are steamed or stewed and require less heat and a longer cooking time, for instance chicken with chestnuts, the glorious pork steamed in lotus leaves, duck with a stuffing made from eight ingredients and the evocatively named "lion head" meatballs.

The cuisine of Beijing has perhaps been subjected to more outside influences than any other major cuisine in China. First came the once-nomadic Mongols, who made Beijing their capital during the Yuan dynasty (1279–1368). They brought with them mutton, the chief ingredient in Mongolian hot pot, one of Beijing's most popular dishes in the autumn and winter. The Manchus, as the rulers of the Qing dynasty (1644–1911), introduced numerous ways of cooking pork. As the capital of China for the last eight centuries, Beijing became the home of government officials who brought their chefs with them when they came from the wealthy southern provinces. But the most important influence comes from nearby Shandong province, which has a pedigree that goes back to the days of Confucius (ca. 550 b.c.). Shandong cuisine features the seafood found along China's eastern seaboard: scallops and squid, both dry and fresh, sea cucumber, conch, crabs and shark's fins, often teamed with the flavors of raw leek and garlic.

such as lemon, curry and Worcestershire sauce. Cantonese chefs excel in preparing roasted and barbecued meats (duck, goose, chicken and pork), and *dim sum*, snacks taken with tea for either breakfast or lunch. *Dim sum* can be sweet, salty, steamed, fried, baked, boiled or stewed, each served in their own individual bamboo steamer or plate. To eat *dim sum* is to "*yum cha*" or drink tea. In traditional *yum cha* establishments, restaurant staff walk around the room pushing a cart or carrying a tray offering their tasty morsels. *Dim sum* restaurants are important institutions where the locals go to discuss business, read newspapers and socialize.

The home of spicy food, Sichuan, is a landlocked province with remarkably fertile soil and a population of over 100 million. The taste for piquant food is sometimes explained by Sichuan's climate. The fertile agricultural basin is covered with clouds much of the year and there is enough rain to permit two crops of rice in many places.

Beijing's most famous dish, Peking Duck, owes as much to the culinary traditions of other parts of China as to the capital itself. The method of roasting the duck is drawn from Hunan cuisine, while the pancakes, raw leek and salty sauce that accompany the meat are typical of Shandong.

Beijing is also famous for its steamed and boiled dumplings (*jiaozi*), which are filled with a mixture of pork and cabbage or leeks, or a combination of eggs and vegetables.

The Food of the People

The proliferation of refrigerators in China today is making inroads on an institution that for centuries has been an essential part of daily life: shopping in the local food market. Many housewives and househusbands go to the market two or three times a day. In some state-run offices in Beijing, half-hour rest periods are allotted to enable its employees to shop for fresh produce.

In addition to fresh food markets, there are shops selling a huge variety of prepared and packaged food. Along with food markets, most cities have areas where snack foods are sold in stand-up or sit-down stalls. Breakfast may be a fried egg wrapped in a pancake; an "elephant ear" plate-sized piece of fried bread; noodles; congee (rice gruel) or bean curd jelly accompanied by a deep-fried cruller (*you tiao*); or a slice of cake and a jar of milk. Lunch or dinner could be noodles from a food stall or careful preparation of the just-bought produce from the market.

Esoteric and often extremely expensive ingredients such as shark's fin, dried scallops and dried oysters go into some of China's prized dishes.

Every region has its own particular snacks, very often sold on the street. Snack food is very inexpensive and includes such regional specialties as Beijing's boiled tripe with fresh cilantro, fried starch sausage with garlic, sour bean soup, and boiled pork and leek dumplings (*jiaozi*). Shanghai is known for its steamed *baozi* dumplings, sweet glutinous rice with eight sweetmeats (*babaofan*) and yeasty sweetened wine lees (the sediment of the wine left after fermentation). Sichuan is noted for spicy *dan dan* noodles, dumplings in hot sauce and bean curd jelly (*dou hua*), while Cantonese *dim sum* is a cuisine unto itself.

The average urban family eats its main meal of the day in the evening. This meal usually consists of a staple such as rice or noodles, one or two fried dishes, at least one of which contains meat or fish, and a soup. Northerners eat more wheat than rice, in the form of steamed buns or noodles, which are fried or simmered in stock.

Beer regularly accompanies meals at home; stronger spirits are reserved for special occasions. The whole family gets involved in the business of shopping and cooking, and friends or relatives may be invited to join in the feast.

Western foods have made tentative inroads into the 6,000-year-old bastion of Chinese cuisine, but fast-food outlets succeed mainly because of their novelty and location in Chinese tourist cities.

China's Gourmet Culture

As the Son of Heaven, the emperor of China enjoyed a status so elevated above the common mortal that it is difficult to conceive of the awe in which he was held and the power that he enjoyed. There are no dining rooms in the Forbidden City; tables would be set up before

the emperor wherever he decided to eat. Every meal was a banquet of approximately 100 dishes. These included 60 or 70 dishes from the imperial kitchens, and a few dozen more served by the chief concubines from their own kitchens. Many of the dishes served to the emperor were made purely for their visual appeal, and were placed far away from the reach of the imperial chopsticks. These leftovers were spirited out of the palace to be sold to gourmets eager to "dine with the emperor."

From the palace, this gourmet culture filtered down to the private homes of the rich and powerful and to the restaurants where the privileged entertained. Banquets are important social and commercial events in China today and many high officials attend banquets five or six nights a week. Almost any event can supply the reason for a banquet: the completion (or non-completion) of a business deal, wedding, graduation, trip abroad, return from a trip abroad, promotion, moving house and so on. One can also give a banquet to save or give "face" in the case of some unpleasant situation or mishap.

Some of the best restaurants in China today are the pre–1949 enterprises that have managed to survive by virtue of the quality of their cooking and by their location. One example is Fangshan Restaurant in Beihai Park in Beijing, set in a former imperial palace on the shores of an artificial lake, where many of the recipes are taken from the late-Qing dynasty Forbidden City. Fangshan is renowned for its Manchu-Chinese Banquet, a three-day dining extravaganza that consists of over 100 different dishes, a souvenir of Qing dynasty court banquets. At another famous restaurant, Listening to the Orioles Pavilion, in the gardens of the famed Summer Palace (known to the Chinese as *Yi He Yuan*), dinners for 10 at around $1,000 per table are reputedly not uncommon.

The Chinese Kitchen and Table

Rice is essential to a Chinese meal. This is particularly true in South China, although this division is not hard and fast. One reason the Grand Canal was built in the sixth century was to transport rice from the fertile Yangtze delta region to the imperial granaries in the rela-

This child seems to be eating with more gusto than finesse. You may need some practice before becoming adept with chopsticks.

tively dry North. And since the Ming dynasty (1368–1644), an annual crop of short-grain rice has been grown in the suburbs of Beijing, originally for the palace and today for the military leadership. Numerous varieties of rice are produced in China, supplemented by the more expensive Thai rice which is available at urban markets throughout the country. Southerners seem to prefer long-grain rice, which is less sticky than other varieties and has strong "wood" overtones when steaming hot.

The basic Chinese diet and means of food preparation were in place about 6,000 years ago, although many imported ingredients entered the Chinese larder and new cooking methods were adopted. From the earliest times, the Chinese have divided their foodstuffs into two general categories: *fan* (cooked rice and staple grain dishes) and *cai* (cooked meat and vegetable dishes). A balanced mixture of grain and cooked dishes has been the ideal of a Chinese meal since time immemorial. Further balances were sought between the *yin* (cooling) and *yang* (heating) qualities of the foods served. The notion of food as both preventative and curative medicine is deeply embedded in the Chinese psyche.

The specific proportion of grain and cooked dishes on a menu depends on the economic status of the diners and the status of the occasion. The grander the occasion, the more cooked dishes and less grain. Even today, this tradition is maintained at banquets, where a small symbolic bowl of plain steamed rice is served after an extensive selection of dishes.

Rice is served steamed, fried (after boiling) or made into noodles by grinding raw rice into rice flour. It is also cooked with a lot of water to produce congee or *zhou* (rice gruel), a popular breakfast food and late-night snack eaten with savory side dishes. Rice is eaten by raising the bowl to the mouth and shoveling the grains in with the chopsticks in a rapid fanning motion.

The Chinese table is a shared table. The average meal would comprise three to four *cai*, *fan* and a soup, served at once, to be shared between the diners who help themselves. The *cai* dishes should each have a different main ingredient, perhaps one meat, one fish and one vegetable. Each dish should complement the other in terms of taste, texture and flavor, and the total effect appeal to both the eye and the tongue.

When cooking Chinese food, prepare all the ingredients and have them ready before you start cooking as trying to juggle a hot wok and chop a chicken at the same time inevitably leads to catastrophe!

Tea is drunk before and after a meal, but rarely during a meal. The most famous of clear-spirits drunk "straight up" in small handle-less cups or glasses during a meal is Maotai, made in the south-west province of Guizhou.

Chinese meals are socially important events, and special menus are presented for weddings and birthdays; important festivals also have their traditional dishes and snacks.

Finally, some tips on etiquette. Don't point with your chopsticks and don't stick them into your rice bowl and leave them standing up or crossed. Don't use your chopsticks to explore the contents of a dish—locate the morsel you want with your eyes and go for it with your chopsticks without touching any other pieces.

If you wish to take a drink of wine at a formal dinner, you must first toast another diner, regardless of whether he or she responds by drinking. If you are toasted and don't wish to drink, simply touch your lips to the edge of the wine glass to acknowledge the courtesy.

It is incumbent upon the host to urge the guests to eat and drink to their fill. This means ordering more food than necessary and keeping an eye out for idle chopsticks. It is polite to serve the guest of honor the best morsels, such as the cheek of the fish, using a pair of serving or "public" chopsticks or with the back end of one's chopsticks. And remember, all food is communal and to be shared.

SUGGESTED MENUS

Family meals

For simple family meals, try serving with steamed jasmine rice:
• Winter Melon Soup (page 32);
• Bamboo Shoots with Mushrooms (page 36);
• Sliced fresh fruit.

Alternatively, you could offer:
• Pork-Stuffed Steamed Bean Curd (page 30);
• Beef with Black Pepper (page 35);
• Red Bean Soup (page 40).

Dinner parties

For a dinner party that is guaranteed to impress, present a selection of appetizers and two main dishes served with noodles instead of rice, such as.
•Marinated Sliced Beef (page 30), Carrot and Radish Rolls (page 30) and Seafood in Bean Curd Skin (page 30);
•Teochew Steamed Pomfret (page 36) or the classy Shrimp-stuffed Lychees (page 37) and Chicken with Dried Chilies (page 39);
• Fried Noodles Xiamen Style (page 33);
•White Fungus with Melon Balls (page 40).

One-pot meals

Many of the noodle soup dishes here are meals-in-a-bowl, and make an ideal lunch or supper. In China, dishes such as the following are often eaten for breakfast and in-between meals:
• Hot and Spicy Hawker Noodles (page 32);
• Cold Chengdu Noodles (page 33).

A melting pot menu

For a festive culinary tour around Asia:
• Shark's Fin Soup (page 32) from China;
• the ubiquitous but always delicious Chicken Rice from Malaysia/Singapore, (page 114);
• Kale with Crispy Pork (page 134) from Thailand served with rice;
• Almond Jelly (from Malaysia and Singapore) in individual servings (page 120).

THE ESSENTIAL FLAVORS OF CHINESE COOKING

Indispensable to the Chinese pantry are **garlic**, **ginger** and **scallions**. A good supply of **fresh jasmine rice** and **dried egg noodles** is also a must. Flavorings you'll need include **soy sauce**, **rice wine**, **sesame oil** and **chili sauce**. **Bamboo shoots** and **bean curd** are a common addition to everything from stir-fries to one-pot braises. **Rock sugar** is frequently used in red-braised dishes. **Sesame paste** is mixed into dipping sauces, and **Sichuan peppercorns** add a subtle heat to dishes.

Some of these appetizers would make very good starters to a formal dinner. Some, like the Seafood in Bean Curd Skin and Pork-Stuffed Steamed Bean Curd, can be served as part of a main meal—just adjust the quantities of the ingredients accordingly.

Nu Er Hong Niu Rou
Marinated Sliced Beef

Red rice is available from many Chinese medicine or specialty food shops.

| 12-ounce top round beef
| Water
| 2 teaspoons red rice (optional)
| 2 tablespoons Chinese rice wine
| 2 teaspoons salt
| 4 bay leaves

Put the beef in a pan with water to cover. Add all other ingredients and simmer, covered, until the beef is tender. Turn the meat from time to time and add a little more water if it looks like it's drying up. Allow to cool.

To serve, slice the beef thinly and arrange on a plate. Serve with a dipping sauce.

Pork-Stuffed Steamed Bean Curd.

Chao Lian Xia Xie Jiao
Seafood in Bean Curd Skin

| 8 ounces peeled shrimp
| 4 ounces crabmeat, fresh or tinned
| 2 water chestnuts, roughly chopped
| 1 tablespoon chopped cilantro
| 1 teaspoon salt
| 3–4 large sheets dried bean curd skin
| 1 teaspoon cornstarch mixed with water
| Oil for deep-frying

Blend the shrimp and crabmeat in a food processor until coarsely chopped. Add water chestnuts, cilantro and salt and process for a few more seconds. Wipe the bean curd skin with a damp cloth to make it pliable, then cut into 5-inch squares. Place a heaped spoonful of filling on the square and spread across. Smear the far end of the bean curd skin with cornstarch paste, then fold over the sides of the skin and roll up to seal firmly.

Heat oil in wok until hot and deep-fry until crisp and golden. Cut rolls into bite-sized pieces before serving.

Dou Fu Rou Jiang Zha
Pork-Stuffed Steamed Bean Curd

| 1 pound bean curd
| 3 teaspoons cornstarch
| 4 ounces ground lean pork
| 3 dried black mushrooms, soaked and finely chopped
| 2 teaspoons chicken broth powder
| 1/2 teaspoon salt
| 1 teaspoon sugar
| 1 teaspoon Chinese rice wine
| 1 1/2 cups leafy greens (spinach, white cabbage or *bok choy*), blanched
| 1/2 cup Chicken Stock (page 41)

Cut the bean curd into squares of about 3 inches x 1 1/2 inches thick. Use a teaspoon to scoop out some of the bean curd from the centre to make a hole for the pork filling. Combine 1 teaspoon cornflour with all other ingredients, except the leafy greens and stock, mixing well. Stuff this into the bean-curd and steam over high heat for 4 minutes.

While the beancurd is steaming, cook the greens in chicken stock. Drain, keeping the stock. Arrange greens on a plate. Blend the remaining 2 teaspoons cornstarch with water and add to the stock, stirring until thickened. Pour over vegetables, arrange the cooked bean curd on top and serve.

Ma La Lian Ou
Lotus Root Salad

It is said that Gautama Buddha likened man striving to achieve goodness to an exquisite lotus bloom rising unsullied from the muddy bottom of a lake—whatever the case, this dish is exquisite!

| 1 x 6–8-inch piece lotus root
| 1 tablespoon white rice vinegar
| 2 tablespoons sugar
| Salt to taste

Peel the lotus root and cut crosswise into slices about 1/4-inch thick. Heat a pan of water until boiling, then drop in the lotus root slices and blanch for about 5 seconds. Drain and rinse in cold water.

Toss the lotus root slices in a bowl with the vinegar, then arrange on a plate. Sprinkle with sugar and salt to taste and serve immediately.

Carrot and Radish Rolls

| 1 large carrot, shredded
| 3-inch piece giant white radish, peeled and sliced lengthwise as thinly as possible
| 3 teaspoons sugar
| 2 teaspoons white rice vinegar
| 2 teaspoons sesame oil
| 1/2 teaspoon salt

Blanch the carrot and radish separately in a little boiling water. Drain well and pat dry with paper towel. Place the slices of radish flat on a board and put some shredded carrot crosswise in the center of each. Roll up to enclose the carrot, then cut each roll on the diagonal into pieces of about 1/2-inch. Arrange on a plate.

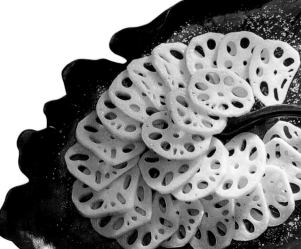

Lotus Root Salad.

Boiled Dumplings in Hot Sauce.

Combine all remaining ingredients, mixing until the sugar dissolves. Pour over the rolls and serve.

Sesame Squid

- 5 ounces squid, skinned and cleaned
- 1 cup water
- 1 teaspoon salt
- 1 tablespoon sesame paste
- 2 teaspoons sesame oil

Cut the squid in 2 inch x $^3/_4$ inch pieces. Score crosswise in a diamond pattern with a sharp knife, cutting about halfway into the squid so that it will curl during cooking. Bring water and salt to a boil and drop in squid. Simmer just until the squid turns white and curls (about 1 minute). Drain.

Combine sesame paste and oil in a mixing bowl and add squid. Toss and serve at room temperature or chilled, if preferred.

Gong Cai Xian Shen Pian
Duck Giblets

Duck or chicken giblets, often discarded by Western cooks or relegated to the stock pot, are favored for their firm texture and flavor in China. The word *gong* in the name of this dish means gratuity to the emperor.

- 10 ounces duck or chicken giblets
- 2 teaspoons salt
- 4 whole star anise
- 4 bay leaves
- 1 cup salted mustard cabbage, soaked, squeezed and sliced

Clean the giblets and drain. Put in a pan with salt, star anise and bay leaves. Cover with water, bring to a boil and simmer for about 30 minutes until tender. Remove giblets, drain and keep refrigerated until required.

To serve, slice the giblets thinly, then mix with salted cabbage and sesame oil. If you like, garnish with a little sliced red chili. Serve cold.

Chuan Wei Hun Tun
Boiled Dumplings in Hot Sauce

Steamed or boiled dumplings are a favorite snack in most of China, from Beijing in the north to Shanghai on the east coast, from the southern province of Guangdong to Sichuan in the far west. The filling differs from one area to another, as well as according to the season. In summer time in Beijing, the basic pork stuffing might be seasoned with fresh dill. The dumplings may be steamed, fried, boiled, served in soup (like the famous Cantonese *wonton* soup) or, as in this Sichuan version, bathed in a tangy sauce.

- 50 fresh wonton wrappers
- 8 ounces ground lean pork
- 1 egg, lightly beaten
- 1$^1/_2$ teaspoons very finely chopped ginger
- 2 tablespoons Chinese rice wine
- 1 teaspoon salt
- $^1/_4$ teaspoon ground white pepper

Hot Sauce
- 1 teaspoon finely chopped garlic
- 4 tablespoons black soy sauce
- $^1/_2$ teaspoon sugar
- $^1/_2$ teaspoon ground cinnamon
- 4 tablespoons Chili Oil (page 41)
- 1 tablespoon finely sliced scallion

Most *wonton* wrappers are 3–4 inches square. Turn a small Chinese soup bowl or a glass upside down on the wrappers and cut around the bowl or rim of the glass with a sharp knife to form circles.

Combine pork, egg, ginger, rice wine, salt and pepper. Put a heaped teaspoonful of this in the center of a wrapper. Use your fingertip to smear a little water around the edge of the circle, then fold across to make a semicircle, pressing firmly to enclose the filling. When all the dumplings are ready, drop in rapidly boiling water and simmer for 2–3 minutes. Drain.

Take 4 bowls and prepare the sauce separately for each portion. Put $^1/_4$ teaspoon garlic, 1 tablespoon black soy sauce, a pinch of sugar and a pinch of cinnamon in the bottom of each bowl. Divide the dumplings among the 4 bowls and pour 1 tablespoon chili oil over each. Garnish with scallion. Stir before serving.

Duck Giblets (below right) and Marinated Sliced Beef (below left).

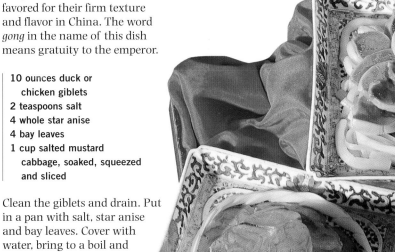

Restorative and satisfying, Chinese soups are usually drunk throughout a meal. Don't despair at the "exoticism" of some of the ingredients; most can be found in Asian food shops.

Dong Gua Tang
Winter Melon Soup

A restaurant classic appreciated for the clear, clean flavor of the stock, usually served in an intricately carved, hollowed-out melon. Winter melon is believed to be very *yin*, cleansing and cooling for the body and good for the skin.

| 1 large winter melon
| 1 teaspoon salt
| 6 cups Gourmet Stock (page 41) or Chicken Stock (page 41)
| 6 dried lotus nuts, soaked in hot water for 2 hours, peeled and hard core removed
| 4 ounces straw mushrooms, halved
| 1/3 cup shredded cooked chicken breast
| 1/3 cup shredded cooked duck meat (or double the chicken)
| 1/3 cup shredded cooked liver (duck, chicken or pork)
| 1/4 cup cooked or canned crabmeat
| 1/2 cup asparagus tips
| Salt to taste

Choose a winter melon that will hold at least 6 cups liquid. Cut off the top or, if the melon is very large, slice it in half. Carve the skin decoratively if you like. Remove the central fiber and seeds. Scrape out some of the flesh, leaving about 3/4 inch flesh on the skin. Sprinkle the inside with salt and put the melon in a large deep pan with boiling water to cover. Simmer for 30 minutes, drain and then put in a large steamer and steam for another 30 minutes.

Bring the stock to a boil, add the asparagus tips and the lotus nuts and pour into the melon. Cover and steam for 25 minutes. Add all other ingredients and serve. Scrape out some of the flesh with a spoon when serving the soup in individual bowls.

Yu Chi Tang
Shark's Fin Soup

Shark's fin is a real gourmet item, enjoyed for its texture and its ability to absorb the flavors of other ingredients. The dried scallops and fish maw are optional. In southern China, a few drops of black rice vinegar are generally added to the soup at the table.

| Shallot Oil
| 1 cup oil
| 8 shallots, peeled and sliced
| 1 ounce shredded dried shark's fin
| 1/3 ounce dried scallops (optional)

Shark's Fin Soup.

| 1 1/2 cups) Chicken Stock (page 41) (optional)
| 1 teaspoon dry sherry (optional)
| 1/2 inch ginger, sliced (optional)
| 1 scallion (optional)
| 1/3 ounce dried fish maw (optional)
| 3 cups gourmet stock or Chicken Stock (page 41)
| 3 teaspoons black soy sauce
| 1 teaspoon shallot oil
| 1/2 teaspoon salt
| 1/4 teaspoon ground white pepper
| 1 1/4 inches ginger, very finely shredded
| 1/3 cup finely shredded cooked chicken
| 2 tablespoons cornstarch, blended with water
| 1 heaped tablespoon finely shredded Yunnan ham

To make shallot oil, heat oil, add shallots and simmer until the shallots are golden. Do not allow the shallots to burn or the flavor will be bitter. Drain and store the oil in a jar with a tight-fitting lid.

Soak the shark's fin in hot water for about 30 minutes until swollen and transparent. Drain.

If using the scallops, place them in a bowl containing chicken stock, dry sherry, ginger and scallion. Steam in a steamer until the scallops are soft.

If using the fish maw, place them in a bowl, pour enough hot water over to cover, put a lid on and set aside until soft.

Heat stock with soy sauce, shallot oil, salt and pepper, then add shark's fin, scallops and fish maw if using, ginger and chicken. Add cornstarch and stir to thicken, then serve. Garnish with shredded Yunnan ham.

Hong Tang Dan Dan Mian
Hot and Spicy Hawker Noodles

A spicy favorite from Sichuan often sold at street-side stalls.

| 1 pound fresh wheat noodles or 1 small packet narrow flat dried noodles
| 1 teaspoon cooking oil
| 8 ounces ground lean pork
| 1/2 cup preserved salted radish, finely chopped
| 2 cups Chicken Stock (page 41)
| 4 tablespoons black soy sauce
| 1 1/2 tablespoons black rice vinegar
| 1 tablespoon very finely chopped garlic
| 2 teaspoons Sichuan Pepper Oil (page 41)
| 2 teaspoons sesame oil
| 1 teaspoon chili oil (page 41)
| 1 teaspoon ground white pepper
| 1 heaped tablespoon finely sliced scallion

Set the noodles aside for blanching later. Heat cooking oil and stir-fry the pork over very high

Winter Melon Soup.

heat for 2–3 minutes, until cooked. Mix well with the preserved radish and then heat with the chicken stock and all other ingredients, except noodles and scallion. Keep stock warm while blanching noodles in rapidly boiling water for 1 minute.

Drain noodles and divide among 4 bowls. Pour over hot pork mixture, garnish with scallion and serve.

HELPFUL HINT
Preserved salted radish is available from Asian stores. If unavailable, use Tientsin preserved vegetables (*tung choy*) instead if you like.

Chao Mian Xian
Fried Noodles Xiamen Style

Very fine fresh wheat-flour noodles, like angel-hair pasta, are used for this dish, which is popular in the southern coastal province of Fujian. Try to get fresh noodles for this dish—the texture is superior to dried noodles.

- 10 ounces small shrimp
- 1 pound fresh wheat-flour noodles
- Oil for deep-frying
- 2 tablespoons very finely chopped garlic
- 1 3/4 cups bamboo shoots, in matchstick shreds
- 4 ounces of lean pork, finely shredded
- 1 small carrot, in matchstick shreds
- 3–4 dried black mushrooms, soaked and finely shredded
- 1/4 cup chopped garlic chives
- 2 tablespoons Chinese rice wine
- 1 teaspoon salt
- 1/2 teaspoon ground white pepper
- 4 shallots, sliced and deep-fried until golden brown

Hot and Spicy Hawker Noodles.

Peel shrimp, remove heads and discard any intestinal tract. Keep shrimp aside and put heads and shells in a pan with 1 cup water. Bring to a boil, then simmer 10 minutes. Strain through a sieve, pressing on heads and shells to extract the maximum stock. Set aside.

Shake the noodles to separate if using fresh noodles, then deep-fry in very hot oil for a few seconds until golden brown. Drain well and set aside, discarding oil. If using dried noodles, blanch in boiling water until just softened.

Put 1 tablespoon of fresh oil into the wok, stir-fry the garlic for a few seconds then add shrimp, bamboo shoots, pork, carrot, mushroom and chives. Stir-fry until the pork and shrimp change color. Pour in 1/2 cup of the reserved shrimp stock, add wine, salt and pepper and simmer, uncovered, for 5 minutes, stirring from time to time. Add the fried or blanched noodles and continue stir-frying, mixing well, for another 5 minutes. Serve garnished with fried shallots.

Chengdu Leng Mian
Cold Chengdu Noodles

Chilled noodles are a popular summer dish in China and Japan. This dish is quick and easy to prepare: cook the noodles in the morning, chill them for a few hours, combine the sauce and you have an almost instant luncheon.

- 1 pound fresh wheat-flour noodles, boiled, drained and chilled
- 3/4 cup bean sprouts, blanched for a few seconds and chilled
- 1 scallion, finely sliced

Sauce
- 2 tablespoons very finely chopped ginger
- 1 tablespoon very finely chopped garlic
- 1 tablespoon sesame paste
- 1 tablespoon peanut butter
- 1 teaspoon peanut oil or cooking oil
- 3 tablespoons black soy sauce
- 2 teaspoons sugar
- 2 teaspoons black rice vinegar
- 1 teaspoon sesame oil
- 1 teaspoon Chili Oil (page 41)

Combine all sauce ingredients in a bowl, mixing well. Add the noodles and stir to coat the noodles with the sauce, then add bean sprouts and mix carefully with chopsticks or a fork, taking care not to break the sprouts. Divide among 4 bowls and sprinkle each portion with a little scallion.

Cold Chengdu Noodles.

Yu Xiang Qie Zi
Fragrant Eggplant with Pork

- 8 ounces eggplant, peeled and cut into 3-inch x 1/2-inch pieces
- Oil for deep-frying
- 2 ounces ground lean pork (1/4 cup)
- 2 tablespoons dried shrimp, soaked and very finely chopped
- 2 teaspoons commercial chili paste
- 1 teaspoon salted soybeans, mashed
- 2 teaspoons very finely sliced scallion
- 1 teaspoon very finely chopped soaked dried black mushroom
- 1 cup Chicken Stock (page 41)
- 1 teaspoon Chinese rice wine
- 1 teaspoon sesame oil
- 2 teaspoons commercial sweet and sour sauce
- 1/2 teaspoon dark soy sauce
- 1/4 teaspoon salt
- 1 teaspoon cornstarch, blended with water
- Cilantro to garnish

Heat oil until very hot and deep-fry the eggplant for 1 minute. Drain and set aside. Pour out all but 2 teaspoons of the oil and stir-fry pork over high heat for 2 minutes. Add dried prawns, chili paste, salted soybeans, 1 teaspoon of the scallion and mushroom. Stir-fry for 30 seconds, then add all remaining ingredients, except remaining scallion, cornstarch and cilantro. Heat, then add eggplant and cook a further 30 seconds.

Add cornstarch and stir to thicken. Serve garnished with the cilantro leaves and remaining scallion.

Ma Po Dou Fu
Spicy Bean Curd with Ground Beef

The dominant ingredient of this dish is meltingly soft bean curd laced with pungent Sichuan seasonings.

- 3 tablespoons oil or Chili Oil (page 41)
- 4 ounces ground lean beef
- 1 tablespoon salted black beans, chopped
- 1 tablespoon salted soybeans, chopped
- 1 tablespoon very finely chopped ginger
- 1 tablespoon very finely chopped garlic
- 2 tablespoons commercial chili paste
- 2–3 scallions, finely sliced
- 1 cup Chicken Stock (page 41)
- 1 pound soft bean curd, cut into 3/4-inch dice
- 1 tablespoon black soy sauce
- Salt to taste
- 2 teaspoons cornflour, blended with water
- 1 teaspoon powdered Sichuan peppercorns

Heat oil and stir-fry beef and black beans for 3–4 minutes. Add salted soybeans, ginger, garlic, chili paste and half the scallions. Stir-fry for another 2 minutes, then add the stock and bean curd.

Simmer for 5 minutes, season with soy sauce and salt, then thicken with cornstarch. Sprinkle with Sichuan pepper and remaining scallions, and serve.

Eggplant with Pork (top) and Stir-fried Mixed Vegetables (bottom).

Jiang Cong Chao Zhu Gan
Stir-Fried Pork Liver

This dish is very easy to make once you have all the ingredients ready and to hand.

- 10 ounces pork liver, thinly sliced
- 2 tablespoons Chinese rice wine
- 2 teaspoons oil
- 2 teaspoons finely chopped garlic
- 1 1/4 inches ginger, finely sliced
- 1 scallion, cut in 1 1/4-inch lengths
- 1/2 red chili, seeded and sliced (optional)
- 1 teaspoon chicken broth powder
- 1 teaspoon light soy sauce
- 1/2 teaspoon sugar
- 1 teaspoon cornstarch, blended with water

Marinate liver with wine for about 5 minutes. Heat oil and fry garlic for a few seconds, then add drained liver, ginger, scallion and chili (if using).

Stir-fry over high heat for a few seconds. Add broth powder, soy sauce and sugar and continue stir-frying for 1–2 minutes, until the liver is cooked.

Add cornstarch, stir to thicken and serve immediately.

Chao Qing Cai
Stir-Fried Mixed Vegetables

- 1/2 cup snow peas, ends trimmed
- 2 teaspoons oil
- Pinch of salt
- 1/4 teaspoon sugar
- 3 ounces bamboo shoots, quartered lengthwise, then cut in 2 inch lengths (3/4)
- 6–8 dried black mushrooms, soaked
- 1 cup chicken stock (page 41)
- 1 teaspoon oyster sauce
- 1/4 teaspoon sesame oil
- 1/4 teaspoon salt
- 1/4 teaspoon dark soy sauce
- Dash of ground white pepper
- 1 teaspoon cornstarch, blended with water

Blanch snow peas in boiling water for 5 seconds, then drain. Heat oil and stir-fry blanched snow peas with salt and sugar for 30 seconds. Remove from wok. Add bamboo shoots, mushrooms, chicken stock and all seasonings and bring to a boil. Simmer 1 minute, add snow peas, then thicken with cornstarch. Serve immediately.

Note: Additional vegetables such as baby corn or sliced carrots and broccoli can be used. Boil for 2 minutes before adding to the other vegetables.

Stir-fried Pork Liver.

Shuan Yang Rou
Mongolian Lamb Hot Pot

This is a popular winter dish in China and Mongolia, and as a reunion dinner, where everyone sits around a table and cooks their own portions of food in the simmering hot pot.

1 pound boneless lamb leg, sliced paper-thin (reserve the bone for stock)
1–2 cakes bean curd, sliced
3 cups coarsely chopped Napa cabbage
4 ounces dried rice vermicelli, soaked in hot water to soften

Stock
$1\frac{1}{4}$ inches ginger, finely sliced
1 scallion, coarsely chopped
2 teaspoons dark soy sauce
6 cups stock made from lamb leg bone boiled with water

Dips and Garnishes
$\frac{1}{2}$ cup sesame paste
2 tablespoons fermented beancurd, mashed
$\frac{1}{2}$ cup light soy sauce
$\frac{1}{2}$ cup red rice vinegar
$\frac{1}{2}$ cup Chinese rice wine
$\frac{1}{4}$ cup chili oil (page 41)
4 tablespoons Pickled Garlic (page 41)
Bunch of cilantro leaves, chopped

Roll up the sliced lamb and arrange on a plate. Put the bean curd and cabbage on separate plates, and divide the soaked vermicelli among 6 soup bowls.

Arrange dips and garnishes in small bowls and place on the table for diners to combine according to taste. Heat all stock ingredients in a pan, then carefully transfer to a hot pot. Bring back to a boil.

Diners cook their own portions of meat, bean curd and cabbage, seasoning them to taste, and eat them with pieces of pickled garlic and cilantro. When all the ingredients are used up, pour the stock into soup bowls over the noodles and eat as a final course.

Note: The hot pot is traditionally heated by charcoal, although electric and gas models are increasingly available.

Mongolian Lamb Hot Pot.

Hei Jiao Niu Rou
Beef with Black Pepper

Do try to get Sichuan peppercorns for this dish—they really do add to the taste.

8 ounces beef fillet, trimmed and cut in 1-inch cubes
2 tablespoons Chinese rice wine
1 tablespoon water
$\frac{1}{2}$ teaspoon salt
$\frac{1}{4}$ teaspoon ground white pepper
Oil for deep-frying
1 tablespoon finely chopped garlic
2 teaspoons coarsely crushed black peppercorns
1 teaspoon crushed Sichuan peppercorns
2 teaspoons oyster sauce
2 teaspoons light soy sauce
1 teaspoon sesame oil
Sliced lettuce (garnish)

Put beef in a bowl and sprinkle with wine, water, salt and white pepper. Massage well for about 30 seconds until all the liquid is absorbed by the beef.

Heat oil and deep-fry the beef over very high heat for 30 sec-

onds. Drain and set aside. Tip out all but 1 teaspoon of oil and stir-fry the garlic for a few seconds, then add the beef and all other ingredients, except for the lettuce. Stir-fry for a few seconds until well mixed. Serve immediately on a bed of shredded lettuce.

HELPFUL HINT

For the hot pot, if using a charcoal hot pot, light charcoal over a gas flame and then use tongs to insert it down the central chimney of the hot pot and into the bottom.

Beef with Black Pepper

Stuffed Vegetables and Bean Curd.

Guang Dong Niang San Bao

Stuffed Vegetables and Bean Curd

This Cantonese and Hakka favorite uses a selection of vegetables and bean curd stuffed with a shrimp filling. The sauce, flavored with salted black beans, gives an emphatic salty tang to the delicate vegetables.

Stuffing
8 ounces peeled prawns, chopped
1/4 cup lard, chopped
1 tablespoon black moss fungus, soaked to soften
1/2 teaspoon salt
Dash of ground white pepper

1 large green bell pepper
1 long thin eggplant
1 square hard bean curd
1 teaspoon cornstarch
Oil for deep-frying

Sauce
1 teaspoon salted black beans, mashed slightly with the back of a spoon
1 teaspoon finely chopped red chili
1 teaspoon very finely chopped garlic
1 teaspoon very finely chopped ginger
1 cup chicken stock (page 41)
1/2 teaspoon black soy sauce
2 teaspoons cornstarch, blended with water

To make the stuffing, blend together all ingredients. Set aside.

Cut the green pepper into four and discard seeds. Cut the eggplant across into 1 1/2-inch lengths and make a lengthwise slit down one side to form a pocket for the stuffing—do not cut through.

Cut the bean curd into four and slit a pocket in each. Sprinkle the inside of the vegetables and bean curd with cornstarch to help make the stuffing stick, then fill.

Heat oil in a wok and deep-fry the stuffed items, a few at a time, until golden and cooked. Remove the vegetables and set aside, leaving 1 teaspoon of oil in the wok.

To make the sauce, stir-fry the black beans, chili, garlic and ginger for a few seconds until fragrant, then add the stock and soy sauce. Bring to the boil, then add the vegetables and bean curd and simmer for 1 minute. Add cornstarch and stir to thicken. Serve immediately.

Xiang Gu Chao Jiao Bai

Bamboo Shoots with Mushrooms

Jiao bai, a special type of bamboo shoot used for this dish in southern China, has an excellent texture and flavour somewhat reminiscent of fresh heart of palm. Canned bamboo shoots can be used if you like.

12 ounces bamboo shoots
2 teaspoons oil
1 heaped teaspoon very finely chopped garlic
10 dried black mushrooms, soaked
1 teaspoon Chinese rice wine
1 teaspoon chicken broth powder
1 teaspoon sugar
1/2 teaspoon salt

If using fresh bamboo shoots, peel off the outer layer, then slice coarsely. If using canned shoots, simmer in boiling water for 5 minutes, drain and slice coarsely.

Heat oil in a wok and stir-fry the garlic and mushrooms until fragrant. Add the shoots and seasonings and stir-fry for 1–2 minutes. Serve immediately.

Chao Zhou Zheng Chang Yu

Teochew Steamed Pomfret

This recipe demonstrates the subtlety of Teochew (Chiu Chow) style of cooking. The trick is not to overcook the fish.

1 1/2-pound pomfret, pompano, butterfish or plaice
1/2 cup salted mustard cabbage, soaked and finely sliced
1 tomato, seeded and cut in strips
2 sour salted plums
1 red chili, seeded and finely shredded
3-inch celery stalk, finely shredded
1 scallion, cut in 1 1/2 -inch lengths
3 inches ginger, finely shredded
1 square bean curd, shredded
1 dried black mushroom, soaked and finely shredded
2 teaspoons chicken broth powder
1/2 teaspoon sugar
1/4 teaspoon salt
Cilantro leaf to garnish

Clean the fish inside and out and wipe dry. Place on an oval plate and arrange over it all the ingredients except chicken broth powder, sugar, salt and cilantro.

Sprinkle with the broth powder, sugar and salt and put inside a large steamer that has been set over boiling water. Steam over high heat for about 8 minutes, until the fish is cooked. Garnish with cilantro leaf.

Teochew Steamed Pomfret.

Yu Xiang Cui Pi Gui Yu
Crispy Fried Mandarin Fish

The Chinese believe that fresh-water fish from lakes, rivers and fish ponds are more delicate in flavor and texture than fish from the sea. Although this recipe calls for freshwater fish, fine-textured ocean fish such as perch, grouper, bream or snapper could be substituted.

1 fresh fish, 1 1/2 –2 pounds,
   cleaned and scaled
3 inches ginger, finely sliced
1 scallion, chopped coarsely
1 teaspoon ground white pepper
1/2 cup Chinese rice wine
Oil for deep-frying
2 tablespoons cornstarch
1 scallion, finely sliced for garnish

Sauce
1–2 tablespoons chili paste
1 1/2 teaspoons finely chopped garlic
1 1/2 teaspoons finely chopped ginger
1 1/2 teaspoons white rice vinegar
1 teaspoon sugar
1/2 teaspoon salt
3/4 cup Chicken Stock (page 41)
1 scallion, finely sliced
2 teaspoons cornstarch, blended
   with water

Cut 4 or 5 deep diagonal slashes on each side of the fish to help it cook more quickly. Marinate the fish for 15 minutes with ginger, scallion, pepper and rice wine. Drain fish and scrape off any marinade. Dry thoroughly.

Heat a wok and add oil. When the oil is hot, sprinkle the fish on both sides with cornstarch, shaking it to remove any excess. Carefully lower the fish into the oil and cook, over moderate heat, for about 5–8 minutes until golden brown and cooked through. Drain and keep warm on a serving dish. Discard all but 1 teaspoon of the frying oil.

To prepare the sauce, stir-fry the chili paste, garlic and ginger for a few seconds until fragrant, then add all other ingredients, except cornstarch. Simmer for 2 minutes, then add cornstarch and stir to thicken. Pour the sauce over the fish and garnish with scallion. Serve immediately.

Shrimp-Stuffed Lychees.

Zeng Cheng Bai Hua Niang Xian Guo
Shrimp-Stuffed Lychees

A fine example of the creativity and delicacy of Cantonese food. The texture of fresh lychees is best. If you cannot obtain fresh lychees, use canned fruit, but rinse well to remove any sugar syrup.

8 ounces peeled shrimp, finely
   chopped or blended (1 cup)
1 teaspoon salt
1 teaspoon cornstarch
1/4 teaspoon ground white pepper
10 fresh or canned lychees, peeled
   and seeded
Lettuce leaves to garnish
Cilantro leaf to garnish
Red pepper flakes to garnish
   (optional)

Sauce
1 cup Chicken Stock (page 41)
1 teaspoon cooking oil
1/2 teaspoon salt
1 teaspoon cornstarch, blended
   with water
2 egg whites

Mix together the shrimp, salt, cornstarch and pepper. Divide mixture into 10 portions. Sprinkle the inside of each lychee with a dusting of additional cornstarch and stuff withthe shrimp paste, pushing it in well. Put the lychees on a plate and steam over high heat for 6–8 minutes, until the filling is firm and cooked.

Arrange lettuce leaves in a shallow bowl and put the lychees on top.

To make the sauce, bring stock, oil and salt to a boil. Lower heat and add the cornstarch mixture, then stir in the egg whites and remove from the heat. Pour over the lychees and serve immediately.

Suan Rong Zheng Dan Cai
Steamed Mussels with Minced Garlic

This way of cooking mussels also works for oysters or clams. Boil the shellfish just until they open, then steam. The shellfish can be cooked in advance and refrigerated until you are ready to steam them.

12 fresh mussels or oysters or
   24 clams
6–8 cloves garlic
1 teaspoon oil
1 teaspoon chicken broth powder
1 teaspoon sugar
1/2 teaspoon light soy sauce
1 red chili, finely chopped
1 scallion, finely sliced
Cilantro leaf (optional)

Bring a wok of water to a boil. Put in mussels or other shellfish and cook until the shells open. Remove, drain, and discard one side of the shell. Put the half-shell with the attached shellfish on a plate.

Slice half the garlic and fry gently in oil until crisp and golden. Drain and set aside. Chop the remaining garlic very finely and scatter a little over each of the mussels. Sprinkle with chicken broth powder, sugar and soy sauce. Put inside a steamer and cook over high heat for 3 minutes.

Garnish with the fried garlic, chili, scallion and cilantro and serve immediately.

Steamed Mussels with Minced Garlic (outside of plate).

You Bao You Yu Juan
Squid with Bamboo Shoots

Squid is very popular in coastal regions of China. Use the freshest you can lay your hands on. Chinese cooks often score the squid so that it has an attractive "pine cone" appearance after cooking.

| 1 pound fresh squid, peeled and cleaned
| 3 ounces bamboo shoots
| 1/4 cucumber
| 1 carrot
| Oil for deep-frying
| 1 teaspoon finely chopped garlic
| 1 scallion, sliced
| 2 tablespoons Chinese rice wine
| 1 teaspoon salt
| 1 teaspoon cornstarch, blended with water

Cut the cleaned squid in half lengthwise and score each piece with a sharp knife in a diamond pattern, taking care not to cut right through the flesh. Cut the scored squid into pieces about 2 1/2 inches x 3/4 inch. Dry thoroughly.

Thinly slice the bamboo shoots, cucumber and carrot lengthwise and cut into 2-inch pieces.

Heat oil and when very hot, deep-fry the squid for 5 seconds only. Drain and set aside. Pour out all but 1 teaspoon of the oil and reheat. Stir-fry the garlic for a few seconds until fragrant, then add the squid and stir-fry for 1 minute. Add the bamboo shoots, cucumber, carrot and scallion and stir-fry for 1 minute. Season with rice wine and salt, and stir in cornstarch to thicken. Serve immediately.

Beggar's Chicken.

Qi Gai Ji
Beggar's Chicken

According to legend, this dish was created by a poor man who stole a chicken. He was about to cook it on a fire when the landowner passed by. To conceal it, he hastily wrapped the chicken in mud and tossed it on the fire. Later, when the danger had passed, he broke open the mud casing to find a succulent cooked bird.

This refined version includes stuffing that the beggar would never have been able to lay his hands on, and encases the chicken in an edible bread dough instead of mud.

Dough
4 teaspoons dried yeast
8 cups flour
2 tablespoons sugar
1 tablespoon salt
2 eggs, beaten
2 cups warm water

Stuffing
5 ounces pork, finely shredded
3 1/2 ounces preserved dried vegetable (*mei cai*), finely chopped
5 dried black mushrooms, soaked and shredded
3 inches ginger, finely shredded
1–2 scallions, finely sliced
2 teaspoons chicken broth powder
2 teaspoons sugar
2 teaspoons light soy sauce
3 tablespoons rice wine
Pinch of powdered ginger

3-pound chicken, cleaned
2 dried lotus leaves

To make the dough, proof yeast according to the manufacturer's instructions. Sift flour into a bowl, add yeast mixture and all other ingredients; mix well until pliable. Add a little more water or flour if necessary to achieve the right consistency. Cover and leave to rise.

To make the stuffing, combine all ingredients and mix well. Stuff the chicken and close each end with a strong toothpick. Wrap in the lotus leaves, overlapping so as to enclose the chicken. Put on a plate and steam over high heat for 30 minutes.

Knead the dough and roll out into a rectangle large enough to enclose the chicken. Put chicken in the dough and close, pinching well to seal. Bake in a 350 ° F oven until the dough is golden brown (about 15 minutes). Cut open at the table and serve the chicken and stuffing. The dough can also be eaten.

Note: Chinese preserved vegetables add rich flavor to Chinese braised dishes and stews. They come in a variety of packaging including cans or plastic packages.

Squid with Bamboo Shoots.

Cui Pi San Dong Ji

Deep-Fried Shandong Chicken

This dish from the province of Shandong involves two methods of cooking: the chicken is first simmered gently, then deep-fried. It is served with a clear, unthickened sauce with a slightly hot and sour edge. This dish can be partially prepared in advance; simmer and dry the chicken and keep for several hours before the final frying.

2¹/2-pound fresh chicken
¹/2 teaspoon salt
Oil for deep-frying
1 scallion, white part only, shredded
4 cloves garlic, finely sliced and deep-fried

Sauce
1 red chili, seeded and sliced
4 cloves garlic, sliced
1 teaspoon commercial chili paste
1 cup Chicken Stock (page 41)
1 tablespoon light soy sauce
¹/4 cup white vinegar
2 tablespoons sugar or honey
Salt to taste

Rub the chicken inside and out with salt and set aside for 30 minutes. Bring a large pot of water to a boil and put in the chicken. Reduce the heat to its lowest setting and simmer the chicken for 30 minutes. Drain the chicken, pat dry and hang in an airy place to dry thoroughly.

Just before the dish is required, heat oil for deep-frying in a wok. To ensure a crisp texture, make sure the chicken is thoroughly dry (a brief session with a hair dryer sometimes helps). Lower the whole chicken, breast side down, into the oil and fry for about 5 minutes until golden brown. Turn and fry the other side for another 5 minutes. Remove chicken from oil, drain, chop into bite-sized pieces and arrange on a serving dish deep enough to contain 1¹/2 cups sauce.

Tip out all the oil from the wok but do not wipe. Add the sauce ingredients and simmer for 2 minutes. Pour over the chicken and garnish with scallion and fried garlic.

HELPFUL HINT

Dried chilies give this dish a smoky finish, so do try to get them. If using fresh chilies, don't dry-fry but add with the garlic and ginger so that they cook through.

Gong Bao Feng Hua

Chicken with Dried Chilies

5-ounce chicken breast
¹/2 teaspoon salt
1 egg white
2 tablespoons Chinese rice wine
2 teaspoons cornstarch
Oil for deep-frying
1 teaspoon finely chopped garlic
1 teaspoon finely chopped ginger
1 tablespoon black soy sauce
1 tablespoon white rice vinegar
1 teaspoon sugar
2–3 dried chilies, cut into ¹/2-inch pieces, dry-fried until crisp and lightly browned
1 tablespoon finely sliced scallion
2 tablespoons fried peanuts, skinned

Score chicken breast with diagonal cuts about ¹/4-inch apart, taking care not to cut right through the flesh. Cut the breast into ¹/4-inch x ³/4-inch pieces. Mix well with salt, egg white, wine and cornflour. Set aside for 2–3 minutes.

Heat oil until very hot and deep-fry chicken for 30 seconds, drain and set aside.

Tip out all but 1 teaspoon of oil from the wok. Stir-fry the garlic and ginger for a few seconds, then add soy sauce, vinegar and sugar. Stir well and return the chicken, dried chilies and scallion and and stir-fry for 3–4 minutes. Stir in the fried peanuts and serve immediately.

Pi Pa Xia

Pi Pa Shrimp

This dish is fancifully named after the *pi pa*, a classical Chinese stringed instrument which the finished shrimp are thought to resemble. They can be prepared ahead of time and deep-fried just before serving. Use 12 small Chinese wine cups or egg cups to mold the paste.

Shrimp Paste
10 ounces shrimp
6 tablespoons diced lard
1 dried black mushroom, soaked and finely chopped
1 tablespoon finely chopped bamboo shoots or water chestnuts
1 teaspoon salt
2 egg whites
2 tablespoons cornstarch

12 medium shrimp, 2¹/2–3 inches long
Oil for deep-frying
2 tablespoons cornflour
1 egg white, lightly beaten

Sauce
1 cup Chicken Stock (page 41)
1 teaspoon Chinese rice wine
Salt to taste
2 teaspoons cornstarch, blended with water

To make the paste, peel the shrimp, discarding heads, tails and shells. Remove intestinal tract. Process shrimp in a blender for a few seconds with the lard. Add all other paste ingredients and process just until well blended.

Grease tiny Chinese wine or egg cups with a little oil, then divide the shrimp paste among these, packing in firmly.

Peel the medium shrimp, discarding heads and shells but leaving on the tail for a more decorative appearance. Push the head end of each shrimp into a paste-filled cup, leaving the tail end protruding. Repeat until all the shrimp are used up, then steam for 20 minutes. Allow to cool, then remove from the cups with the tip of a knife.

Just before the dish is required, make the sauce by bringing stock, wine and salt to a boil. Add cornflour, stir to thicken and keep the sauce warm.

Heat oil for deep-frying in a wok. Dust each steamed shrimp with a little cornstarch, dip into the egg white and deep-fry until golden brown.

Put on a serving dish and pour the sauce over the top.

Deep-Fried Shandong Chicken.

Chicken with Dried Chilies.

The most popular Chinese dessert is a platter of sliced, fresh fruits. For more formal banquets one of the desserts in this section may be served; however, these are more commonly eaten as snacks or as a late-night supper.

Bing Tang Yin Er
White Fungus with Melon Balls

White fungus is virtually tasteless but prized for its texture as well as its health-giving properties. This soup can be served warm or chilled.

1¹/₂ ounces dried white fungus

3 ounces rock sugar

3 cups water

3 ounces Hami melon,
     rock melon or honeydew

Wash the fungus well, then soak in warm water for 1 hour. Remove the stems and any tough portions and cut into bite-sized pieces. Set aside.

Heat rock sugar and water in a pan, stirring until sugar dissolves. Pour into a bowl and add the white fungus. Cover the bowl and put in a steamer. Steam for 1¹/₂ hours until the fungus is soft. Leave to cool, then chill.

Just before serving, scoop out small balls of melon flesh. Add to the chilled fungus and serve in small bowls.

Lian Zi Hong Dou Sha
Red Bean Soup

1¹/₂ ounces dried or canned lotus
     nuts

8 ounces dried red azuki beans (1
     cup)

1 strip dried or fresh orange peel

4 cups water

¹/₂–³/₄ cup sugar

White Fungus with Melon Balls.

If using dried lotus nuts, soak in hot water for 2 hours, drain, peel and use a toothpick to push out the bitter core. If using tinned nuts, drain and discard liquid.

Soak the red beans in warm water to cover for 30 minutes. Drain and combine with orange peel and water and simmer gently, covered, for 1 hour. Add the lotus nuts and cook for 1 more hour. Add sugar to taste and stir until dissolved. Serve warm.

Red Bean Pancakes.

Dou Sha Wo Bing
Red Bean Pancakes

Light pancakes enclose a filling of red bean paste. If canned red bean paste is not available, soak ¹/₂ cup red beans for 2 hours. Boil until soft with a strip of dried orange peel. Mash, adding sugar to taste.

1¹/₄ cups white flour, sifted

¹/₄ teaspoon custard powder

1 egg

Water to mix

Oil for frying-pan

4 ounces red bean paste

Combine flour, custard powder, egg and sufficient water to make a pancake batter the consistency of thin cream.

Heat wok and grease with 1 teaspoon oil, swirling the wok around so that the oil covers all sides. Pour in about ¹/₄ cup of the batter and swirl the wok around to make a thin pancake. Cook until the top of the pancake has set and the underside is slightly brown. Remove, set aside and repeat until the batter is used up.

Place the pancakes, browned side up, on a flat surface. Spread the center of each pancake with bean paste and fold in the edges to enclose the paste. Heat a little oil in a wok and fry the stuffed pancake until golden. Cut into bite-sized pieces and serve.

Ba Si Ping Guo
Candied Apples

Make sure that you have everything laid out before you start cooking.

Batter

1 cup white flour

2 tablespoons cornstarch

1 teaspoon baking soda

¹/₂ beaten egg

Syrup

¹/₂ cup sugar

2 tablespoons water

Oil for deep-frying

4 large green apples, peeled, cored
     and cut into 8 slices

To make the batter, combine all ingredients, adding enough water to achieve the consistency of a thick cream. To make the syrup, heat the sugar and water over moderate heat, stirring, until the syrup turns golden brown. Keep warm. Have a bowl of iced water and a greased serving dish ready. Heat oil for deep-frying. When it is very hot, dip slices of apple, a few at a time, into the batter and fry until golden brown. Remove from oil, drain, and dip into the syrup, turning to coat thoroughly. Plunge apple slices immediately into iced water to set coating, then put on the serving dish. Serve immediately.

Chili Oil

- 3/4 cup peanut oil
- 1 tablespoon Sichuan peppercorns
- 2 dried chilies, sliced

Heat wok and add oil, peppercorns and chilies. Cook over low heat for 10 minutes. Allow to cool, then store in a covered jar for 2–3 days. Strain and discard peppercorns and chilies. Store oil in a tightly sealed jar and keep in a cool place for up to 6 months.

Sichuan Pepper Oil

- 2 tablespoons Sichuan peppercorns
- 3/4 cup peanut oil

Stir-fry peppercorns in dry wok until fragrant. Add the oil and cook over low heat for 10 minutes. Allow to cool, then store in a covered jar for 2–3 days. Strain and discard peppercorns. Store oil in a tightly sealed jar and keep in a cool place for up to 6 months.

Gourmet Stock

- 1 pound pork ribs, blanched
- 12 ounces chicken pieces, blanched
- 12 ounces duck pieces, blanched
- 12 ounces smoked ham hock
- 2 scallions, coarsely chopped
- 2 inches ginger, sliced
- 1/4 cup Chinese rice wine
- 20 cups water

Combine all ingredients and simmer, uncovered, for 2 hours. Strain stock through cheesecloth.

Chicken Stock

- 1 stewing hen or 3 pounds chicken pieces
- 1 stalk celery, with leaves still attached, chopped
- 2 inches ginger, bruised
- 10 cups water

Plunge the hen or chicken pieces into a large pan of boiling water and simmer for 1 minute. Discard water and refill pan with fresh water and all other ingredients. Bring to a boil and simmer gently, uncovered, for 2 hours. Keep skimming any scum or impurities as they rise to the top of the pan. Strain stock through cheesecloth. This can be made in large quantities and frozen in smaller portions for future use.

Pickled Garlic

- 3 cups water
- 6–8 bulbs garlic, skins on
- 1 cup white rice vinegar
- 3 tablespoons sugar
- 1 teaspoon salt
- 1 bay leaf

Bring water to a boil in a pan, add garlic and remove from the heat. Add remaining ingredients and leave to cool.

Put garlic in a jar, cover with liquid, cover the jar and marinate for 3 days before using. Drain and serve as an accompaniment or appetizer.

Ginger Garlic Sauce

- 4 inches young ginger
- 6 cloves garlic
- 1 teaspoon salt
- 1 teaspoon sugar
- 1 teaspoon sesame oil
- 1 tablespoon cooking oil

Blend ginger and garlic. Combine with all other ingredients. Put in a covered jar and shake just before serving. Good with boiled meats.

Chili Garlic Sauce

- 5 red chilies, chopped
- 3 cloves garlic, chopped
- 3 tablespoons white rice vinegar
- 1 teaspoon sugar
- 1/2 teaspoon salt

Process all ingredients in a blender until fine. Keep refrigerated in a covered jar. Serve as a dipping sauce with steamed poultry or with rice and other cooked dishes.

Soy and Ginger Dip

- 2 teaspoons light soy sauce
- 2 tablespoons very finely chopped ginger
- 1 tablespoon finely sliced scallion
- 1/2 teaspoon sugar
- 2 tablespoons peanut oil
- 1 tablespoon sesame oil

Combine soy sauce, ginger, scallion and sugar. Heat both oils together until they smoke, then pour over the ginger mixture and stir. Serve immediately with steamed chicken or fish.

Ginger and Black Vinegar Dip

- 3-inch piece young ginger, scraped and finely shredded
- 3 tablespoons black rice vinegar

Combine ginger and vinegar. Serve with dumplings and other *dim sum* dishes.

Sesame Sauce

- 4 tablespoons sesame paste
- 4 tablespoons cold Chicken Stock (page 41)
- 1 teaspoon sesame oil
- 1/2 teaspoon salt
- 1/2 teaspoon sugar

Mix all ingredients well and serve with any seafood dish.

Ginger Garlic Sauce (top), Chili Garlic Sauce (above left) and sliced chilies in soy sauce (no recipe).

"Cooking and eating Indian cuisine is a discovery of the culture, the richly varied history and the spicy treasures of this fascinating land."

INDIA

Three thousand years of tradition and change are reflected in the cuisine of the subcontinent.

Left: The ultimately in Indian dining, an elegantly laid antique table set with thalis of Rajasthani food, while attentive retainers hover nearby.

Right: One of the peaceful canals that crisscross the southern state of Kerala.

India is a vast and ancient land, with a recorded history that dates back over three thousand years. It is divided into many provinces that stretch from the snowy mountains of Kashmir to the southern tip of verdant Kerala, from the harsh arid deserts of Rajasthan in the west across to the remote tribal region of Assam along the Burmese border. Thus India has it all—from palm-fringed beaches to desert, and bustling cities to small one-ox towns.

This is also the land that gave rise to two of the world's major religions, Buddhism and Hinduism, and produced Jainism and Sikhism. Caste, too, plays its role in influencing the food of the people.

With all these differences Indian cuisine may seem undefinable, but there are enough common strands that combine to form a thrilling and exciting tapestry.

The Land and its People

Located in southern Asia, India ranges from the Himalayas in the north to the great Gangetic plain with its immense and sacred waters, to the lush tropical splendor of Kerala in the south. With its considerable land area—it is the seventh largest country in the world—India naturally encompasses four defined seasons.

In the cooler north and in the Gangetic plain of the middle and eastern part of India, rice and wheat are the main staples; while in the deserts of Rajasthan and Gujarat, it is millet and corn. Rice is also a basic food in the eastern belt of India, where its large and fertile alluvial lands make it an ideal rice-growing region. Along the coastal area of Kerala, fish and meat are the basic foods in the people's diet.

Spices, the foundation of Indian cooking, are widely cultivated according to region. Cardamom, cloves and peppers are harvested mainly in the south, while Rajasthan, Kashmir and Gujarat are known for their chilies and turmeric. One of the

Above: **Nutmeg being weighed in the wholesale spice market of Cochin.**
Right: **A southern Indian thali with an array of vegetables, pickle, soup, rice, bread, banana and dessert.**

those which were absorbed into the flesh, and those which were transformed into thought or mind. The last were the finest and rarest of foods and referred to as *manas*. The term *prasad* was used for food left over from offerings to the gods, food which was considered nectar, left no trace, and which maintained man's spirituality.

Food was classified into different categories: cereals, legumes, vegetables, fruit, spices, milk products, animal meats and alcoholic beverages. This was the time when ghee or clarified butter emerged as a popular cooking medium because of its associations with purity, as it was used in religious sacrifices and offerings. Most traditional Indian cooking in the north still uses cholesterol-high ghee, although modern Indians have switched to cooking oil

Ancient food habits were altered by religion and trade, through occupation and invasion, with Indian cuisines becoming more varied and vibrant. Religion was a major influence in changing food habits, with Buddhism and Jainism starting the first indigenous movements which challenged Hindu practices. Abstinence, austerity and simplicity were the tenets of changes which questioned, among other things, the eating of meat. Jainism underlined the importance of innocent foods and vegetarianism was born. Sikhism followed to reaffirm simplicity, with tobacco and alcohol becoming inscribed targets.

Geography also plays a role in what is served. In Gujarat, Nasto is made from Bengal gram flour (*besan*) mixed with an assortment of spices and fried. Chevda or beaten rice is fried and mixed with salt, spices, almonds, raisins and peanuts. The Parsis brought with them a strong meat-eating tradition and a love of egg dishes, raisins, nuts, butter and cream. They inevitably absorbed Gujarati influences and a hybrid cuisine developed. One of the most famous of these dishes is the Parsi fish steamed in banana-leaf packets. Another is Dhansak, a one-pot meal that combines several types of dal with spices, meat and vegetables.

glorious sights of Kashmir is the fields of purple-blue crocuses, source of the world's most expensive spice, saffron.

Islam has been in India since the 8th century, but it was not until the 16th century that the Muslims gained control over large parts of India. The Mughal dynasties, which ruled various independent states of pre–Independence India, upstaged the mainstream Hindu culture and cuisine significantly.

Besides the Muslims and Hindus, Jewish settlers also came to Kerala in 7 a.d., bringing with them the notion of kosher meat. The Christians, on the other hand, only settled here during the fourth century a.d. Zoroastrians came and settled in large numbers when they were hounded out of Persia as far back as 850 a.d. Parsis, as they are now known, settled largely in Gujarat.

Besides the British, other Europeans who established themselves in India were the Portuguese, who remained largely in Goa, north of Kerala, from the 16th century until after Indian independence from the British.

The Making of a Cuisine

The Vedas, ancient historical and religious texts dating from 1700–1500 b.c., set the framework for what is broadly known as Hindu culture. They record the civilization of the Aryans or nomadic tribes from the upper Urals, who traveled as far east as India on one side and as far west as Ireland on the other. Most Hindu food practices were influenced by the Aryans, beginning in the north and the northwest of India and gradually spreading all over the country.

The Aryans did not treat food simply as a means to physical sustenance but saw it as part of a cosmic circle, their dictum being that "food that man eats and his universe must be in harmony." Food, they believed, can be grouped into three types: those which needed expulsion,

New flavors, rich relishes, meats with cream and butter sauces, dates, nuts and delectable sweets were the hallmarks of Mughal cuisine, which is widely known and famed for its exotic non-vegetarian food.

Finally, the period of British colonial rule in India—the Raj—has left an indelible mark on both the food and eating practices of this country. In middle-class homes, the dining table replaced the kitchen floor and porcelain, the banana leaf. Cutlery was introduced.

The blending of eastern spices into "western" food began at this time, and some of these "crossings" have endured to this day: kedgeree (a rice and lentil mixture, known as *kichidee* in India), mulligatawny soup (literally, pepper water or *mooloogoo thani*), and the ubiquitous curry. Curry is a catch-all term used initially by the Raj to refer to any sauced dish of spicy meat, fish or vegetables and is probably a corruption of the Tamil word for sauce "*kari.*"

The Food of the People

In temperate Kashmir, tucked into the Himalayas, the food is characterized by a subtle blend of fragrant spices, richness and pungency. Some of the most popular dishes include lamb marinated in yogurt; mutton simmered in milk and scented with nutmeg; and rich meat curries.

In the Ganges, plain rice is usually accompanied by vegetables sautéed with spices, *dal*, unleavened bread, plain yogurt and a sweet. Chutneys and pickles are commonplace.

Bengali cuisine is considered elaborate and refined: Bengal being the only place in India where food is served in individual courses, the sequence of which is based on ancient beliefs relating to the aiding of the digestive process. Fish plays a large part in this cuisine, as do rice, *dal* and chutney.

In the south, where rice is the staple, it appears in many guises: steamed, puffed, made into paper-thin crêpes known as *dosay* (page 49) or steamed to form *idli*, which are served with a variety of chutneys, vegetables and light *dal* broths known as *sambar*.

In Karnataka, the central southern state, the basic meal consists of vegetables which accompany *dosay*, *idli* or steamed rice. Popular southern vegetables include eggplants and bitter gourd, and lots of relishes are served to punctuate a meal.

Goans are known for their use of vinegar and kokum fruit (other Indians add sourness with tamarind, lime juice or dried mango powder), and, of course, for their love of fiery chilies. Classic examples of Goan dishes include the pork curry Vindaloo, which gets its name from the Portuguese words for vinegar and garlic, and Sorpotel, a sour hot curry of pork, liver and pig's blood.

We can't leave the food of the people without making mention of the food of the Raj. The culinary fusion has yielded piquant dishes that pay homage to their roots; the spiced chutneys and curries of today have their humble beginnings in the Indian kitchen.

The Indian Table and Kitchen

At the heart of Indian cuisine is spice—carefully overlaid, one on the other, into dishes, with care. The use of spices in India was recorded in Sanskrit texts three thousand years ago.

Walk into an Indian home at meal time or into a good Indian restaurant and you will be engulfed by a wave of heavenly aromas. So great was the importance of spices for seasoning, as preservatives and as medicine that the search for their source pushed the Europeans into the Age of Exploration in the 15th century.

The Indian kitchen's range of spices is hard to beat in terms of

Offerings of coconut, bananas, flowers and incense on display at a market stall in a typical southern Indian village.

variety, color and aroma—from the sweetness of cumin and coriander to the pungency of *asafoetida* and turmeric. In a culinary sense, "spices" as used in India embraces dried seeds, berries, bark, rhizomes, flowers, leaves and chilies. These may be used dried or fresh, come in the form of pods or seeds, be roasted, ground or put into hot oil to expel their flavors. Certain spices are used whole, others always ground; some are used only with meat, since they would overpower more delicate seafood and vegetable dishes. Some, such as cardamom, saffron and cinnamon, are also used for desserts.

Any combination of spices is referred to as a *masala*. The most widely used is *garam masala*, a fragrant combination of cinnamon, cloves, black pepper and cardamom, with the optional addition of nutmeg, mace and saffron in northern regions. The spices are then combined with fresh rhizomes and leaves such as ginger, garlic, turmeric, garlic, mint and chilies.

The medicinal properties of spices are always taken into account when food is prepared, as well as the interaction of each spice with the natural properties of a particular vegetable or *dal*.

The Indian kitchen is a place of surprising simplicity: it has a stove, often heated by charcoal, and a few implements such as the *kadai* (a wok-like utensil), straight-sided pots, and pans.

The house guest is looked on as a visiting god in India, and treated with attendant respect. By and large, home food is influenced by such factors as climate, nutritional balance and religion, and is usually simple fare, where rice, bread and *dal* constitute the core of the meal. Each region and household then adds its distinctive touch with the vegetables, meat and fish, and the palate teasers: the pickles, *pappadums*, *raita* or chutneys.

All Indian food is served with either rice or bread, or both. In the cooler north, breads are commonplace; in the south, rice is the sta-

The richness of Mughal cuisine—the food of emperors—has seen its popularity spread throughout India and the rest of the world.

ple. Food is generally served on a banana leaf or a stainless steel *thali*. Washing the hands before meals is an important ritual, since Indians generally use their fingers to eat and the meal is eaten squatting down, usually on the kitchen floor. A small straw mat is placed for sitting and the *thali* or banana leaf is laid in front of the mat, either on the floor or on a low stool.

Families eat together, except for the mother or wife who serves the meal. In middle-class homes, this role is taken over by the household help. The family usually sits in a straight line and the women of the household serve and refill the *thali* repeatedly.

The *thali* contains all the courses of the meal, but there is usually an order in which the food is eaten. The first mouthfuls of rice are eaten with ghee or chutney and spicy additives. *Dal* is served with a variety of dry-cooked vegetables seasoned with different spices and garnishes. Pappadums and relishes are replenished, as are the *dal* and rice. The best portions of fish and meat are always offered to the guest. *Roti* or unleavened bread, *puri* and *paratha* are common in the north and eaten with *dal* and vegetables.

The sweet, which is milk-based, completes the meal, although in the south it is followed by rice with curds or buttermilk which are believed to soothe the stomach after a spicy meal.

A very Indian end to a meal is the betel leaf and its seasonings or *paan*. The leaf is chewed along with a slice of areca nut, a dab of slaked lime and a smear of *katha* paste (another wood extract). The betel quid can mean many things: hospitality, moral and legal commitment, a digestive and a fitting end to the remarkable hospitality displayed during a meal.

Many of the curries in this chapter store very well—indeed many people believe that curries taste better the day after they are made, since the flavors are allowed to mature. You may wish to double the quantities of whatever you're making and freeze a batch in an airtight container—very convenient for quick meals and if unexpected guests turn up!

If properly stored, many of the condiments will keep for up to a month in the refrigerator. Just make sure you use a clean, dry spoon when taking any from the jar and seal the top with a thin film of vegetable oil before refrigerating. It is worthwhile roasting and grinding spices for the *garam masala* as you need it, however. Ground spices lose their aroma very quickly.

SUGGESTED MENUS

A family meal

What's so good about this menu, apart from how delicious everything is, is that most of it can be cooked ahead and served at room temperature if you like.
- Samosa (page 48) and some Pakora (page 48);
- Spiced Chickpeas (page 51) and Chicken Tikka (page 53) with a fresh green salad and a selection of breads (or just one type);
- fresh fruit with Kulfi (page 57).

A dinner party

For a dinner party that mixes the familiar with the more exotic, serve the following foods:
- Plantain and Potato Balls (page 49);
- Stuffed and Skewered Homemade Cheese (page 51) and skewered pieces of Tandoori Chicken (page 52); with these you should serve a selection of raitas and chutneys (page 58) (you may wish to buy the latter if you do not want to make your own);
- Gulab Jamun (page 57) that have been gently dusted with edible gold or silver foil.

A regional menu

For a gastronomic tour around the country, offer curries from the different regions in India:
- Lemon Rice (page 50) and some bread (the Puris [page 48] are particularly elegant);
- Spiced Potatoes in Yogurt (page 51), Mild Chicken Curry (page 52), some Goan Pork Curry (page 55), and Creamy Shrimp Curry (page 54);
- Cream Cheese Balls in Syrup (page 57).

A melting pot menu

An all-Asian menu:
- from Indonesia, Karedok, the Indonesian raw vegetable salad (page 68), accompanied by Crisp Peanut Wafers (page 67);
- Indian Crab Curry (page 54) served with lots of plain rice or, for a change, *dosay* (page 49);
- Thai Rice Balls in Coconut Milk (page 138).

THE ESSENTIAL FLAVORS OF INDIAN COOKING

Spices are the backbone of Indian cooking, so buy the freshest you can to roast and grind—**cardamom**, **cumin**, **nutmeg**, **cinnamon**, **fennel seeds** and **fenugreek**—as you need. **Chilies**, dried and fresh, are pounded and sliced into cooking pastes with **garlic**, **onions** and **ginger**. **Lentils** and **beans**, **breads** and **basmati rice** are eaten with curries. **Saffron** and **turmeric** are used to add flavor and color to dishes. **Yogurt** is not only used in both sweet and savory dishes but is also the main ingredient in *lassi*, a popular drink.

Here are the recipes for all those tasty morsels you see at the local Indian corner store or restaurant. The fried items such as *samosas* and *pakoras* are ideal for parties, and the breads are ideal for mopping up all those curry juices. And don't think that all fried foods are fatty and greasy—as long as you keep the oil hot and drain the items well, they are truly delicious and will not leave you feeling heavy.

Chapati
Unleavened Bread

For the best results, *chapati* should be properly kneaded. A plastic blade in a food processor set on slow is an acceptable alternative to 10–15 minutes of hand-kneading.

- 2 cups very fine wholewheat flour (*atta*) or fine white flour
- 1/2 cup warm water
- 2 teaspoons softened *ghee* or butter

Mix the flour and water in a bowl to make a dough that is pliable yet not too sticky. Add *ghee* or butter and turn the mixture out onto a floured board or put in a food processor. Knead by hand for 10–15 minutes or process at low speed for 5 minutes. Roll into a ball, cover with a damp cloth and set aside for at least 1 hour.

Knead the dough again for 3–4 minutes, then break into pieces the size of a golf ball. Flatten into a circle with your hands, then roll out into circles about 8 inches in diameter. Heat a heavy griddle or frying pan until very hot. Put on a *chapati* and cook until brown spots appear underneath. Turn over and cook the other side, pressing on the top of the *chapati* with a clean cloth to help make air bubbles form and keep the *chapati* light. As each *chapati* is cooked, wrap in a clean cloth to keep warm. Serve with curries, *dal* or vegetables.

Puri
Deep-Fried Bread

Puri are a delicious alternative to *chapati* and use exactly the same dough. To ensure they puff up when cooking, keep flicking the oil over the top while the *puri* are frying.

- 1 quantity *chapati* dough
- Oil for deep-frying

Roll out the dough as for *chapati*, then roll out into 8-inch circles and cover with a cloth.

Heat plenty of oil in a wok until very hot. Put in a *puri* and immediately start flicking hot oil over the top of it with a spatula so that it will swell up like a ball. This should take only a few seconds. Flip the *puri* over and cook on the other side until golden brown. Serve immediately with curries, *dal* or vegetables.

Samosa
Vegetable-Stuffed Pastries

- 7 tablespoons *ghee* or butter (firm to touch)
- 2 cups white flour
- 1/2 teaspoon carom seeds (*ajwain*)
- 1/2 teaspoon salt
- Oil for deep-frying

Filling
- 3 tablespoons oil
- 1/2 teaspoon cumin seeds
- 1 large potato, boiled in salted water and very finely diced
- 1/3 cup green peas, cooked
- 1/2 teaspoon salt
- 1 teaspoon ground coriander
- 1/2 teaspoon ground turmeric
- 1/2–1 teaspoon cayenne
- 1 green chili, seeded and finely chopped
- 1 teaspoon dried mango powder

Rub *ghee* or butter into the flour until the mixture is crumbly. Mix in the carom seeds and salt, then add sufficient water to make a firm but pliable dough. Leave for 30 minutes, covered with a damp cloth.

To make the filling, heat oil in a pan and sauté the cumin seeds until they crackle. Add remaining ingredients and sauté for 1 minute. Cool.

Roll out the pastry thinly, then cut into circles 3 inches in diameter. Cut each circle in half. Put a spoonful of filling on one semicircle of pastry and fold in the sides, pressing the edges firmly to seal. Repeat until all the filling is used up.

Heat oil and deep-fry the *samosas* until golden brown. Drain and serve with a chutney or chili sauce.

Pakora
Batter-Coated Vegetables

- 1 potato, peeled
- 1 small eggplant
- 1 large onion
- 2 cups Bengal gram flour (*besan*) or chickpea flour
- 1 teaspoon salt
- 1 teaspoon cayenne
- 1/2 teaspoon baking soda
- Oil for deep-frying

Cut the potato in half lengthwise, then into 1/4-inch-thick slices.

Do not peel the eggplant but cut into slices the same size as the potato.

Peel the onion and slice to the same thickness. Set the vegetables aside.

Combine flour, salt, cayenne and baking soda, mixing well. Add enough cold water to make a very thick batter of coating consistency.

Heat oil and dip the vegetables, one at a time, into the batter, coating thoroughly. Deep-fry until half-cooked (about 2–3 minutes), then drain and set aside.

Just before the *pakoras* are needed, reheat the oil and deep-fry until golden brown and cooked through. Serve hot.

Deep-Fried Bread.

Plantain and Potato Balls.

Naan
Tandoor-Baked Bread

This bread gets its characteristic teardrop shape from the way the dough droops as it cooks on the wall of a tandoor.

- 4 cups white flour
- 1/2 teaspoon baking powder
- 1 teaspoon salt
- 1/2 cup milk
- 1 tablespoon sugar
- 1 egg
- 4 tablespoons oil
- 1 teaspoon nigella seeds

Sift the flour, baking powder and salt together into a bowl and make a well in the middle.

Mix the milk, sugar, egg and 2 tablespoons of the oil in a bowl. Pour this into the center of the flour and knead, adding more water if necessary to form a soft dough. Add the remaining oil, knead again, then cover with a damp cloth and allow the dough to stand for 15 minutes.

Knead the dough again, cover and leave for 2–3 hours. About half an hour before the *naan* are required, turn on the oven to the maximum heat.

Divide the dough into 8 balls and allow to rest for 3–5 minutes.

Sprinkle a baking sheet with the nigella seeds and put it in the oven to heat while the dough is resting.

Shape each ball of dough with the palms to make an oval shape. Bake the *naan* until puffed up and golden brown. Serve hot.

Kele Ka Tikka
Plantain and Potato Balls

If plantains are not available, use 3 1/3 cups potatoes.

- 12 ounces plantains, steamed until soft
- 1 1/2 cups mashed potatoes
- 1 teaspoon *Chaat Masala* (page 58)
- 1 teaspoon coriander seeds, toasted and ground
- 1/4 teaspoon *Garam Masala* (page 58)
- 1/2 teaspoon salt
- 3/4 inch ginger, finely chopped
- 1 heaped tablespoon chopped cilantro
- 2 green chilies, seeded and finely chopped
- 1 heaped tablespoon cornstarch
- 4 ounces fine wheat vermicelli, broken into small pieces
- Oil for deep-frying

Grate the steamed plantains, then combine with the potato and all other ingredients, except vermicelli and oil. Mix well, then shape into balls and roll in the vermicelli, pressing to make sure the vermicelli adheres.

Heat oil and deep-fry the balls until golden brown. Drain and serve with Mint and Cilantro Chutney (page 58).

Dosay
Southern Indian Rice-Flour Pancakes

A southern Indian breakfast favorite, these tangy pancakes are often served with fresh coconut chutney and tomato chutney, with *dal* as a dip. Alternatively, they can be stuffed with spiced potato to make Masala Dosay.

- 3 cups long-grain rice
- 1 cup husked blackgram *dal* (*urad dal*)
- 1 teaspoon salt
- 1 onion, cut in half
- 3 tablespoons oil

Put the rice and *dal* into separate bowls, cover each with water and soak overnight.

Grind the rice and *dal* separately in a food processor, adding a little water if necessary to obtain a smooth consistency. Mix the ground rice and *dal* together and leave at room temperature for up to 24 hours to ferment. The dough can now be refrigerated for up to 24 hours until required.

Stir the dough, adding salt and sufficient water to achieve the consistency of a very thick cream.

Heat a nonstick pan or heavy griddle and rub with half an onion. Grease lightly with a little of the oil and pour in a ladle (about 1/4 cup) of the batter, smearing it quickly with the back of the ladle to form a thin pancake about 5–6 inches in diameter. Cook for about 2–3 minutes until the bottom is golden and the top is starting to set. Turn over and cook on the other side. If you like, stuff the *dosay* with hot spiced potato or, for a non-vegetarian treat, with boneless Chicken Masala.

Vecchu Paratha
Flaky Fried Bread

These wonderfully light breads are normally flung out in circles, like a fisherman throwing his net (*vecchu*) until paper thin. They can be hand-pulled like strudel for a similar result.

- 4 cups white flour, sifted
- 3 eggs, lightly beaten
- 1 cup water
- 1 teaspoon salt
- 3/4 cup oil

Make a very soft dough with flour, eggs, salt and water, kneading well. Divide into 12 balls, cover with a damp cloth and leave to stand for 30 minutes. Spread out each ball on a well-oiled table top, pulling the edge gently with the hands to stretch it out as wide and as thin as possible, as for a strudel. Dust the surface with flour and fold over and over to make a fan. Roll up the pleated dough to make a curled ball and leave to rest for 15 minutes. Use your hands to pat the ball into circles about 6 inches in diameter, or use a rolling pin.

Oil a griddle or heavy frying pan and cook the bread, turning so that it is golden brown on each side. Serve hot with *dal* or curries.

Flaky Fried Bread.

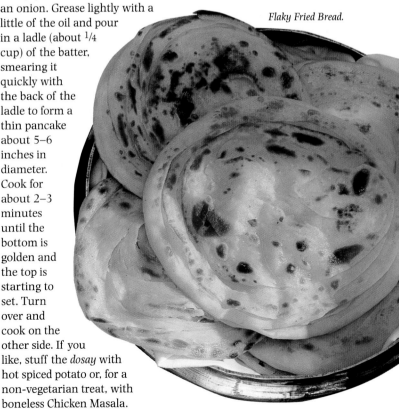

Lemon Rice.

Don't forget the rice and breads when you make the recipes here, or you'll miss out on the wonderful flavors of the juices. These dishes are a testament to Indian ingenuity with blending spices: a little more of this and a little less of that, and you'll end up with something else. Enjoy!

Dal Maharani
Bean and Lentil Stew

- 1/2 cup whole blackgram dal (*urad dal*), skins on
- 2 tablespoons dried pinto or kidney beans
- 1 inch ginger, sliced
- 1 teaspoon salt
- 1 tablespoon *ghee* or butter
- 1 teaspoon cumin seeds
- 1–2 green chilies, slit lengthwise
- 2 medium-sized tomatoes, chopped
- 2 teaspoons *Garam Masala* (page 58)
- 1/2 cup cream

Rinse and soak *dal* and beans overnight. Combine *dal* and beans in a pan with ginger, salt and water to cover. Bring to a boil, cover the pan and simmer until just soft.

Heat the *ghee* or butter, add cumin and chilies and sauté until the cumin crackles.

Add to the cooked *dal* with the tomatoes and half the *garam masala*, and simmer until the tomatoes soften. Reserve 1 tablespoon of the cream for garnish and add the rest to the pan. Stir and heat through. Garnish the soup with the reserved cream and the remaining *garam masala*. Serve with any of the Indian breads.

Chitrannam
Lemon Rice

Try serving this on a platter with some of the soupier dishes in this section, such as Creamy Shrimp Curry (page 54).

- 1 1/2 cups long-grain rice, washed and drained
- 1 tablespoon oil
- 1 teaspoon black mustard seeds
- A pinch of asafoetida powder
- 1 sprig curry leaves
- 1/2 teaspoon finely chopped ginger
- 1/2 green chili, finely chopped
- 2–3 dried chilies, broken into 1-inch pieces
- 1 tablespoon split raw cashews, lightly toasted
- 1 teaspoon husked blackgram dal (*urad dal*)
- 1 teaspoon split Bengal gram (*channa dal*), lightly toasted
- 1/2 teaspoon turmeric powder
- 2 1/2 tablespoons lemon juice
- 1 teaspoon salt
- 1 tablespoon water
- Cilantro leaf to garnish

Boil the rice in plenty of water until the grains are just tender. Drain thoroughly and set aside.

Heat oil in a pan and add the mustard seeds. When they begin to pop, add *asafoetida*, curry leaves, ginger, green chili, dried chilies, cashews, blackgram *dal*, Bengal gram and turmeric powder. Sauté for a few seconds, then add lemon juice, salt and water. Simmer for 2–3 minutes, then toss in the rice and heat through.

Garnish with cilantro leaves.

Undiya
Spiced Mixed Vegetables

This Gujarati dish is served as part of a main meal. If yam or plantains are unavailable, increase the amounts of potato, eggplant and sweet potato.

- 1/3 cup red *dal* (*masoor dal*), soaked for 4 hours in warm water
- 2 tablespoons oil
- 1 teaspoon cumin seeds
- 1/2 teaspoon carom seeds (*ajwain*)
- A pinch of *asafoetida* powder
- 1/3 cup coarsely chopped tomatoes
- 1/3 cup peeled, diced potatoes
- 1/3 cup diced eggplant
- 1/3 cup peeled and diced sweet potatoes
- 1/3 cup peeled and diced purple or white yam, (optional)
- 1/3 cup peeled and diced plantain (optional)
- 2 tablespoons freshly grated or moistened dried coconut

Spiced Mixed Vegetables.

Masala

- 2 tablespoons coriander seeds
- 1 teaspoon cumin seeds
- 1/2 teaspoon carom seeds (*ajwain*)
- 2 tablespoons raw peanuts
- 3–4 green chilies, chopped
- 2 tablespoons chopped cilantro leaves
- 1 teaspoon crushed garlic
- 1 teaspoon crushed ginger
- 1 tablespoon freshly grated coconut or moistened dried coconut
- 1 tablespoon chopped palm sugar
- 1 teaspoon salt
- 2/3 cup water

Drain the soaked *dal*.

To make the *masala*, toast the coriander, cumin, carom seeds and peanuts together until the spices crackle, then grind to a paste with water. Combine with all other *masala* ingredients and blend or process until fine.

Heat oil in a pan and sauté the cumin, carom and *asafoetida* until the spices start to crackle. Add the ground *masala* and cook for about 5 minutes. Put in the tomatoes and continue cooking until they soften, then add the drained *dal* and prepared vegetables. Cover the pan and cook gently until the vegetables are tender. Sprinkle with coconut and serve.

Pindi Channa
Spiced Chickpeas

- 1 cup chickpeas
- 1 tea bag or 1 tablespoon black tea leaves tied in cheesecloth
- 6 cups water
- 2 1/2 inches ginger, 3/4 inch of it shredded finely for garnish
- 2–3 tablespoons oil
- 2 onions, chopped
- 2 teaspoons finely crushed garlic
- 2 green chilies, sliced
- 3 medium-sized tomatoes, chopped
- 2 teaspoons ground coriander
- 1 1/2 teaspoons ground cumin
- 1/2 teaspoon ground turmeric
- 1 teaspoon cayenne
- 1 teaspoon salt
- 2 teaspoons chopped cilantro leaves
- 1/2 teaspoon *Garam Masala* (page 58)

Soak chickpeas for 1 hour, drain and discard liquid. Put chickpeas, tea bag and water into a pan and simmer until chickpeas are tender. Drain, reserving 1 cup of the cooking liquid.

Finely chop the remaining ginger. Heat oil and sauté onions until golden, then add garlic, chopped ginger and chilies. Sauté for 5 minutes.

Add tomatoes, cilantro, cumin, turmeric and cayenne and sauté over low heat until the oil separates.

Add the chickpeas, the reserved cooking liquid, salt and half the cilantro leaves. Simmer, uncovered, until the liquid has been absorbed. Add a pinch of *garam masala* and serve the chickpeas sprinkled with the remaining *garam masala*, cilantro leaves and ginger shreds.

Dum Aloo
Spiced Potatoes in Yogurt

The melon seeds or cashews add a nutty finish to foods, and the thick, clinging sauce makes this an ideal dish to serve with breads. Try these spicy potatoes in place of roast potatoes with your next roast dinner for an exotic accent.

- 1 pound baby new potatoes
- 3 tablespoons oil
- 2 onions, sliced and fried until brown
- 1 cup plain yogurt
- 4 black cardamom pods
- 1 teaspoon fennel seeds
- 2-inch stick cinnamon
- 1 1/2 inches ginger, finely chopped
- 4 cloves garlic, finely chopped
- 1 1/2 teaspoons ground coriander
- 1 teaspoon ground cumin
- 1 teaspoon ground turmeric
- 1/2 teaspoon chili powder
- 2 tablespoons melon seeds or cashews, soaked and ground to a paste with water
- 1 cup water
- 1 teaspoon salt

Parboil the potatoes, peel and sauté in oil until golden. Drain and set aside, leaving oil in the pan.

Purée the onions and half the yogurt in a blender.

Toast the cardamom, fennel and cinnamon in a dry pan until the spices start to smell fragrant, then blend or grind to a powder. Set aside.

Skewered Home-made Cheese.

Sauté the ginger and garlic in the oil left from frying the potatoes, then add coriander, cumin, turmeric and cayenne and stir for 1 minute. Whisk the remaining yogurt and add together with the nut paste.

Heat through, then put in the potatoes, water and salt and simmer, uncovered, until the potatoes are tender. Stir in the reserved ground spices and serve.

Paneer Shashlik
Skewered Homemade Cheese

Paneer is a delicious soft cheese often used in Indian vegetarian dishes.

- 1 pound *Paneer* (page 59), cut into 1/2-inch-thick slices
- 2 green or red bell peppers
- 2 onions
- 2 tomatoes
- 1 cup pineapple wedges
- 8 button mushrooms
- Oil

Marinade

- 3 tablespoons plain yogurt
- 1 tablespoon oil
- 1 teaspoon tomato paste
- 1 teaspoon salt
- 1 teaspoon cayenne
- 1/2 teaspoon ground coriander
- 1/2 teaspoon ground cumin

Cut the *paneer*, peppers, onions and tomatoes into 1 1/4-inch-squares and set aside.

Combine all marinade ingredients and mix with the *paneer*, vegetables, pineapple and mushrooms. Leave for 1 hour, then thread onto skewers.

Cook in a tandoor, under a broiler or over a hot grill until done, brushing with oil half way through cooking.

HELPFUL HINT

Other fruits and vegetables can be used—try making these with zucchini, baby eggplant and cubed mango—not authentic, but delicious all the same!

Bhindi Bharwan
Stuffed Okra

You can try making this dish with zucchini—scrape out a little of the central core first before stuffing. Again, another dish that works as well in a Western-style meal.

1 pound okra, washed and dried
3 tablespoons oil
1 teaspoon cumin seeds
1 medium-sized onion, chopped
2 green chilies, seeded and chopped
3/4 inch ginger, finely chopped
A pinch of *asafoetida* powder
1 tomato, chopped

Stuffing
3 teaspoons ground coriander
2 teaspoons ground turmeric
2 teaspoons ground fennel
2 teaspoons dried mango powder
1 teaspoon cayenne
1/2 teaspoon salt

Cut the stalk off each okra and make a lengthwise slit.

Combine stuffing ingredients and mix well. Stuff each okra with the mixture.

Sauté cumin with a little oil until it starts to crackle. Add onion, chilies and ginger and sauté until the onion turns transparent, then put in the *asafoetida* and cook for a few seconds. Add tomato and cook until it turns pulpy.

Add the okra and cook for 5 minutes until tender and well coated with the sauce. Serve with rice.

Murgh Korma
Mild Chicken Curry

A *korma* is a Mughal creation, rich in fragrant spices and nuts. Chicken *korma* is probably the best-known dish prepared in this style, although vegetable, mutton and lamb are frequently used.

1 1/2 pounds boneless chicken
2 onions, finely chopped
4–6 cloves garlic, chopped
1 1/2 inches ginger, chopped
4 tablespoons *ghee* or butter
4 green cardamom pods, bruised
1 black cardamom pod, bruised
1 1/2 inches cinnamon stick
2 cloves
2 bay leaves
1/2 teaspoon ground cumin
1/2 teaspoon ground coriander
1 cup Whipped Yogurt (page 59)
1/4 teaspoon freshly grated nutmeg
1 1/2 teaspoons ground white pepper
2 tablespoons cream
1 teaspoon salt
1 teaspoon *Garam Masala* (page 58)
1 teaspoon chopped cilantro leaves to garnish

Nut paste
3 tablespoons white poppy seeds, soaked and simmered 30 minutes
3 tablespoons unsalted melon seeds, soaked
2 tablespoons *chironji* nuts or blanched almonds
3 tablespoons raw cashews, soaked

Cut the chicken into bite-sized pieces and set aside. Sauté onions, garlic and ginger until the onions are transparent and very slightly browned. Blend together the onions, garlic and ginger with 1/4 cup water to obtain a paste and set aside.

Blend the nut paste ingredients with just enough water to make a paste and set aside.

Heat the *ghee* and sauté both types of cardamom, cinnamon, cloves and bay leaves for a couple of minutes, then add the cumin, coriander and blended onion paste.

Sauté over very low heat, stirring constantly, until the oil separates. Add the yogurt and continue cooking for 15 minutes, stirring from time to time. Add the nutmeg, pepper and chicken and simmer over low heat, uncovered, for 10–15 minutes, until the chicken is tender. Add the nut paste and simmer gently for 3–5 minutes.

Add 1 tablespoon of the cream, salt and half of the *garam masala*, stirring well. Remove from the heat and garnish with the remaining cream, *garam masala* and cilantro. Serve with steamed rice.

Murgh Tandoori
Tandoori Chicken

Originally from the northwest of India, food baked in a tandoor or clay oven heated with charcoal is very popular in restaurants all over the country. Marinated chicken cooked in a tandoor achieves an unrivaled succulence and flavor. The result is also very good with gas or electric ovens. The chicken can be marinated as much as 24 hours in advance. An alternative method of cooking is to grill the chickens over hot charcoal.

Two 1 1/2-pound spring chickens
1 tablespoon chili paste
2 teaspoons lemon juice
1 teaspoon salt
1 teaspoon *Chaat Masala* (page 58)
Melted butter

Marinade
2 cups Hung Yogurt (page 59)
1 1/2 tablespoons chili paste
1 tablespoon crushed garlic
1 tablespoon crushed ginger
1 tablespoon oil
2 teaspoons lemon juice
1 teaspoon *Garam Masala* (page 58)
Few drops red and yellow food coloring (or pinch of turmeric)

Make deep gashes on the breast, thighs and drumsticks of each chicken, both inside and outside, to allow the marinade to penetrate. Combine the chili paste, lemon juice and salt and rub all over the chickens.

Refrigerate for 30 minutes. To make the marinade, combine the yogurt with all other ingredients. Rub this well into the chickens, saving some marinade to rub inside the chest cavity. Marinate for 3–4 hours.

Heat an oven to maximum heat. Put the chickens on a wire rack in a baking dish and baste with a little melted butter. Cook for about 15 minutes, until the chickens are brownish-black and cooked. Sprinkle with *chaat masala* and serve with Mint and Cilantro Chutney (page 58), onion rings and lemon wedges.

Stuffed Okra (left) and Mild Chicken Curry (right).

Murgh Tikka
Chicken Tikka

1 1/2 cups Hung Yogurt (page 59)
1 1/2 teaspoons crushed garlic
1 teaspoons crushed ginger
2 teaspoons chili paste
1 1/2 tablespoons oil
2 teaspoons lemon juice
1 teaspoon salt
1 teaspoon *Garam Masala* (page 58)
Few drops of red and yellow food coloring
1 1/4 pounds boneless chicken thighs, cut into 1 1/4-inch cubes

Combine all the marinade ingredients and mix in the chicken. Leave in the fridge to marinate for 2–3 hours.

Thread the chicken onto skewers and brush with additional oil.

Cook over charcoal or under a very hot broiler for 6–8 minutes, turning once, until the chicken pieces are cooked and golden brown. Serve with Mint and Cilantro Chutney (page 58), onion rings, lemon wedges and Indian bread, such as *Naan* (page 49).

Keema Kofta
Spicy Meatballs

A specialty of Uttar Pradesh region, these meatballs are bathed in a sauce enriched with pounded cashews and almonds. In India, the meat would be bought in one piece, mixed well with the seasonings and then taken to a shop to be put through a mincer. A food processor will also do the job.

1 pound lean lamb, cubed
3 green chilies, sliced
1 tablespoon chopped cilantro leaves
1/2 inch ginger, finely chopped
1/4 teaspoon ground cloves
1/4 teaspoon ground mace
A pinch of *Garam Masala* (page 58)
1/2 teaspoon salt
1 tablespoon *ghee* or butter

Sauce
2 tablespoons raw cashews
2 tablespoons blanched almonds
1 heaped tablespoon *ghee* or butter

3 onions, finely chopped
3/4 teaspoon crushed garlic
3/4 teaspoon crushed ginger
1/4 teaspoon ground turmeric
1/2 teaspoon cayenne
3 tomatoes, finely chopped
1/4 cup Whipped Yogurt (page 59)
1 tablespoon chopped mint leaves
1 teaspoon salt
A pinch of *Garam Masala* (page 58)

Spicy Meatballs.

Mix lamb with the chilies, cilantro, ginger, spices and salt. Blend seasoned meat in a food processor until very finely ground. Shape into balls about 3/4 inch in diameter and sauté in ghee or butter until browned. Keep aside.

To make the sauce, soak the cashews and almonds in hot water to cover for about 10 minutes, then pound or process to make a paste.

Heat the ghee and sauté the onions until golden. Add the garlic, ginger, turmeric and cayenne and sauté until the oil separates.

Add the tomatoes and cook until they become pulpy. Add the yogurt and nut paste and simmer over low heat until the oil separates.

Add the meatballs, cover the pan and simmer for 5–7 minutes, stirring gently from time to time. Add half the chopped mint and salt to taste, then garnish with the remaining mint and *garam masala*.

HELPFUL HINT

Yogurt is frequently hung to drain off some of the whey and obtain thicker curds. Although this is done using cheesecloth or muslin fabric in India, cooks elsewhere may find an easier method is to put the yogurt in a paper-lined coffee filter and set the cone-shaped device over a jar. The whey will drip through, leaving the curds in the filter. This is **hung yogurt**, which is preferred for cooking, as it does not change its texture.

Chicken Tikka.

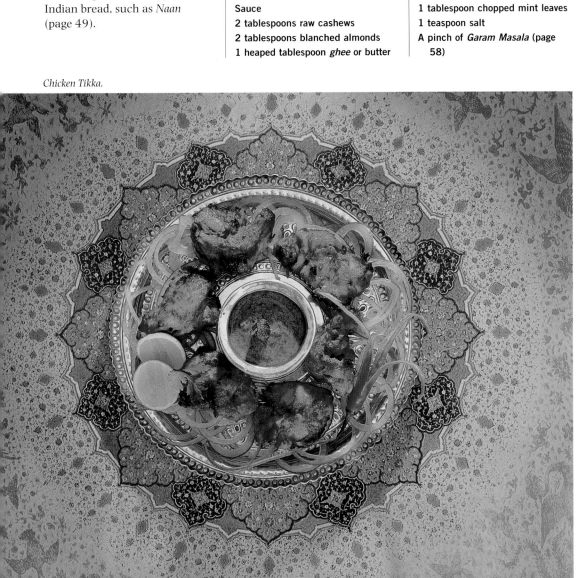

Creamy Shrimp Curry.

Chingdi Macher
Creamy Shrimp Curry

Thick coconut milk gives this succulent curry a creamy texture and flavor.

```
3/4 inch ginger
6 cloves garlic
1/2 teaspoon cumin seeds
3 tablespoons mustard oil
1 bay leaf
4 cloves
2 inches cinnamon stick
4 green cardamom pods, bruised
1 large onion, chopped
4 green chilies, seeded and chopped
Salt to taste
1/2 cup water
1 pound shrimp, peeled and
   deveined
1 cup thick coconut milk
1 teaspoon sugar
Chopped cilantro leaf to garnish
```

Pound the ginger, garlic and cumin together.

Heat oil and sauté the bay leaf, cloves, cinnamon and cardamom until fragrant. Add onion and sauté gently for 5 minutes.

Add green chili and ginger-garlic-cumin paste, and sauté for 2 minutes, then add salt and water. Simmer, uncovered, for 5 minutes, then put in the shrimp and simmer for 3 minutes. Add coconut milk and simmer gently, stirring occasionally, until the shrimp are tender. Add sugar, stir and serve garnished with cilantro leaves.

Nandu Kari
Crab Curry

This dish comes from Mangalore, a city on the southwest coast which is an area renowned for its prolific use of fish and coconuts.

```
Four 8–10 ounce live crabs
2 tablespoons oil
1 teaspoon black mustard seeds
3 sprigs curry leaves
2 bay leaves
3 green chilies, halved lengthwise
A pinch of asafoetida powder
3 onions, chopped
1/4 teaspoon ground turmeric
1 teaspoon cayenne
2 tomatoes, chopped
1 cup coconut milk
Salt to taste
1/4 cup freshly grated or moistened
   dried coconut
```

Plunge crabs in a large pan of boiling water for 2–3 minutes. Drain and chop into large pieces. Discard the spongy grey matter. Crack the shell to allow the flavorings to penetrate.

Heat oil in a wok and fry mustard seeds until they start popping. Add the curry and bay leaves and green chilies and sauté gently for 1 minute, before adding the *asafoetida*.

Add onions and cook until the onion is transparent, then sprinkle in turmeric and cayenne. Sauté for 1 minute, then add the crab and tomatoes.

Cover the wok and cook, without adding water, stirring occasionally. When the crab is cooked (about 10 minutes), add the coconut milk and salt. Bring just to a boil, stirring constantly, then add the grated coconut and serve with plain steamed rice.

Aatirachi
Kerala Lamb Curry

A meat curry from the southern coastal state of Kerala in which shallots are sautéed with the spices.

```
Masala
2 onions, chopped
3/4 inch ginger, chopped
4–6 cloves garlic, chopped
1/4 inch fresh turmeric or 1/2 tea
```

Crab Curry.

```
spoon ground turmeric
2 ripe tomatoes, chopped
4–6 dried chilies, broken and
   soaked to soften
2 green chilies, chopped
6 green cardamom pods
1 teaspoon black mustard seeds
1/2 teaspoon black peppercorns
2 tablespoons oil
6 green cardamom pods, bruised
1/2 teaspoon black peppercorns
8–10 shallots, sliced
11/4 pounds boneless lamb,
   cut into 1-inch cubes
1/2 teaspoon salt
3/4 cup water
Fresh cilantro leaf
```

Process or blend the *masala* ingredients to make a paste. Keep aside.

Heat oil and fry the green cardamoms and peppercorns for 2 minutes. Add the shallots and sauté until they turn golden brown.

Put in the meat and sauté until brown, then add the *masala* and sauté on low heat for 10–15 minutes.

Add the salt and water, cover the pan and cook gently until the meat is tender. Garnish with cilantro leaf and serve with rice or Vecchu Paratha (page 49).

Goan Pork Curry.

1 pound pork, cut into 3/4 -inch
  cubes
8 cloves garlic
3 teaspoons cayenne
4 green chilies
1 teaspoon black peppercorns
1 inch fresh ginger, finely chopped
1 teaspoon cumin seeds
1 cup coconut vinegar
2 onions, chopped
1/2 teaspoon salt
1 teaspoon sugar
2 tablespoons *feni* or brandy

Cut about 1 tablespoon of fat
from the pork and set aside.

Grind or blend the garlic,
cayenne, chilies, pepper, ginger
and cumin seeds with the vinegar. Marinate the pork in the
vinegar and spice mixture for
1/2 hour.

Fry the tablespoon of fat
until the lard comes out of it,
then sauté the onions until
golden brown. Add the pork,
marinade and salt. Simmer until
the pork is tender and the gravy
is thick. Pour off excess oil.
Then add sugar and *feni* or
brandy. Stir through, and serve
with bread or rice.

HELPFUL HINT
If you cannot obtain coconut
vinegar, use rice vinegar, or
cider vinegar diluted with
1 part of water to 4 parts of
vinegar.

Macher Jhol
Bengali Fish Curry

1 1/2 pounds white fish cutlets
  or fillets
2 teaspoons salt
1 teaspoon ground turmeric
Mustard oil for pan-frying
1 large potato, cut into wedges
1 small eggplant, sliced
1 cup water
4 green chilies, seeded and slit
  lengthwise

Masala
1 teaspoon cumin seeds
1 teaspoon fennel seeds
1 teaspoon black mustard seeds
1/2 teaspoon fenugreek seeds
1/2 teaspoon nigella seeds

Wipe the fish dry, sprinkle both
sides with salt and turmeric
and set aside to marinate for
about 5 minutes.

Heat oil in a pan and sauté
the fish until golden brown on
both sides and cooked through.
Set aside.

Using the same oil, sauté the
masala spices until they start to
crackle. Add the potato and eggplant and sauté until well coated with the spices. Put in the
water and simmer until the vegetables are tender. Add fish and
chilies and heat through. Serve
with steamed rice.

Kesari Murgh
Saffron Chicken

2-pound chicken
1 teaspoon salt
3 tablespoons ghee or butter
3 inch cinnamon stick
4 green cardamom pods, bruised
3 whole cloves
2 large onions, peeled, boiled
  whole, then puréed
1 teaspoon crushed garlic
2 teaspoons crushed ginger
1 cup Whipped Yogurt (page 59)
A pinch of saffron, soaked in 1
  tablespoon warm milk
3 1/4 cup cashew nuts, soaked and
  ground to a paste
1/2 cup cream
Cilantro leaves

Debone the chicken and sprinkle with salt. Set aside.

Heat ghee and sauté cinnamon, cardamom and cloves
for a minute, then add
puréed onions, garlic and
ginger and continue sautéing
until they begin to take color.

Add the yogurt and saffron
and cook for 15 minutes, stirring occasionally. Add the
chicken, simmer for 5 minutes,
then add the cashew nut paste
and blend well. Simmer until
the chicken is tender. Add the
cream, heat through and serve
garnished with cilantro leaves.

Vindaloo
Goan Pork Curry

This dish was once carried on
sea voyages because it kept well.
No water is used in the preparation and the layer of fat on the
top helps seal and preserve the
meat. Vindaloos can be very
pungent, although this recipe
should cause just a gentle
sweat. Choose pork that has
some fat on it.

Saffron Chicken.

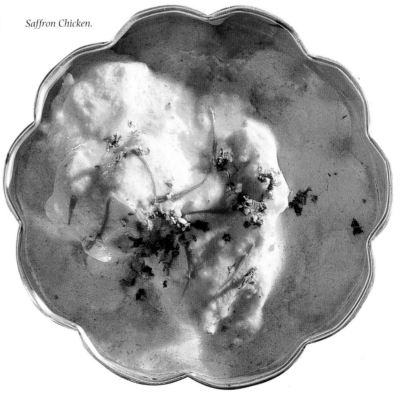

Once again, nothing quenches the heat of a fiery curry quicker than a plate of sliced fresh fruit. That is not to say that desserts are not eaten—they are, with much relish, especially among the Bengalis. Here are some of the more popular Indian treats.

Kheer
Rich Rice Pudding

A northern favorite, this rice pudding is very different from the Western version.

- 1/2 cup long-grain rice, washed and drained
- 3 cups milk
- 2–3 green cardamom pods, bruised
- 2 tablespoons blanched slivered almonds
- A pinch of saffron threads, soaked in a little hot milk
- 1 tablespoon skinned pistachio nuts, chopped
- 1 tablespoon raisins (optional)
- 2–3 tablespoons sugar

Sweet Yogurt with Saffron.

Put the rice, milk and cardamom into a pan, bring to a boil and simmer gently until the rice is soft and the grains are starting to break up.

Add the almonds, saffron, pistachios and raisins (if using) and simmer for 3–4 minutes. Add the sugar and stir until completely dissolved. Remove from heat and serve either warm or chilled.

Rich Rice Pudding.

Shrikand
Sweet Yogurt with Saffron

In India, this Gujarati favorite is always served with deep-fried bread (*puri*). As it is so rich and substantial, you may prefer it on its own. The saffron can be omitted and about 1/2 cup concentrated mango pulp added for a different flavor.

- 6 cups plain yogurt
- 1/4 cup superfine sugar
- 1 tablespoon skinned pistachio nuts, chopped
- 2 teaspoons *chironji* nuts, hazelnuts or almonds, chopped
- 1/4 teaspoon cardamom powder
- A pinch of saffron threads, soaked in a little hot milk

Put the yogurt into a large sieve or colander lined with wet cheesecloth and allow to drain for 6–8 hours, until it is relatively firm.

Sprinkle the drained yogurt with sugar, stirring to dissolve, then push through a fine sieve to obtain a silken smooth texture. Add half of the pistachios, the nuts, cardamom and saffron or mango pulp. Mix and chill.

Before serving garnish with the remaining pistachios.

HELPFUL HINT

If the Sweet Yogurt with Saffron is made a day in advance and refrigerated, the flavor of the saffron and cardamom will be much stronger.

Channa Dal Payasam
Southern Indian Dessert

Payasam is made of sweetened milk with a variety of nuts, *dal*, pearl sago or even wheat-flour vermicelli added. This version is enriched with coconut milk.

- 2 tablespoons split Bengal gram
- 2 cups milk
- 1/2 cup thick coconut milk
- 3 tablespoons palm sugar
- 1 tablespoon *ghee*
- 1–2 green cardamom pods, bruised
- 1 tablespoon raw cashew nuts, coarsely chopped
- 1 tablespoon raisins or sultanas

Wash the Bengal gram and simmer with 1 cup of water until half cooked.

Add the milk and simmer until the gram is very soft, then add the coconut milk and palm sugar. Cook, stirring frequently, until the mixture thickens.

Heat the ghee and sauté the cardamom pods, cashews and raisins until golden brown, then add to the cooked mixture.

Although Payasam is normally served warm or at room temperature, it can be chilled.

Rasgulla
Cream Cheese Balls in Syrup

Soft homemade cream cheese or *chenna* is shaped into balls and simmered in syrup to make a simple but richly satisfying dessert. An extravagant touch in the form of pure silver beaten into the finest possible sheets is sometimes added as a garnish on special occasions in India.

Syrup
4 cups sugar
3 cups water
8 ounces *Chenna* (page 59)
1 teaspoon flour

Make the syrup by bringing the sugar and water to a boil. Turn off the heat and set aside.

Combine the *chenna* and flour and shape into balls. Reheat the syrup and when it is boiling, add the balls and simmer for about 20 minutes. Add another 2 tablespoons of water to the syrup every 5 minutes to replace water lost by evaporation; this is essential to avoid having the syrup become too thick. When the cream cheese balls are cooked, remove from the syrup, drain and keep covered in water until required. Serve with a spoonful or two of the syrup poured over the top.

Kulfi
Indian Ice Cream

8 cups whole milk
1/2 cup sugar
1–2 tablespoons skinned pistachio nuts, chopped
2 tablespoons almond, finely ground (optional)

Falooda
1 1/2 cups cornstarch
4 cups water

To make the ice cream, put the milk into a wide, heavy pan and cook over very low heat. Stir constantly until the milk has thickened and is reduced to about 2 cups, or until the milk is the color of the *kulfi* in the photo. Stir the sides of the pan constantly to prevent the milk from scalding. Add the sugar and nuts, and allow to cool. Freeze in individual metal containers such as jelly molds.

To make the *falooda*, dissolve the cornstarch in 1 cup water. Heat the remaining water in a pan, add the blended cornstarch and cook to make a thick jell.

While the mixture is still hot, put into a press capable of making fine threads the size of vermicelli noodles.

Cream Cheese Balls in Syrup.

Fill a bowl full of cold water right up to the brim and set the press over the water so that when the *falooda* is pushed through the press, it immediately touches the water. Push all the jell through the press. Store the *falooda* in water until required.

To serve unmold the ice-cream and garnish with *falooda*.

Gulab Jamun
Fried Milk Balls in Syrup

Syrup
6 cups water
11 cups sugar
2 pounds *Khoa* (page 58)
7 ounces *Chenna* (page 59)
2 tablespoons white flour
A pinch of baking soda
2 tablespoons skinned pistachio nuts, chopped
Oil for deep-frying

Make the syrup by boiling the water and sugar together, stirring from time to time, for about 10 minutes until thickened slightly. Keep aside.

Crumble the *Khoa* and mix with *Chenna*, flour, baking soda and pistachios to make a soft dough. Make one very small ball for testing the consistency.

Heat oil until moderately hot and add the ball. If it breaks apart, the mixture is too moist and a little more white flour should be mixed into the dough. When the mixture is of the correct consistency, shape into balls about 2 1/2 inches in diameter and deep-fry, a few at a time, until golden brown. Drain the fried balls and put into the warm syrup. Serve warm or at room temperature.

Indian Ice Cream (left) & Fried Milk Balls in Syrup (right).

Saunth Ki Chatni
Tamarind and Ginger Chutney

Serve with appetizers such as *Pakora* or *Samosa* (page 48), or serve with simple vegetable dishes for extra tang.

> 5 tablespoons dried tamarind pulp
> 5 dates, stones removed (optional)
> 1 teaspoon cayenne
> 3/4 teaspoon ginger powder
> 1/4 teaspoon nigella seeds, toasted and ground
> 3/4 teaspoon fennel seeds, toasted and ground
> 1 teaspoon cumin seeds, toasted and ground
> 1/4 cup palm sugar
> 1 teaspoon white sugar or more to taste
> Salt to taste

Soak the tamarind pulp in 2 cups of water for a minimum of 4 hours. Put pulp and liquid together with dates (if using) into a nonreactive pan, cover and simmer for 30 minutes. Push through a sieve, discarding the seeds and fibrous matter.

Return the sieved pulp to the pan and add cayenne, ginger, nigella, fennel and cumin. Cook over low heat for 10 minutes, then add palm sugar and stir until dissolved. Add white sugar and salt to taste. Keeps refrigerated for about 1 week.

Hussaini Tamatar Qoot
Tomato Chutney

> 1 tablespoon oil
> 3/4 teaspoon black mustard seeds
> 1/2 teaspoon nigella seeds
> 1 sprig curry leaves
> Pinch of *asafoetida* powder
> 1 teaspoon crushed garlic
> 3/4 teaspoon crushed ginger
> 4 green chilies, slit lengthwise and seeded
> 4 medium-sized ripe tomatoes, chopped coarsely
> 1/2 teaspoon ground turmeric
> 1 teaspoon cayenne
> 2 teaspoons sugar
> Salt to taste

Heat oil and fry mustard seeds, nigella seeds, curry leaves and *asafoetida* until the spices start to crackle. Add the garlic, ginger and green chilies and sauté gently for a couple of minutes,

then put in the tomatoes and cook for about 10 minutes until the tomatoes turn pulpy. Add the turmeric, cayenne and sugar and stir until the sugar dissolves. Add salt to taste and serve hot. This chutney keeps for 3–4 days if refrigerated in a covered jar.

Pudina Ki Chatni
Mint and Cilantro Chutney

> 1 cup cilantro leaves
> 1/2 cup mint leaves
> 2 green chilies, chopped
> 1/2 inch ginger, chopped
> 3 cloves garlic, chopped
> 2 tablespoons plain yogurt
> 1 teaspoon sugar
> 1/2 teaspoon cayenne
> Salt to taste
> 1 teaspoon *chaat masala*
> Lemon juice to taste

Put all ingredients in a blender and process until very fine. Serve with snacks or tandoori dishes.

Mangga Thuvial
Green Mango Chutney

> 3 unripe green mangoes, about 1 pound
> 1/2 teaspoon sesame seeds
> 3–4 dried chilies, broken into 1-inch lengths
> 2 medium-sized onions, chopped
> 2 tablespoons freshly grated or dried coconut
> 1 sprig curry leaves
> 1 tablespoon chopped cilantro leaves
> 1 teaspoon oil
> 1 teaspoon black mustard seeds
> 1 1/2 teaspoons split Bengal gram (*channa dal*)
> Salt to taste

Peel the mangoes, discard the seeds and chop the flesh coarsely. Gently sauté the sesame seeds and chilies until crisp. Combine the mango flesh, sesame seeds, chillies, onion, coconut, curry leaves and coriander leaves and grind or blend coarsely. Heat the oil and fry mustard seeds and *dal* until the mustard seeds start to pop. Pour into the other ingredients, mix and add salt to taste and serve.

Garam Masala

> 1/2 cup cumin seeds
> 2 tablespoons coriander seeds
> 4 sticks cinnamon, each 2 inches long
> 10–12 green cardamom pods, bruised
> 4–5 black cardamom pods, bruised
> 10 cloves
> 1/2 nutmeg, broken
> 3–4 blades of mace
> 1 tablespoon black peppercorns
> 4 whole star anise
> 5 bay leaves

Put all the spices in a dry pan (preferably nonstick) and heat over a very low fire, shaking the pan from time to time. When the spices give off a fragrance, allow to cool slightly, then grind finely in a coffee mill or electric blender. Store in an airtight bottle. (If stored in the deep-freeze portion of the fridge, spices keep fresh almost indefinitely.)

Rasam Masala

This is used to flavor the southern Indian soup, Rasam.

> 2 teaspoons coriander seeds
> 1/2 teaspoon cumin seeds
> 1 teaspoon fenugreek seeds
> 1 teaspoon black peppercorns
> 1 teaspoon black mustard seeds
> 6 dried chilies, broken into several pieces
> 1 sprig curry leaves
> 1/2 teaspoon husked blackgram dal (*urad dal*)
> 1/2 teaspoon split Bengal gram (*channa dal*)
> A pinch of *asafoetida* powder

Put all ingredients except *asafoetida* in a pan over low heat and cook until the chillies become crisp and the spices smell fragrant, taking care not to burn them. Cool slightly, then grind all ingredients together, then mix with the *asafoetida* powder.

Kadai Masala

> 6 dried chilies, broken into several pieces
> 2 tablespoons coriander seeds
> 1/4 teaspoon *Garam Masala*

Heat chilies and coriander in a pan, shaking from time to time, until they smell fragrant. Grind and add *garam masala*.

Chaat Masala

This salty, sour *chaat masala* (the approximate translation is "finger licking") is sprinkled over cooked food for additional flavor.

> 1 tablespoon cumin seeds
> 1 tablespoon black peppercorns
> 5 cloves
> 3 peppercorns or long pepper (optional)
> 1/2 tablespoon dried mint leaves
> 1/4 teaspoon carom seeds (*ajwain*)
> 1/4 teaspoon *asafoetida* powder
> 1 tablespoon rock salt
> 2 1/2 tablespoons dried mango powder
> 1 teaspoon ginger powder
> 1 teaspoon cayenne
> 1/4 teaspoon tartaric acid
> 2 teaspoons salt

Put first seven ingredients in a dry pan and heat gently, shaking the pan from time to time, until the spices begin to smell fragrant. Remove from heat, add the rock salt and grind while still warm. Mix in all other ingredients, cool and store tightly bottled.

Khoa
Condensed Milk

This makes about 3 ounces *khoa*.

> 4 cups fresh milk

Bring the milk to a boil in a wide, heavy-bottomed pan, stirring constantly. Continue stirring over high heat until the milk changes to a doughy consistency, which will take about 25 minutes.

Dahi
Plain Yogurt

- 4 cups fresh milk
- 2 tablespoons full-cream powdered milk
- 1 tablespoon plain yogurt

Combine the fresh and powdered milks, stirring to dissolve, then put over moderate heat and bring almost to a boil, stirring from time to time.

Remove from the heat and allow to cool to a little over 100 ° F. You should be able to hold your finger in the milk up to the count of 10 without it stinging at all.

Put the plain yogurt starter in a clean container and stir in the hot milk. Cover with a cloth and leave in a warm place until set. In cooler temperatures, a wide-mouth insulated jar or thermos flask should ensure that the temperature stays warm enough for the yogurt to set. Refrigerate the yogurt as soon as it has set and use some of this as a starter for the next batch you make.

Note: Before it is used in Indian cuisine, yogurt is often vigorously stirred to ensure the whey is reincorporated with the curds; this is referred to as **whipped yogurt**.

Yogurt that is drained for several hours to remove the whey is called **hung yogurt**. To make, put yogurt in a paper-lined coffee filter and set the cone-shaped device over a jar. (In India cooks use cheesecloth or muslin.) The whey will drip through, leaving the curds.

Chenna/Paneer
Homemade Cream Cheese

- 4 cups fresh milk
- 1 tablespoon of lemon juice or
    - 1 tablespoon vinegar mixed with
    - 1 tablespoon water

Put the milk into a heavy-bottomed pan and bring slowly to a boil, stirring occasionally. Remove from heat and add the lemon (or vinegar and water) while the milk is still hot, stirring vigorously until the milk starts to curdle. Strain through a muslin or cheese-cloth-lined sieve until all the whey has drained off. The curds left are known as *chenna* and should be kneaded lightly to make a smooth mixture, then refrigerated until needed for various desserts.

To obtain *paneer*, wrap the cheese in the same cheesecloth and shape into an oblong or square. Wrap tightly and place it under a heavy weight for about 2 hours to compress it. Remove the weight and cut into desired shapes.

Clockwise, from the top left: chili pickle (no recipe), Lemon Mango Pickle, Mixed Vegetable Pickle, green chili pickle (no recipe) and Onion Mustard Pickle.

Pyaz Ka Achar
Onion Mustard Pickle

- 1 cup mustard oil
- 4 tablespoons black mustard seeds
- 2 teaspoons cayenne
- 1 teaspoon ground turmeric
- 3 tablespoons vinegar
- 2 1/2 tablespoons sugar
- 1/2 tablespoon salt
- 3 tablespoons dried mango powder
- 15–18 green chilies
- 30 cloves garlic, peeled and left whole
- 1 1/2 tablespoons crushed ginger
- 1 1/2 tablespoons crushed garlic
- 2 pounds onions, sliced
- 1/2 teaspoon ascorbic acid

Heat oil to smoking point, then set aside to cool. Grind or blend the mustard seeds, chilli powder, turmeric, vinegar, sugar, salt and mango powder together to make a paste.

Add paste to the oil, then all the other ingredients. Stir to mix well and store in sterilised jars, covered with a film of oil. Keeps for 3–4 weeks refrigerated.

Nimbu Aur Aam Ka Achar
Lemon Mango Pickle·

- 2 pounds lemons, quartered
- 10–15 green chilies, halved lengthwise
- 3–4 unripe green mangoes, peeled and diced
- 1 cup lemon juice
- 1 1/2 tablespoons ground cumin
- 1 tablespoon ground turmeric
- 1 1/2 teaspoons cayenne
- 4 1/2 tablespoons salt
- 2 1/2 tablespoons sugar
- 1 1/2 cups mustard oil

Combine the lemons, chilies, mangoes and lemon juice in a bowl and sprinkle with the spices, salt and sugar.

Put into a large glass jar, cover loosely with a cloth and leave in the sun for 6 days.

Heat the oil to smoking point, allow to cool and then stir into the lemon mixture. Leave in the sun for another 4 days, then cover the jar with a lid and store in a cool, dry place away from the light. Keeps for several months refrigerated.

Sabzi Achar
Mixed Vegetable Pickle

- 8 ounces each of carrots, green mangoes, green chilies and lotus root
- 4 lemons, quartered
- 1 cup mustard oil
- 2 teaspoons fennel seeds
- 1 teaspoon nigella seeds
- 1 teaspoon black mustard seeds
- 2 1/2 teaspoons cayenne
- 2 1/2 teaspoons ground turmeric
- 2 teaspoons *Garam Masala* (page 58)
- 1 onion, chopped and puréed
- 1 1/2 tablespoons crushed ginger
- 1 1/2 tablespoons crushed garlic
- 1/2 teaspoon ascorbic acid
- 4 1/2 tablespoons salt

Peel and cut the carrots and mango into small wedges. Peel and slice the lotus root. Leave the chilies whole. Heat the mustard oil to smoking point, then add the fennel, nigella and mustard seeds and sauté until the spices crackle. Add cayenne, turmeric, *garam masala*, onion, ginger and garlic and stir, then add the vegetables and lemons. Take off the heat and add ascorbic acid and salt. Stir to mix well. Put the pickle into sterilized jars, making sure it is covered with oil. If necessary, heat more oil until smoking, pour over the pickle, and cool. Keeps for 3–4 months refrigerated.

"*Silahkan makan*" or "please eat" are two of the most welcome words you will hear in Indonesia.

INDONESIA

As the languages, religions and cultures of the archipelago are many and varied, so too its cuisines.

Left: Chilies, whether sold whole or ground into a paste, are an indispensable part of Indonesian cuisine.

Right: A Javanese man on his way to the market, his bike loaded with terra cotta cookware.

Indonesia is the world's largest archipelago, consisting of literally thousands of islands. With terrain that ranges from snow-capped mountains and lush rainforests to arid savannah, swamps and irrigated rice fields, it's hard to imagine a more appropriate national motto than "*Bhinneka Tunggal Ika*"—Unity in Diversity.

Over the past two thousand years, Buddhist, Hindu and Muslim kingdoms rose and fell in Sumatra, Java and Borneo, attracting merchants from China, the Middle East and India, as well as Siam and Malacca. Their quest was spice—not surprising, since some of the archipelago's eastern isles were the original Spice Islands.

With its geographic and cultural diversity, it is to be expected that the cuisines of Indonesia are so varied. Indigenous styles have been influenced degrees over the centuries by the introduction of ingredients and cooking styles from China, India, the Middle East and Europe.

Tanah Air: Land and Water

Stretching some 5,000 miles Indonesia's 18,000 or so islands (home to some 190 million people) range from roughly six degrees north of the equator to 11 degrees south. Indonesia is within the so-called "Ring of Fire," the meeting point of two of the earth's tectonic plates, which gives rise to frequent seismic activity. Smoldering volcanoes periodically shower fertile ash on the land.

To a large extent, the western islands of Indonesia are lush and evergreen. While Borneo has rainforests and swampy coastlines, Java and Sumatra abound with fertile gardens, coconut groves and paddy fields.

All of Indonesia enjoys tropical warmth and relatively high humidity, although the temperature drops significantly on the mountains. Most parts of the archipelago experience a definite dry season followed by life-giving monsoon rains. However, the eastern islands of the archipelago, especially

Nusa Tenggara, the chain of islands in between Lombok east to Timor, are often rocky and semi-arid. The dry seasons there are longer and harsher than elsewhere in Indonesia, and the land often degraded by tree felling and subsequent erosion.

Different parts of Indonesia receive their monsoon rain at different times of the year. The Maluku islands conform to the image of the lush tropics, while Irian Jaya, the western portion of the island of New Guinea, has everything from swamps to rainforest to the highest mountain east of the Himalayas, the almost 16,000-foot Mount Jaya.

The preferred staple throughout Indonesia is rice, which is grown both in irrigated paddies—where up to three crops a year can be achieved by using special strains of rice and fertilizers—and in non-irrigated fields, which depend on the monsoon rains. In areas where insufficient rainfall or unsuitable terrain make rice-growing impossible, crops such as sweet potato, tapioca (cassava or manioc), corn and sago are the staple.

The most popular accompaniment to rice is fish, which is often simply fried with a seasoning of sour tamarind, turmeric and salt, or simmered in seasoned water or coconut milk. Although vegetables are grown throughout Indonesia, they do not always figure prominently in the diet. Some wild leaves and plants, as well as the young leaves of plants grown for their fruit or tubers, such as starfruit, papaya, sweet potatoes and tapioca, are cooked as a vegetable. These are supplemented with water spinach (kangkung), long beans, eggplants, pumpkins and cucumbers. Elevated areas, especially in islands with rich volcanic soil, have proved perfect for temperate-climate vegetables introduced by the Dutch.

A Culinary Tour of the Islands

Over the centuries Indonesia's cuisines, especially in the major islands, have borrowed ingredients and cooking styles from many sources. Arab and Indian traders brought their spices and sweet rose water. The Spanish were responsible for the introduction of chillies. The Chinese introduced the now-ubiquitous noodles (mie); soy sauce, which the Indonesians modified to suit their taste by adding sugar (kecap manis); mung peas; bean curd and soybeans, which the Indonesians fermented to make tempeh.

Despite their long period as colonial rulers, the Dutch did not really have an enormous impact on the local cuisine, apart from, per-

Special Indonesian es (ice) drinks, both refreshing and delicious, are sold at stalls and mobile carts throughout Indonesia.

A sambal served in *daun mangkokan*, a decorative leaf used as a herb in Sumatra.

haps, the *rijstaffel*. This colonial invention is a larger-than-life adaptation of the Indonesian style of serving rice with several savory side dishes and condiments—only the Dutch modified it to a "rice table" where as many as 18 to 20 dishes might be served.

The Javanese of the sultanates of Yogyakarta and nearby Surakarta have a very refined culture. Theirs is a highly structured society where harmony depends upon consideration for others, the group being more important than the individual. Ritual events are marked by a communal feast (selamatan). Centerpiece of the selamatan may be a cone-shaped mound of yellow rice, with at least a dozen dishes accompanying, including gudeg (young jackfruit cooked in coconut milk); fried chicken, which had first been simmered in spiced coconut milk; fermented soybean cakes (tempeh) fried with shrimp and sweetened with palm sugar; red chili sambal and crisp shrimp wafers (krupuk).

Less subtle is the food of the west Sumatran region of Padang—ideal, however, if you like it hot and spicy! Most of the food in restaurants are served as a smorgasbord: portions are taken from ten to as many as twenty different dishes and carried from their display counter to the restaurant table. You help yourself to whatever you desire and pay only for what you consume. Vital to Padang food are the herbs, rhizomes and other seasonings that include chilies, ginger, garlic, shallots, galangal, turmeric, lemongrass, basil, fragrant lime and salam leaves and pungent dried shrimp paste. Coconut flesh is squeezed to make the rich, creamy milk that soothes (if only slightly) the impact of much Padang food. Steaming white rice is served to counterbalance the emphatic flavors.

Sulawesi (Celebes) is renowned for its fish. Ikan bakar, fish roasted over charcoal and served with a variety of dipping sauces, is a regional favorite.

Feasts are commonplace in Bali, and, as the island did not turn to Islam when the rest of the nation did, pork is a popular meat.

Game from the interior highlands of the so-called wilds of Borneo include wild boar, used to make the famous roast pig babi guling. Many leafy greens are gathered wild, such as the young shoots of trees found in the family compound (starfruit is a favorite), or young fern tips and other edible greens found along the lanes or edges of paddy fields. Immature fruits like the jackfruit and papaya are also used as vegetables. Mature coconut is used almost daily: grated to add to vegetables, fried with seasonings to make a condiment, or the grated flesh squeezed with water to make coconut milk.

The Food of the People

To properly savor the diversity of Indonesian cuisine, take a walk along local streets and do as the locals do—frequent the *warung* (simple food stall). The social center of most villages and small towns, the *warung* is usually made of either woven bamboo or wood, open-fronted with dirt or cement floors, and offers everything you might need for the home—mosquito coils, laundry powder or the ubiquitous clove-scented cigarettes.

Warungs also sell a colorful array of packaged snacks, cakes, biscuits, bottles of drink and whatever fresh fruit is available that day: fresh bananas, avocados, papayas or guavas gathered from a nearby garden.

Eating out for many Indonesians is usually a necessity rather than a luxury, and basic food stalls selling cooked food at very reasonable prices are found in any large village as well as in towns and cities. Stalls are often a good source of regional favorites. You can find *soto Makassar* (a rich beef soup) and grilled fish (*ikan bakar*) along Ujung Pandang's waterfront in Southern Sulawesi. Lombok's favourite chicken, which is grilled over coals and served with a spicy sauce (*ayam taliwang*) is found at many foodstalls in the capital, Mataram, and almost any market in Bali will feature the famous roast pig (*babi guling*).

Market foodstalls often sell *nasi campur* (literally "mixed rice") with small portions of several "dishes of the day," the various vegetables, meat, poultry or fish dishes are often cooked in the regional style.

Hawkers on rumbling pushcarts, makeshift wooden contraptions resting on a couple of bicycle wheels, are also a popular sight, offer-

Indonesia is blessed with an abundance of luscious fruit: the giant jackfruit, notorious durian and spiky rambutan are only a few.

ing *mie bakso* (noodle and meatball soup), or bowls of shaved ice with the syrups, jellies and fruits of your choice added. Another hawker with a charcoal fire will grill satay on request.

What Westerners may consider desserts are eaten as snacks throughout the day, and may include treats such as fermented rice or cassava (*tape*), slivers of young coconut, chunks or strips of colorful jelly, sweet corn kernels or vivid green "noodles" of transparent mung pea flour.

Coffee is more popular than tea in many areas of Indonesia. Finely ground coffee is put straight into the serving glass and mixed with boiling water. The trick of drinking the coffee (known as *kopi tobruk*) without getting a mouthful of grounds is to stir it a little so that the grounds settle. Indonesians love sugar and coffee is served sweet unless one asks for it *pahit* (literally "bitter").

Stronger drinks can be found, except in conservative Islamic areas (Muslims are forbidden to drink alcohol). Two popular local brands of beer, Bintang and Anker, are made to Dutch specifications and are similar to any European lager. In many non-Muslim areas, a local brew is made from either rice or the sap of the coconut or lontar palm. Bali is noted for its *brem*, a sweetish type of rice beer. Palm wine (toddy) is made by tapping the sap that flows from the inflorescence of the coconut or lontar palm. It is enjoyed fresh the day it is gathered, or left to mature for a few days; leftovers are distilled to made a fierce *arrack*.

The Indonesian Table and Kitchen

"*Silahkan makan*" is the Indonesian invitation that precedes any meal served to guests, and a phrase foreigners should wait for before beginning even as much as a snack served by their Indonesian hosts. But in countless homes throughout the archipelago, meals are usually an informal affair and often eaten alone.

The most popular staple food is rice, and Indonesians eat large quantities of it with savory side dishes and condiments. Only small amounts of savory dishes—which may include fish, poultry, meat, eggs, vegetables, bean curd or *tempeh*—are eaten. Variety is preferred over quantity; a little of four or five side dishes rather than large helpings of only one or two.

Condiments are as important as savory dishes and will usually include a chilli *sambal* and something to provide a crunchy contrast. This could be deep-fried *tempeh*, peanuts, deep-fried tiny anchovies (*ikan teri*), *krupuk* (wafers made of tapioca flour seasoned with anything from shrimp to melinjo nuts), a seasoned fried coconut concoction such as *serundeng* or fried peanut wafers (*rempeyek*).

The rice and accompanying dishes are normally cooked early in the day, immediately after a trip to the market. The prepared food is left in the kitchen, and members of the family help themselves to whatever they want whenever hungry, or take a container of food to the fields. Evening meals, taken at the end of the day when family members return from the fields, school or their work in the towns and cities, are often based on food left over from the main midday meal, with one or two extra dishes cooked if necessary.

As food is often served some time after it has been prepared, it is usually eaten at room temperature. Where meals are communal, the rice and all the accompanying dishes are placed in the middle of the table or on a mat on the floor for everyone to help themselves. It is considered impolite to pile one's plate with food at the first serving; there's plenty of opportunity to take more food as the meal progresses.

Indonesians traditionally eat with the right hand (the left is considered unclean by Muslims), although serving spoons are used to transfer the food to individual plates or bowls from the serving dishes. Many modern homes and almost all restaurants provide a spoon and fork, while chopsticks can be expected in Chinese restaurants.

In more affluent homes, the choice of dishes to accompany the rice is made with a view to achieving a blend of flavors and textures. If one of the savory dishes has a rich, creamy coconut-milk sauce, this will be offset by a dry dish with perhaps a sharper flavor. There may well be a pungent *sambal goreng* (food fried with a spicy chili seasoning), but this will be balanced with other mild or even sweet dishes using *kecap manis* (sweet black soy sauce) or palm sugar.

For a family celebration, food is prepared by the family involved. Larger feasts involve the whole *banjar*, or local community, the work supervised by a ritual cooking specialist, invariably a man. There is a strict division of labor along gender lines, with men being responsible for butchering the pig or turtle, grating coconuts and grinding spices. The women of the community perform the more fiddly tasks of peeling and chopping the fresh seasonings, cooking the rice and preparing the vegetables.

The Indonesian kitchen is a combination of simplicity and practicality. The gleaming modern designer kitchen is unknown to the majority of Indonesians; meals are usually cooked over a wood fire or a *kompor*, a kerosene burner.

A little known fact: despite the Moluccas's reputation as the Spice Islands—islands literally responsible for starting the Age of Exploration and for the discovery of the Americas by Christopher Columbus—cloves and nutmeg are rarely used in cooking in the Moluccas. A little grated nutmeg may be added to a rich beef soup at a pinch, but in the main, nutmeg and cloves are regarded more as medicinal plants. Nutmeg fruit, the fleshy covering of the hard nut which is used as a spice, is usually pickled and eaten as a snack.

The most widely used spice is coriander, a small round beige seed with a faintly orange flavor, commonly partnered with peppercorns and garlic to flavor food, especially in Java.

SUGGESTED MENUS

Family meals

For an easy but elegant family meal, serve the following selection of small dishes with Yellow Rice (page 72):
• Marinated Sour Shrimp (page 66);
• Grilled Fish in Banana Leaf (page 66);
• Fern Tips in Coconut Milk (page 73);
•Coconut Pancakes (page 79) as a sweet.

Or, you may like to consider:
• Spicy Sparerib Soup (page 71);
• Vegetables with Spicy Coconut (page 72) and Simmered River Fish (page 75) with steamed rice;
• Sago Flour Rolls (page 78) for a good make-ahead dessert.

Dinner party (1)

Many of the dishes in this chapter make very good dinner-party nibbles:
• Grilled Fish in Banana Leaf (page 66), Dry Spiced Beef (page 74) and Spicy Fried Sardines (page 75);
• Buginese Chicken (page 76) or Yogya Fried Chicken (page 77) and Hot Spicy Fried Tempeh (page 73) served with rice to follow the appetizers;
• Black Rice Pudding (page 79) makes a dramatic ending.

Dinner party (2)

Other great dinner party suggestions are:
• Beef or Seafood Satays (page 67);
• Yogya Fried Chicken (page 77) and Padang-Style Eggs in Coconut Milk (page 72) with Gado Gado (page 68);
• Rice Flour Cake with Palm Sugar (page 78) completes the meal.

Salad meals

The salads in this chapter are a vegetable lover's delight, and easy to assemble once you've prepared all the ingredients. They make an ideal lunch, served with bread or rice.

A melting pot menu

For a mixed dinner menu serve:
• Green Papaya Soup (page 70) from Indonesia;
• Spicy River Prawns (page 154) from Vietnam and Chinese Stuffed Vegetables and Bean Curd (page 36);
• Sago with Honeydew from Malaysia/Singapore (page 120) makes an excellent finale.

THE ESSENTIAL FLAVORS OF INDONESIAN COOKING

For making the Indonesian *rempah*, **garlic**, **ginger**, **galangal**, **chilies** and **shrimp paste** are a must. You'll also need freshly squeezed **lime juice** and **salam leaf**. Unique to Indonesian cuisine is the use of **tempeh**. **Coconuts**—the milk and flesh—are an integral part of Indonesian cooking, and are used in salads, curries and desserts. **Palm sugar** is used in sweet and savory dishes. **Noodles** and **rice** are the main staples.

Marinated Sour Shrimp (upper left) and Tuna Sambal (lower right).

In Indonesia these dishes would be used as side dishes to accompany rice. If you like you can increase the quantities slightly and serve as part of a shared main meal with rice.

Asam Udang
Marinated Sour Shrimp

Belimbing wuluh, small sour carambola fruits, grow abundantly in many kitchen gardens throughout Indonesia, as well as in other areas of Southeast Asia. They add a delicious tang to this North Sumatran salad, although sour grapefruit or sour oranges can be used as a substitute.

- 2 pounds large shrimp (with shell)
- 6 shallots, peeled and finely chopped
- 3 red chilies, seeded and finely sliced
- 4 sour carambola, sliced, or 1 sour grapefruit, peeled and chopped
- 1/2 teaspoon salt

Put shrimp in a pan with 8 cups water and bring to a boil. Simmer for 4 minutes, drain and plunge shrimp in iced water for 30 seconds. Drain, then peel shrimp.

Grind or blend shallots, chilies and carambola or grapefruit to a fine paste. Add salt to taste and a little lime or lemon juice if not sour enough. Combine with shrimp and serve.

Sambal Tappa
Tuna Sambal

This recipe comes from Ambon, in Maluku, where tuna is abundant. Drained canned tuna can be used as a substitute if fresh tuna is not available.

- 5 sour green mangoes, peeled and coarsely shredded
- 2 teaspoons salt
- 1 1/4 pounds fresh tuna, grilled and flaked
- 3 shallots, peeled and sliced
- 1 teaspoon ground white pepper
- 1/4 cup thick coconut milk

Mix mangoes with salt and leave aside for 10 minutes. Squeeze to remove any excess liquid. Mix with tuna, shallots, pepper and coconut milk and serve.

Otak-otak
Grilled Fish in Banana Leaf

This Kalimantan recipe calls for steamed bundles of minced seasoned fish to be cooked directly on hot charcoal. The result is a slightly smoky flavor.

- 1 1/4 pounds boneless white fish fillets such as snapper, skinned and chopped
- 15 shallots, peeled and sliced
- 3 cloves garlic, peeled and sliced
- 3 scallions
- 1 teaspoon white peppercorns, crushed
- 1/2 cup thick coconut milk
- 1 tablespoon lime juice
- 1 teaspoon salt
- 3 eggs
- 5-inch square pieces of banana leaf or aluminium foil

Put fish in a blender and process for a few seconds. Add all other ingredients, except for banana leaf, and process until well blended.

Put 3 heaped tablespoons of fish in the center of each square of banana leaf. Roll over firmly and secure both ends of the roll with toothpicks. Steam the parcels for 15 minutes, then place directly onto charcoal or under a broiler for 5 minutes, turning from time to time, until the leaves are charred.

Serve banana leaf parcels and allow diners to unwrap their own.

Grilled Fish in Banana Leaf.

Sate Sapi
Beef Satay

The spice paste for this satay can be kept for up to four days. The satay can also be made with diced lamb, duck or seafood.

Spice Paste
10 shallots, peeled and sliced
6 cloves garlic, peeled and sliced
4 inches galangal, peeled and sliced
2 inches ginger, peeled and sliced
6 red chilies, sliced
7 bird's-eye chilies, sliced
10 candlenuts
1 tablespoon ground black pepper
1 tablespoon ground coriander seeds
4 tablespoons chopped palm sugar
2 *salam* leaves
4 tablespoons oil

1 1/4 pounds top round beef, in 1 1/2-inch cubes
3–5 bird's-eye chillies
2 tablespoons brown sugar

To make the spice paste, blend all ingredients except *salam* leaves and oil. Sauté blended mixture in oil with *salam* leaves for 5 minutes until golden brown. Cool, then combine with meat, chilies and sugar. Marinate in the refrigerator for at least 24 hours.

    Thread meat onto satay skewers and grill over high heat until cooked. Serve with peanut sauce (page 81).

Beef Satay.

Raw Vegetables (left) and Cooked Vegetables in Peanut Sauce (right), recipes on page 68.

Sate Lilit
Minced Seafood Satay

This is probably the most delicious satay you'll ever encounter. The delicate flavors of the shrimp and fish are greatly improved if you can find spears of fresh lemongrass to use as skewers, and if you can cook them over a fire of coconut husks rather than charcoal. Nonetheless, even with wooden skewers and a standard charcoal grill, you'll have people coming back for more.

10 ounces skinned boneless snapper fillet
10 ounces raw shrimp, peeled
2 cups freshly grated coconut or

1 1/2 cups dried coconut, moistened
1/2 cup Spice Paste for Seafood (page 80)
5 fragrant lime leaves, cut into hair-like shreds
1 teaspoon black peppercorns, finely crushed
2 teaspoons salt
3–5 green bird's-eye chilies, very finely chopped
2 tablespoons brown sugar
Lemongrass, cut into 6-inch lengths, or satay skewers

Combine fish with shrimp and mince very finely in a food processor or with a chopper. Add all other ingredients and mix well.

    Mold a heaped tablespoonful of this mixture around a stalk of lemongrass or skewer and grill until golden brown.

HELPFUL HINT
Soak skewers for at least 30 minutes before use.

Rempeyek Kacang
Crisp Peanut Wafers

1 1/2 cups raw peanuts
14 tablespoons rice flour
3/4 cup white flour
1 cup coconut milk
Oil for deep-frying

Spice Paste
1 teaspoon coriander seeds
2 candlenuts
2 cloves garlic
1/2 inch fresh turmeric, peeled and sliced
5 kaffir lime leaves, shredded (optional)
1 teaspoon salt

Dry fry the peanuts in a wok over low heat for 5 minutes. Rub to remove the skins and set aside.

To make the spice paste, grind or blend all ingredients, then combine with the flours. Mix well, stirring in the coconut milk to blend. Add the peanuts.

    Heat plenty of oil in a wok and drop in a tablespoonful of batter at a time, cooking until golden brown. Drain and cool thoroughly before storing.

Vegetable Salad with Peanut Sauce.

The Indonesian salad may come as a bit of a palate surprise if you're expecting the cooling properties of Western-style salads. Be prepared for the sweet, sour, hot, salty and spicy assailing your senses all at once!

Karedok
Raw Vegetables

The Sundanese of West Java are renowned for their love of vegetables, both raw and cooked, and often eat them as between-meal snacks. They can, of course, be served with rice as part of a main meal.

Spice Paste
4 cloves garlic, peeled and sliced
8 red chilies, seeded and sliced
2 inches *kencur*, peeled and sliced
1 teaspoon dried shrimp paste, toasted
1 tablespoon tamarind juice
4 tablespoons chopped palm sugar
2 teaspoons salt

1/4 medium-sized round green cabbage, shredded
1 small cucumber, peeled, halved lengthwise and sliced
2 cups bean sprouts, cleaned
4 tiny round eggplant, or 1 small long eggplant

finely sliced
1 cup diced young long beans
4 sprigs basil
Fried shallots
Shrimp wafers (*krupuk*)

Arrange vegetables in a bowl.
To make the spice paste, grind or blend the ingredients together, adding a little water if necessary. Pour over vegetables.
Mix well and garnish with basil, fried shallots and *krupuk*.

Lotek
Cooked Vegetables in Peanut Sauce

8 ounces water spinach (*kangkung*) or spinach, steamed
8 ounces pumpkin or chayote (*choko*), cut in chunks and steamed
8 ounces long beans, cut in 1 1/2-inch lengths and steamed
8 ounces young jackfruit, cubed and simmered in water until tender
1 cup bean sprouts, blanched
1 large potato, boiled, peeled and diced
5 bird's-eye chilies, sliced
3/4 inch *kencur*, sliced
1/2 teaspoon dried shrimp paste, toasted
1 teaspoon chopped palm sugar
1/4 teaspoon salt
1/2 cup fried peanuts, ground

Prepare the vegetables and set them aside.
Grind or blend the chilies, *kencur*, shrimp paste, palm sugar and salt. Mix well to make a sauce. Adjust seasoning to taste. Pour the sauce over the vegetables and sprinkle with the ground peanuts.

Gado Gado
Vegetable Salad with Peanut Sauce

Peanut Sauce
3 cups deep-fried peanuts
4 cloves garlic, peeled
10 bird's-eye chilies, sliced
3 inches *kencur*, peeled and chopped
3 kaffir lime leaves
1/2 cup) sweet soy sauce
2 teaspoons salt
6 cups water
3 tablespoons Fried Shallots (page 81)
1 tablespoon lime juice

1 cup long beans, cut and blanched
1 cup beansprouts, blanched
2 cups spinach, blanched
1/4 small cabbage, chopped and blanched
1 medium-sized carrot, thinly sliced and blanched
4 squares hard bean curd, deep-fried and sliced
4 hard-boiled eggs, quartered
2 tablespoons Fried Shallots (page 81)

To make the sauce, blend the first four ingredients until coarse. Put in a pan with all other sauce ingredients, except fried shallots and lime juice. Simmer over very low heat for 1 hour, stirring to prevent sticking. Stir in shallots and lime juice just before use. Arrange all vegetables on a dish and pour the sauce over. Garnish with bean curd and eggs, sprinkle with shallots and serve.

Timun Mesanten
Cucumber with Coconut Sauce

The spicy coconut and chili sauce is a wonderful contrast to the bland, cooling flavor of the cucumber in this salad.

| 2 tablespoons oil
| 3 shallots, peeled and sliced
| 2 cloves garlic, peeled and sliced
| 2 large red chilies, seeded and sliced
| 1/2 teaspoon dried shrimp paste
| 2 cups coconut milk
| 2 medium-sized cucumbers, peeled, seeded and sliced
| 1 teaspoon salt
| 1/4 teaspoon black peppercorns, crushed
| Fried Shallots (page 81)

Heat oil in heavy saucepan. Add shallots, garlic and chilies and sauté for 2 minutes over low heat. Mix in shrimp paste and sauté for another minute. Pour in coconut milk and bring to a boil. Reduce heat and simmer for 5 minutes.

Add cucumbers and bring to the boil. Reduce the heat and simmer until cucumbers are cooked and sauce thickens. Season to taste with salt and pepper. Garnish with fried shallots and serve.

HELPFUL HINT

If possible, use Japanese cucumbers which have a better flavor.and texture.

Green Bean Salad with Chicken.

Lawar
Green Bean Salad with Chicken

No big religious or private celebration in Bali would be held without this ritual dish, and only the eldest and most experienced men are allowed to mix the ingredients. The chicken can be replaced by beef, pork or shredded young jackfruit.

| 3 cups blanched long beans, cut in 1/4-inch slices
| 1/2 cup grated coconut, roasted
| 6 cloves garlic, peeled, sliced and fried
| 6–8 shallots, peeled, sliced and fried
| 2 large red chilies, seeded and cut in fine strips
| 4–6 bird's-eye chilies, finely sliced
| 3 teaspoons Fried Bird's-Eye Chilies (page 81)
| 2 tablespoons Spice Paste for Chicken (page 80)
| Fried Shallots (page 81)

| **Dressing**
| 1/2 pound boneless chicken, minced
| 2 tablespoons spice paste for chicken (page 80)
| Banana leaf, cut in 12-inch square
| 1 teaspoon salt
| 1/2 teaspoon black peppercorns, crushed
| 1 teaspoon freshly squeezed lime juice

Combine beans, coconut, garlic, shallots, all the chilies and spice paste in a large bowl and mix well. To make the dressing, combine mince with 2 tablespoons spice paste and mix well.

Place chicken lengthwise in the center of a banana leaf and roll up very tightly. Place banana leaf roll on aluminum foil and roll up again very tightly. Turn sides simultaneously in opposite directions to tighten the roll.

Set up a steamer over boiling water and steam the roll for 20 minutes. Remove aluminum foil and banana leaf and break up the meat with a fork.

Combine chicken with bean mixture, season to taste with salt, pepper and lime juice. Garnish with fried shallots.

Shredded Chicken with Chilies and Lime.

Ayam Pelalah
Shredded Chicken with Chilies and Lime

Leftover chicken—roast, steamed or fried—is perfect for this tangy chicken salad.

| 2 1/2-pound whole chicken
| 1 cup Spice Paste for Chicken (page 80)
| 1/2 cup Tomato Sambal (page 80)
| 3 tablespoons freshly squeezed lime juice

Preheat oven to 350°F.

Rub the chicken outside and inside with the spice paste. Place on wire rack in oven and roast until done, approximately 40 minutes. When cool, remove and discard the skin.

Remove meat from bones and tear into fine strips. Combine chicken strips with remaining ingredients. Mix well and season to taste.

Serve at room temperature with steamed rice.

HELPFUL HINT

Mix any leftover chicken with mashed potato and make into patties. Pan-fry in a little hot oil until golden. The use of potato is not strictly Balinese, but the result is very good.

Rujak
Vegetable and Fruit Salad with Palm Sugar Sauce

| **Sauce**
| 6 tablespoons tamarind pulp
| 1 cup palm sugar syrup (page 81)
| 1 teaspoon dried shrimp paste, roasted
| 6 bird's-eye chilies, left whole
| 1/2 teaspoon salt
| 1/2 cup water

| 1 small pineapple, peeled and sliced evenly
| 1 sour mango, peeled and sliced
| 1 pomelo or grapefruit, peeled and cut into segments
| 1 small cucumber, peeled, seeded and sliced
| 3 water apples (*jambu*), quartered (optional)
| 1 medium-sized starfruit, sliced
| 1/2 small papaya, peeled, cut in half, seeded and sliced in even segments
| 1 green apple, peeled and sliced

To make the sauce, combine all ingredients in a heavy pan and bring slowly to a boil. Stir well and simmer for 10 minutes. When cool, squeeze to extract all the juice from the tamarind and strain through a sieve.

Combine all ingredients in salad bowl and mix well. Serve at room temperature.

Spicy Sparerib Soup.

Daging Belacang
Beef Soup with Chilies and Tamarind

This sweet-sour soup from Timor in eastern Indonesia is an excellent way of dealing with tough cuts of beef.

2 pound top round beef, in 1 piece
8 cups water
3 tablespoons oil
5 shallots, peeled and sliced
1 clove garlic, peeled and sliced
1/2 teaspoon dried shrimp paste, toasted
3/4 tablespoon chopped palm sugar
1 teaspoon sweet soy sauce
1 tablespoon tamarind juice
Salt to taste
2 red chilies, seeded and sliced in fine strips
2 scallions, cut in 1-inch lengths

Simmer the meat in water until half-cooked, then cut into 3/4 inch cubes, reserving the stock. Sauté beef in 2 tablespoons oil, then set aside.

Grind or blend the shallots, garlic, shrimp paste and palm sugar, then sauté in 1 tablespoon oil until fragrant. Add fried meat and sweet soy sauce and sauté for a couple of minutes. Add beef stock, tamarind juice and salt and simmer until the beef is tender. Garnish with chilies and scallions.

Konro Makasar
Spicy Sparerib Soup

The Makasarese of Southern Sulawesi are renowned for their hearty beef soups, such as this one with coconut.

2 pound beef spareribs, cut in 2-inch lengths
16 cups water
4 shallots, peeled and sliced
2 cloves garlic, peeled and sliced
3 candlenuts

3 cups freshly grated or dried coconut, fried until golden then pounded

5 stems lemongrass, bruised and tied
1 inch galangal, peeled and sliced
3 kaffir lime leaves
1/2 teaspoon white peppercorns, crushed
1 teaspoon salt
1 tablespoon Fried Shallots (page 81)
2 tablespoons sliced Chinese Napa cabbage leaves

Put the ribs and water in a large pan and simmer, uncovered, until tender.

Grind or blend the shallots, garlic, candlenuts and add to the pounded coconut. Put into the stock with all remaining ingredients except the fried shallots and cabbage.

Simmer until the meat is very tender, but not falling from the bone. Serve garnished with fried shallots and cabbage.

Sop Kepala Ikan
Fish-Head Soup

This dish can be made with either one large fish head or a couple of smaller ones. The head is used to flavor the soup rather than to provide a substantial meal in itself.

Spice Paste
7 red chilies, seeded and sliced
6 shallots, peeled and chopped
3 cloves garlic, peeled and chopped
2 inches ginger, peeled and chopped
1 1/2 inches fresh turmeric, peeled and sliced
1 tablespoon oil

4 cups water
1 teaspoon salt
3 stems lemongrass, bruised
5 kaffir lime leaves
1 pound snapper heads, cleaned and well rinsed
1 tablespoon Fried Shallots (page 81)

To make the spice paste, grind or blend all ingredients except the oil, then sauté in oil for 2–3 minutes. Add water, salt, lemongrass and lime leaves and bring to a boil. Put in the fish, return to a boil and then simmer, uncovered, until the fish is cooked. Serve garnished with fried shallots.

Gedang Mekuah
Green Papaya Soup

If you can't get hold of unripe papayas, try this soup with any summer squash or Chinese winter melon.

1 unripe papaya, weighing 1 1/2 pounds
4 cups Chicken Stock (page 81)
1 cup Spice Paste for Vegetables (page 80)
2 *salam* leaves
1 stem lemongrass, bruised
1/4 teaspoon ground white pepper
1 teaspoon salt
Fried Shallots (page 81)

Peel the papaya and cut in half lengthwise and remove the seeds. Cut the papaya lengthwise into 4 or 6 pieces, then crosswise into 1/4-inch-thick slices.

Heat stock, add spice paste and bring to a boil. Simmer 2 minutes, then add the *salam* leaves, lemongrass and papaya. Simmer gently until the papaya is tender. If the stock reduces too much, add more. Season to taste with pepper and salt and garnish with fried shallots.

HELPFUL HINT

To save time, you can use chicken broth cubes in place of homemade chicken stock, although the flavor will not be as good.

Fish-Head Soup.

Gulai Tempeh
Tempeh Stew

Any leafy green vegetable, such as spinach or water spinach (*kangkung*), can be substituted for tapioca (cassava) leaves.

Spice Paste
4 cloves garlic, peeled and sliced
1 teaspoon white peppercorns, crushed
1 inch ginger, peeled and sliced
1 1/2 inches fresh turmeric, peeled and sliced
1 tablespoon chopped palm sugar

2 cups coconut milk
2 whole cloves
4 fermented soybean cakes (*tempeh*), cut in cubes
1 bunch (about 8 ounces) tapioca leaves or substitute
Salt to taste
Fried Shallots (page 81) to garnish

To make the spice paste, grind or blend all ingredients. Bring coconut milk to the boil, then add the spice paste, cloves, *tempeh* and tapioca leaves. Simmer, uncovered, until tender and the sauce has thickened. Season to taste with salt and garnish with fried shallots.

Cram Cam
Clear Chicken Soup with Shallots

This dish is traditionally prepared after a cockfight, when the winner receives the losing chicken as a reward.

4 cups Chicken Stock (page 81)
1/2 cup Spice Paste for Chicken (page 80)
1 teaspoon crushed black pepper
1 *salam* leaf
1 stem lemon grass, bruised
12 ounces boneless, skinless chicken, minced
Salt and pepper to taste
2 tablespoons Fried Shallots (page 81)

Bring chicken stock to a boil in stockpot or large saucepan. Wrap spice paste and black pepper in a piece of cotton cloth and tie with string. Add the spice paste bundle, the *salam* leaf and lemongrass to the soup and simmer for 10 minutes.

Add minced chicken and simmer for 15 minutes. Remove spice paste bundle from the soup and discard. Season soup to taste with salt and pepper.

Garnish with fried shallots.

Clear Chicken Soup with Shallots.

Tempeh Stew

Soto Babat
Clear Tripe Soup

This is usually served with Sambel Tomat as a condiment. The sugar cane is used to soften the tripe rather than to add any sweetness to the soup; if this is not available, extend the cooking time.

1 1/4 pounds beef tripe, cleaned
12 cups water
4 cups commercial beef stock
2 inches sugar cane stem, split lengthwise (optional)
1 inch ginger, peeled and sliced lengthwise
4 cloves garlic, peeled and sliced
1 tablespoon distilled white vinegar
6 ounces giant white radish, peeled and cut into 1/2-inch cubes
5 sprigs celery leaf, chopped
1 tablespoon Fried Shallots (page 81)

Rinse tripe well under running water until very clean. Bring water to a boil in a large pan, add tripe and simmer until soft, approximately 1 hour.

Strain water and cool tripe in iced water. Cut into 1-inch x 1/2 inch pieces.

Bring beef stock, sugar cane, ginger, garlic and vinegar to a boil. Add tripe and radish. Simmer until vegetables are soft. Garnish with celery leaf and fried shallots.

HELPFUL HINT

Any variety of summer squash or Chinese winter melon can be used instead of giant white radish.

To take the grind out of making the spice pastes, make enough for several meals and store, covered with a film of oil, in a jar in the refrigerator. Make sure you use a clean spoon each time you take some out, and it should keep for at least 2 weeks.

Nasi Kuning
Yellow Rice

Rice colored with turmeric and shaped into a cone is often presented on festive occasions in Indonesia. The shape echoes that of the mythical Hindu mountain, Meru, while yellow is the color of royalty and one of the four sacred colors for Balinese Hindus.

1 1/2 cups long-grain rice, washed thoroughly
2 inches fresh turmeric, peeled and scraped
1 1/2 cups coconut milk
1/2 cup) chicken stock (page 81)
1 *salam* leaf
1 pandan leaf, tied in a knot
1 stem lemongrass, bruised
3/4 inch galangal, peeled and sliced
2 teaspoons salt

Drain the rice in a sieve or colander.

Put the fresh turmeric in a blender with 1/4 cup water and process until fine.

Strain through a sieve, pushing to extract all the juice. Measure 2 tablespoons of juice and discard the rest. If fresh turmeric is not available, mix 2 teaspoons turmeric powder with 2 tablespoons water.

Put rice, turmeric water and all other ingredients in a heavy saucepan. Cover and bring to a boil over moderate heat. Stir, lower heat to the minimum and cook until the rice is done.

Remove all leaves and galangal before serving. Press into a cone shape in a conical sieve, if desired.

HELPFUL HINT

If the rice seems to be too dry before the grains are soft and swollen, sprinkle with a little more hot chicken stock and continue cooking.

Yellow Rice.

Gulai Telur
Padang-Style Eggs in Coconut Milk

A full-bodied dish often served at a typical West Sumatran or Padang-style meal.

Spice Paste
5 shallots, peeled and sliced
3 cloves garlic
4 bird's-eye chilies, chopped
1 inch ginger, peeled and chopped
1/2 inch fresh turmeric, peeled and sliced
1 inch galangal, peeled and chopped

2 cups coconut milk
1/2 turmeric leaf, shredded (optional)
8 hard-boiled eggs, peeled
1 tablespoon tamarind juice
Salt to taste
Fried Shallots (page 81) to garnish

To make the spice paste, grind or blend all ingredients until coarse. Bring coconut milk gradually to a boil and add the spice paste, turmeric leaf and eggs. Simmer until the sauce thickens, then add tamarind juice and salt and simmer for another minute.

Garnish with fried shallots and serve.

Jangan Olah
Vegetables with Spicy Coconut

Sauce
7 bird's-eye chilies, sliced
8 red chilies, seeded and sliced
1 tablespoon dried shrimp paste, toasted
4 cloves garlic, peeled and sliced
4 shallots, peeled and sliced
1 inch fresh turmeric, peeled and sliced
1 tablespoon chopped palm sugar
3 cups freshly grated or dried coconut
4 cups water
3 *salam* leaves
Salt to taste

2 cups chopped long beans
2 cups young fern tips (fiddle heads) or spinach
1 cup bean sprouts, blanched
Fried Shallots (page 81) to garnish

To make the sauce, grind or blend the chilies, shrimp paste, garlic, shallots, turmeric and palm sugar. Simmer with other ingredients until the sauce thickens. Cool to room temperature.

Lightly boil or steam the long beans and fern tips or spinach. Drain thoroughly and arrange on a plate. Add blanched bean sprouts. Pour the sauce over and garnish with fried shallots.

Padang-Style Eggs in Coconut Milk.

Pork in Sweet Soy Sauce.

Sambal Goreng Tempeh
Hot Spicy Fried Tempeh

Sweet with palm sugar and tangy with chilies, this Javanese favorite is often served with rice and other dishes.

- 2 cakes fermented soybean cake (*tempeh*), cut in long narrow strips and deep-fried
- 1 tablespoon oil
- 2 shallots, peeled and sliced
- 3 cloves garlic, sliced
- 2 red chilies, sliced
- 1 inch galangal, peeled and sliced
- 1/2 teaspoon dried shrimp paste
- 5 tablespoons chopped palm sugar
- 3 tablespoons water
- 1 tablespoon tamarind juice
- Salt to taste
- 8 bird's-eye chilies, chopped

Prepare the *tempeh* and set aside.

Heat the oil and sauté the shallots, garlic, chilies, galangal and shrimp paste for 2–3 minutes. Add palm sugar, water and tamarind juice and stir until the sugar has dissolved. Put in the *tempeh* and cook, stirring frequently, until the sauce has reduced and caramelized.

Season to taste with salt and stir in the bird's-eye chilies just before serving.

Gulai Daun Pakis
Fern Tips in Coconut Milk

The young tips of several varieties of wild fern are enjoyed in many parts of Indonesia. They can often be found in markets throughout Southeast Asia and have an excellent flavor.

Spice Paste
- 3 shallots, peeled and sliced
- 2 cloves garlic, peeled and sliced
- 10 red chilies, seeded and sliced
- 1 inch galangal, peeled and sliced
- 1 inch fresh turmeric, peeled and sliced
- 1 inch ginger, peeled and sliced

- 3 cups coconut milk
- 1 pound fern tips or fiddleheads, cleaned
- 2 turmeric leaves (optional)
- 1 tablespoon tamarind juice
- Salt to taste

To make the spice paste, grind or blend all ingredients together.

Put spice paste in a saucepan with the coconut milk and bring to the boil, stirring. Simmer for one minute, then add the fern tips, turmeric leaves and tamarind juice. Simmer, stirring frequently, until the fern tips are tender. Season to taste with salt.

Fern Tips in Coconut Milk.

Be Celeng Base Manis
Pork in Sweet Soy Sauce

The heat of the ginger and whole chilies make this subtle dish very appetizing. Serve with steamed rice and a simple vegetable dish.

- 2 tablespoons oil
- 5 shallots, peeled and sliced
- 5 cloves garlic, peeled and sliced
- 1 1/4 pounds boneless pork shoulder or leg, cut in 3/4-inch cubes
- 3 inches ginger, peeled and sliced lengthwise
- 4 tablespoons sweet soy sauce
- 2 tablespoons thin soy sauce
- 1 teaspoon black peppercorns, crushed
- 2 cups Chicken Stock (page 81)
- 6–10 bird's-eye chilies, left whole

Heat oil in a wok or heavy saucepan. Add shallots and garlic and sauté for 2 minutes over medium heat or until lightly colored. Add pork and ginger and continue to sauté for 2 more minutes over high heat. Add both types of soy sauce and black pepper and continue sautéing for 1 minute.

Pour in chicken stock and chilies, and simmer over medium heat for approximately 1 hour. When cooked, there should be very little sauce left and the meat should be shiny and dark brown. If the meat becomes too dry during cooking, add a little chicken stock.

Babi Masak Tomat
Pork Cooked with Tomatoes

A simple recipe from Kalimantan, where pork (particularly wild boar from the jungle) is popular among the Dyak people.

Spice Paste
- 4 shallots, peeled and sliced
- 4 red chilies, sliced
- 1 inch ginger, peeled and sliced
- 1 teaspoon salt

- 1 pound pork, cut in 3/4-inch cubes
- 4 tomatoes, sliced
- 4–6 garlic chives or scallions
- 1 stem lemongrass, bruised
- 1 cup water

To make the spice paste, grind or blend all ingredients together. Combine in a saucepan with all other ingredients and simmer until the pork is tender. Add more warm water if the sauce looks like it is drying out.

HELPFUL HINTS

Pork in Sweet Soy Sauce: For a thicker sauce, pound the shallots, garlic and ginger together and fry them before adding the pork.

Fern Tips in Coconut Milk: If you are unable to find fern tips, spinach or asparagus is an acceptable substitute.

Be Sampi Mesitsit
Dry Spiced Beef

This dish is so wonderful that it's worth making a large amount. Do not be tempted to use a food processor to shred the meat; you will obtain the correct texture only by shredding the meat with your fingers or a fork.

2 pounds top round beef,
    cut into four 8 ounce steaks
8 cloves garlic, peeled
2 teaspoons coriander seeds, crushed
1 tablespoon chopped palm sugar
2 large red chilies, seeded
2 tablespoons galangal, peeled
    and sliced
2 teaspoons dried shrimp paste
2 cloves, ground
1 teaspoon salt
1 teaspoon black peppercorns,
    coarsely ground
2 tablespoons oil
2 teaspoons fresh lime juice

Bring 20 cups of lightly salted water to a boil in a stockpot. Add beef and boil for approximately 1 hour, until very tender. Remove from stock. The meat must be so tender that its fibers separate very easily. Keep stock. Pound meat until flat and shred by hand into fine fibers.

Place garlic, coriander, palm sugar, chilies, galangal, dried shrimp paste, cloves, salt and pepper in a food processor and purée coarsely, or grind in a stone mortar.

Heat oil in a heavy saucepan and sauté the marinade for 2 minutes over medium heat. Add shredded beef, mix well and sauté until dry. Season with lime juice.

Remove from heat and allow to cool. Serve at room temperature with steamed rice.

HELPFUL HINT

If you have leftover beef, deep-fry until very crisp. Drain thoroughly and store in an airtight container. This makes an excellent finger food with cocktails, and a tasty accompaniment to rice-based meals.

Beef in Coconut Milk.

Rendang Sapi
Beef in Coconut Milk

A popular Padang dish from West Sumatra.

Spice Paste
8 red chilies, sliced
12 shallots, peeled and sliced
10 cloves garlic, peeled and sliced
2 inches ginger, peeled and sliced
5 cm (2 in) galangal, peeled and
    sliced
1 teaspoon black peppercorns,
    crushed

2 pounds top round beef
8 cups coconut milk (made from 2
    coconuts if using freshly grated
    coconut)
3 *salam* leaves
3 kaffir lime leaves
3 fresh turmeric leaves (optional)
3-inch cinnamon stick
5 whole star anise
5 cardamom pods, bruised
1 teaspoon salt

To make the spice paste, grind or blend all ingredients finely.

Cut the beef into $1/4$ -inch-thick slices about 1 inch square. Put the beef, spice paste and all the other ingredients into a wok and bring to the boil slowly. Keep stirring constantly to prevent the coconut milk from separating.

Cook over low heat, stirring from time to time, until the meat is very tender and all the sauce has evaporated. Continue cooking the beef, which will fry in the oil that has come out of the coconut milk, until rich brown.

Sambal Udang
Shrimp in Hot Sauce

The distinctive and somewhat bitter flavour of twisted cluster beans (*petai*) is an excellent counterpart to the shrimp in this spicy dish. Even if *petai* are not available, these shrimp partnered with potatoes and a rich sauce are excellent.

1 pound shrimp
5 pods (about 20 beans)
    twisted cluster beans
    (petai), podded (optional)
2 cups coconut milk
4 potatoes, peeled and cut
    in wedges
1 tablespoon tamarind juice
1 teaspoon salt

Spice Paste
5 shallots
2 cloves garlic
5 red chilies, sliced
$1/2$ teaspoon dried shrimp
    paste
2 tablespoons oil

Peel the shrimp and remove the intestinal tract.

To make the spice paste, grind or pound all ingredients together except the oil. Heat the oil and sauté the spice paste until fragrant.

Add the shrimp and sauté until they change color. Put in the beans and coconut milk and bring to a boil, stirring. Add the potatoes and tamarind juice and simmer, uncovered, until potatoes and shrimp are cooked and the sauce has thickened. Season with salt and serve.

Shrimp in Hot Sauce.

Udang Pantung Kuning
Lobster in Yellow Sauce

Large shrimp can be used in place of lobsters. In Bali, coconut chunks are roasted directly on charcoal, then the charred skin is scraped off and the flesh grated for making the coconut milk.

Spice Paste
5 red chilies, seeded and chopped
3 cloves garlic, peeled and chopped
7 shallots, peeled and chopped
2 inches fresh turmeric, peeled and chopped
2 inches ginger, peeled and chopped
5 candlenuts
1 1/2 teaspoons coriander seeds
1/2 teaspoon dried shrimp paste, toasted
1 small tomato, peeled and seeded
2 tablespoons oil
1 1/2 tablespoons tamarind pulp
1 *salam* leaf
1 stem lemongrass, bruised

4 small lobsters, weighing about 1 pound each, or 2 pounds large shrimp
5 cups water
2 stems lemongrass, bruised
2 fragrant lime leaves
Few drops white vinegar
4 cups coconut milk
Fried Shallots (page 81) to garnish

To make the spice paste, grind or blend all ingredients except oil, tamarind, *salam* leaf and lemongrass. Heat oil, add spice paste and all other ingredients. Cook over moderate heat for about 5 minutes, then cool.

Wash lobsters and leave whole. Bring water to a boil, add lobsters and simmer for 15 minutes. Remove lobsters, plunge in iced water for 1 minute, then drain and remove meat. Return shells to the pot of water, keeping lobster meat aside.

Add spice paste, lemongrass, lime leaves and vinegar to the water with the shells and simmer until 4 cups of stock remain.

Add coconut milk and simmer for 10 minutes. Strain stock and return to pan. Add lobster and simmer for 1 minute. Garnish with fried shallots and serve with white rice.

Arsin Ikan Mas
Simmered River Fish

1 1/2 pounds freshwater fish, either 1 large fish or 2–4 smaller fish, cleaned and gutted
1/2 teaspoon salt
Large pinch of ground white pepper
2 cups water
2 stems lemongrass, bruised
2 tablespoons tamarind juice
3 scallions, chopped (garnish)
1/2 small pineapple, peeled and sliced (garnish)
2 fresh limes or lemons, cut in wedges (garnish)

Spice Paste
8 shallots, peeled and chopped
3 cloves garlic, peeled and chopped
1/2 teaspoon salt
6 candlenuts
1 inch ginger, peeled and sliced
1 inch fresh turmeric, peeled and sliced
1 inch galangal, peeled and sliced
15 red chilies, seeded and sliced

Season fish inside and out with salt and pepper.

To make the spice paste, grind or blend all ingredients finely. Put in a pan with the water and all other ingredients, except fish and garnishes. Bring to a boil, reduce the heat and simmer, uncovered, for 10 minutes. Add a little more water if the stock evaporates too much.

Add fish and continue to simmer until cooked, turning fish over from time to time. Remove fish carefully from stock, arrange on platter and pour stock over. Garnish with scallions, pineapple and lime.

Spicy Fried Sardines.

Ikan Bumbu Acar
Spicy Fried Sardines

Small fresh fish, such as sardines, are ideal in this typical seafood dish from the fishing villages near Pekalongan, on the northern coast of central Java.

Spice Paste
1 inch fresh turmeric, peeled and chopped
1/2 inch ginger, peeled and chopped
2 candlenuts
2 shallots, peeled and sliced
2 cloves garlic, peeled and chopped
1 teaspoon white peppercorns, crushed
1/2 teaspoon coriander seeds, crushed
2 tablespoons vegetable oil

1 1/4 pounds sardines or other small fish, cleaned
2 teaspoons salt
6 tablespoons oil
2 red chilies, seeded and sliced
13 green bird's-eye chilies, sliced
2 cloves garlic, peeled and sliced
7 shallots, peeled and sliced
1/2 inch ginger, peeled and sliced
1/2 inch galangal, peeled and sliced
1 large tomato, cut in wedges
2 tablespoons tamarind juice
1 *salam* leaf
1/2 teaspoon brown sugar
3 tablespoons water
Basil sprigs (optional)

To make the spice paste, grind or blend all ingredients except the oil. Heat oil and gently sauté the spice paste for 3–5 minutes until fragrant, then set aside.

Wash the sardines, drain and sprinkle with salt. Heat 3 tablespoons of the oil and sauté the chilies, garlic, shallots, ginger, galangal, tomato, tamarind juice and *salam* leaf over high heat for 1 minute, stirring constantly. Add sugar, then the spice paste and fry for another 2 minutes, stirring frequently.

In another pan, heat remaining oil and fry the fish until golden brown. Drain, then combine with the spicy sauce in the wok and add water. Cook for another minute, stirring to mix well. Serve garnished with fresh basil.

Lobster in Yellow Sauce.

Pesan Be Pasih
Grilled Fish in Banana Leaf

This is the Balinese equivalent of a popular Javanese dish, *ikan pepes*. If banana leaves are not available, replace with greased aluminum foil. Small whole fish are often used in Bali instead of fillets cut from a large fish; just adjust the size of the banana leaf wrapping.

- 1 pound skinned boneless snapper fillet, cut in 4
- 1 teaspoon salt
- 1 cup Spice Paste for Seafood (page 80)
- 4 banana leaves, cut into 6 inch squares
- 8 sprigs lemon basil
- 4 *salam* leaves

Season fish fillet with salt and cover evenly with seafood spice paste. Cover and leave to marinate in cool place for 6 hours.

Place each fillet in the center of a banana leaf, top each with 2 sprigs of lemon basil and 1 *salam* leaf. Fold banana leaves over fillet and fasten both ends with toothpicks. Steam parcels for 15 minutes, then place on charcoal grill or under a broiler and cook for 5 minutes until banana leaves are evenly browned.

> **HELPFUL HINT**
> You can steam the fish packets several hours before actually grilling.

Kenus Mebase Bali
Balinese Squid

The refreshing flavors of lemon basil and lime juice combine beautifully with the baby squid. This recipe also works well with large cuttlefish or any other firm fish fillets, such as snapper or sea bass.

- 1¼ pounds baby squid
- 1 tablespoon freshly squeezed lime juice
- ⅓ teaspoon ground white pepper
- ½ teaspoon salt
- 3 tablespoons oil
- 5 shallots, peeled and sliced
- 2 large red chilies, seeded and sliced
- ½ cup Spice Paste for Seafood (page 80)
- 1 cup Chicken Stock (page 81)
- 5 sprigs lemon basil, sliced
- Fried Shallots (page 81)
- Lemon basil sprigs (extra)

Remove skin of squid and pull out the tentacles and head. Cut off and discard the head and beak, but reserve the tentacles, if preferred. Clean the squid thoroughly inside and out. Marinate squid with lime juice, pepper and salt. Heat oil in wok, add shallots, chilies and squid and sauté for 2 minutes over high heat. Add spice paste and continue to sauté for 1 more minute. Pour in chicken stock, add the sliced basil and bring to a boil. Reduce heat and simmer for 1 minute. Season to taste and garnish with fried shallots and lemon basil.

Buginese Chicken.

Ayam Masak Bugis
Buginese Chicken

A Buginese favorite from Southern Sulawesi, a whole chicken is simmered in seasoned stock and coconut milk. To vary the recipe, vegetables such as long beans, spinach leaves, tomato and corn kernels can be added 5–10 minutes before the end of cooking time.

- 1 whole, 2½–3½ pound chicken
- 4 cups chicken stock (page 81)
- 2 cloves garlic, peeled and sliced
- 12 shallots, peeled and sliced
- 1 tablespoon dried shrimp paste, toasted
- 2 tablespoons tamarind juice
- 2 teaspoons white peppercorns, crushed
- 2 *salam* leaves
- 3-inch cinnamon stick
- 4 cloves
- ¼ teaspoon freshly grated nutmeg
- 1 teaspoon salt
- 1 teaspoon chopped palm sugar
- 1 tablespoon white vinegar
- 4 cups coconut milk
- Fried Shallots (page 81)

Leave chicken whole. Bring chicken stock to the boil in a heavy saucepan then add all other ingredients, except chicken, coconut milk and fried shallots. Bring back to a boil, lower heat and simmer, uncovered, for 5 minutes.

Add the chicken and coconut milk. Bring back to a boil, stirring frequently, then lower heat. Simmer uncovered, turning chicken from time to time, until it is tender. Remove chicken and continue simmering the stock until reduced by half. Garnish with fried shallots.

> **HELPFUL HINT**
> Balinese Squid: If you are using frozen squid, plunge in boiling water for 30 seconds to seal the squid. This will ensure that the squid sautés rather than stews.

Balinese Squid.

Ayam Goreng Yogya
Yogya Fried Chicken

Seasoned chicken is simmered until almost cooked, then deep-fried to make this central Javanese favorite.

2³/4-pound fresh chicken, cut into 8 pieces
2 cups water
Oil for deep-frying

Spice Paste
1 tablespoon coriander seeds
3 cloves garlic, peeled and sliced
³/4 inch fresh turmeric, peeled and sliced
³/4 inch ginger, peeled and sliced
¹/2 inch galangal, peeled and sliced
1 tablespoon chopped palm sugar
2 tablespoons oil
2 *salam* leaves

To make the spice paste, grind or blend all ingredients except oil and *salam* leaves until fine. Heat oil in a wok and sauté the spice paste and *salam* leaves for 3 minutes. Add chicken and cook, stirring, until well coated. Add water and simmer, uncovered, until chicken is almost cooked and sauce is dry. Leave to cool.

Just before chicken is required, heat oil and deep-fry chicken until it is crisp, and golden brown in color.

Bebek Menyatnyat
Duck Curry

Ducks waddling along the banks of the rice fields or following the flag held by their owner (or his children) are a common sight in Bali. On festive occasions, duck is a great favorite. Spiced stuffed duck baked in banana leaf is one popular recipe; this curry-like dish is another. Chicken could be used as a substitute for duck, if preferred.

4-pound whole duck
8 cups coconut milk
2 stems lemongrass, bruised
2 *salam* leaves
1 tablespoon salt
1 teaspoon black peppercorns, crushed
Fried Shallots (page 81)

Spice Paste
12 shallots, peeled and sliced
6 cloves garlic, peeled and sliced
4 red chilies, sliced
1 inch galangal, peeled and sliced
1 inch *kencur*, peeled and sliced
2 inch fresh turmeric, peeled and sliced
2 teaspoons coriander seeds, crushed
3 candlenuts
1 teaspoon dried shrimp paste

¹/4 teaspoon black peppercorns, crushed
Pinch of freshly grated nutmeg
2 cloves
3 tablespoons oil

Cut the duck into 12 pieces and pat dry. To make the spice paste, grind or blend all ingredients for the paste together except the oil.

Heat the oil and sauté the spice paste for 2 minutes. Add the duck, increase heat and sauté for 3 minutes, stirring frequently. Add the coconut milk and all other ingredients except fried shallots and simmer, uncovered, until the duck is tender and the sauce has thickened.

Garnish with fried shallots and serve with steamed rice.

Chicken with Green Tomatoes.

Ayam Cincane
Chicken with Green Tomatoes

This recipe comes from west and south Kalimantan, where it is usually made with a free-range or *kampung* chicken. As this is often as tough as it is flavorful, the meat is simmered in water first. If you are using a normal tender chicken, this preliminary step is very brief.

2¹/2 x 3¹/2–pound chicken, cut in 8–12 pieces
1 teaspoon salt
1 tablespoon lime or lemon juice
2 cups water
10 red chilies, seeded and sliced
12 shallots, peeled and sliced
4 green tomatoes, sliced
1 sprig basil
3 kaffir lime leaves
2 scallions, sliced
¹/2 inch ginger, peeled and sliced
5 bird's-eye chilies, sliced

Season the chicken with salt and lime juice and set aside for 20 minutes. Put the chicken in a wok, add water and simmer, uncovered, until the chicken is just tender.

Add all remaining ingredients, except bird's-eye chilies, and continue cooking for another 5 minutes. Sprinkle with bird's-eye chilies and serve.

Duck Curry.

Indonesian desserts are usually very colorful, and you'll notice that coconut, palm sugar and pandan (screwpine) leaves are indispensable.

Es Campur
Mixed Ice

Fermented tapioca and palm fruit are available in cans in Asian food stores.

$^1/_4$ ripe papaya, peeled and diced
$^1/_2$ avocado, peeled and diced
1 tomato, diced
$^1/_4$ ripe pineapple, peeled and diced
8 tablespoons agar-agar jelly cubes
8 tablespoons diced fermented tapioca (*tape*) (optional)
8 tablespoons diced palm fruit
1 young coconut, flesh removed with spoon (optional)
1 cup coconut water from the young coconut
$^1/_2$ cup condensed milk
$^1/_2$ cup Palm Sugar Syrup (page 81)
4 cups crushed ice

Cut all fruits into $^1/_4$ inch dice. Combine with all other ingredients, except ice, and mix well. Add crushed ice and serve immediately.

Ongol-ongol
Sago Flour Roll

1 cup sago flour
1 cup chopped palm sugar
2 pandan leaves
$3^1/_2$ cups water
Large square of banana leaf or parchment paper
Freshly grated coconut or moistened dried coconut
$^1/_2$ teaspoon salt
Palm Sugar Syrup (page 81)

Combine flour, sugar, pandan leaves and water in a heavy pan and bring to a boil. Simmer over low heat for 30 minutes until thickened, then leave until cool enough to handle.

Place the mixture on a large square of banana leaf and roll up in a cylinder. Fasten the ends with toothpicks and allow to cool. Serve the *ongol-ongol* sliced, sprinkled with a little coconut mixed with salt, and pour palm sugar syrup over.

Sago Flour Roll.

Kue Nagasari
Steamed Banana Cakes

Bananas are the most widely available fruit throughout Indonesia, and find their way into a great many mouthwatering desserts and cakes.

$1^1/_2$ cups mung pea flour or rice flour
$^1/_3$ cup white sugar
$2^1/_4$ cups coconut milk
Pinch of salt
6-inch squares of banana leaf
6 small or 2 large bananas, cut in $^1/_2$-inch-thick slices about $2^1/_2$-inches in length

Combine the flour and sugar in a bowl and stir in coconut milk, mixing well. Add salt and slowly bring the mixture to a boil in a heavy pan (preferably non-stick). Simmer until the mixture is very thick, then leave to cool.

Put 1 heaped tablespoon of the mixture onto a square of banana leaf. Top with a piece of banana and cover with another tablespoonful of mixture. Wrap up the banana leaf, tucking in the sides first and then rolling it over envelope style.

Steam the cakes for about 20 minutes, let cool and serve at room temperature.

HELPFUL HINT

Mung pea flour (*tepong Koen Kwe*) is sold in paper-wrapped cylinders. The flour is sometimes colored pink or green and the paper wrapper correspondingly colored. This flour gives a more delicate texture than rice flour.

Wajik
Rice Flour Cake with Palm Sugar

There are a couple of variations on this delicious steamed rice cake, which can be stored in the refrigerator for several days. It is normally served at room temperature, but can also be served warm topped with the always popular coconut milk. Another variation is to add ripe diced jackfruit (or sultanas) after the rice has been partially cooked.

1 cup glutinous white rice
1 cup water
1 pandan leaf
$^1/_2$ cup palm sugar syrup (page 81)
$^1/_4$ cup thick coconut milk
Pinch of salt

Rinse rice very well under running water for 2 minutes and soak for 4 hours. Rinse again until water becomes clear. Place rice, 1 cup of water and pandan leaf in rice cooker or steamer and cook for approximately 20 minutes, or until liquid has evaporated.

Add palm sugar syrup, coconut milk and salt, and steam for 15 minutes. Spread rice evenly to 1 inch thickness on tray and cool to room temperature. Wet a sharp knife with warm water and cut into even squares to serve.

HELPFUL HINT

To speed up the soaking process, pour boiling water over the rice and let stand for 1 hour. Drain, then add more boiling water and soak for another 30 minutes. If you are using a steamer to cook the rice, line the bottom with a wet cloth to prevent the rice grains from falling through.

Dadar
Coconut Pancake

These pancakes, with a sweet coconut filling known as *unti*, are a popular snack food and are sometimes eaten for breakfast. Both pancakes and filling can be made in advance and refrigerated; allow both to come to room temperature before filling.

Pancakes
²/₃ cup rice flour
2 tablespoons sugar
¹/₄ teaspoon salt
3 eggs
1 cup fresh coconut milk
2 tablespoons coconut oil

Filling
¹/₂ cup Palm Sugar Syrup
   (page 81)
1 cup freshly grated coconut
1 pandan leaf

To make the pancakes, combine rice flour, sugar, salt, eggs, coconut milk and coconut oil in a deep mixing bowl. Stir well with whisk until all lumps dissolve. Strain through strainer. Batter should be very liquid in consistency. Heat nonstick pan over low fire. For each pancake, pour in 4 tablespoons of the batter and cook for about 2 minutes, until the top is just set. Turn the pancake over and cook another minute. Repeat until all the batter is used up. Allow pancakes to cool to room temperature.

To make the filling, combine sugar syrup and grated coconut and mix well. Add pandan leaf and fry over low heat in frying pan for 2 minutes, stirring continuously. Cool and use at room temperature.

Place 1 tablespoon of coconut filling in the center of each pancake, fold and roll tightly into a cigar shape.

Pisang Goreng
Fried Banana Cakes

6 medium-sized bananas, peeled
1 tablespoon white sugar
1 tablespoon white flour
Oil for deep frying

Mash bananas finely and mix with sugar and sifted flour. Heat oil in a wok and drop in a large spoonful of batter. Cook several at one time, but do not overcrowd the wok or the temperature of the oil will be lowered. When cakes are crisp and golden brown, drain on paper towels and serve while still warm.

Black Rice Pudding.

HELPFUL HINT
As fresh coconut milk turns rancid fairly quickly, add a pinch of salt to the milk to help preserve it for a few hours.

Bubuh Injin
Black Rice Pudding

It's hard to find a foreign visitor to Bali who does not fall in love with the wonderful nutty flavor and meltingly smooth texture of this pudding, served with a swirl of creamy coconut milk on top.

1 cup black glutinous rice
³/₄ cup white glutinous rice
2 pandan leaves
5 cups water
¹/₂ cup Palm Sugar Syrup
   (page 81)
Pinch of salt
1¹/₂ cups freshly squeezed thick
   coconut milk

Rinse both types of rice thoroughly for 2 minutes under running water. Drain. Put water, rices and pandan leaf into a heavy pan. Simmer over medium heat for approximately 40 minutes.

Add palm sugar syrup and continue to cook until most of the liquid has evaporated. Season with a pinch of salt. Remove from heat, allow to cool. Serve at room temperature, topped with freshly squeezed coconut milk.

Coconut Pancake.

Base be Siap
Spice Paste for Chicken

14 shallots, peeled
26 cloves garlic, peeled
1 inch *kencur*, peeled and
    chopped
1½ inch galangal, peeled and
    chopped
10 candlenuts
5 inches fresh turmeric,
    peeled and chopped
4 tablespoons chopped palm sugar
4 tablespoons vegetable oil
2 stems lemongrass, bruised
2 *salam* leaves
10 bird's-eye chilies, finely sliced

Put shallots, garlic, *kencur*, galangal, candlenuts, turmeric and palm sugar into a food processor and grind coarsely.

Heat oil and fry all ingredients until very hot, stirring frequently, until the marinade changes to a golden color. Cool before using.

Spice Paste for Beef.

Base be Sampi
Spice Paste for Beef

To maximize the flavor of meat, make sure it is thoroughly coated with this marinade and refrigerate for 24 hours before using.

10 shallots, peeled and chopped
6 cloves garlic, peeled and chopped
2 inches ginger, peeled and
chopped
4 inches galangal, peeled and
    chopped
6 large red chilies, seeded and
    chopped
7 bird's-eye chilies
10 candlenuts
1 tablespoon coriander seeds
1 tablespoon black peppercorns
4 tablespoons chopped palm sugar
4 tablespoons oil
2 *salam* leaves

Combine all ingredients except oil and *salam* leaves, place in food processor and grind coarsely. Heat vegetable oil in heavy saucepan or wok until very hot. Add ground ingredients together with *salam* leaves and cook over medium heat for 5 minutes, stirring frequently, until marinade changes to a golden color. Set aside and let cool before using.

Base be Pasih
Spice Paste for Seafood

The basic seasoning for many seafood dishes.

10 large red chilies, seeded and
    chopped
6 cloves garlic, peeled and chopped
15 shallots, peeled and chopped
4 inches ginger, peeled and
    chopped
4 inches fresh turmeric, peeled
    and chopped
1 medium-sized tomato, skinned
    and seeded
1 tablespoon coriander seeds
10 candlenuts
1 teaspoon dried shrimp paste
4 tablespoons oil
3 tablespoons tamarind pulp
2 *salam* leaves
2 stems lemongrass, bruised

Process all ingredients, except oil, tamarind pulp, *salam* leaves and lemongrass, until coarsely ground.

Heat oil, add ingredients, except tamarind. Stir-fry over moderate heat for 5 minutes, until fragrant and golden. Add tamarind, stir through, and let cool before using.

Base Jukut
Spice Paste for Vegetables

8 shallots, peeled and chopped
10 cloves garlic, peeled and chopped
12 inches galangal, peeled
    and thinly sliced
1 teaspoon coriander seeds
4 inches fresh turmeric,
    peeled and sliced
6 large red chilies, seeded and
    chopped
3–5 bird's-eye chilies
2 inches *kencur*, peeled and
    chopped
1 teaspoon dried shrimp paste
2 tablespoons oil
1 teaspoon salt
¼ teaspoon ground white pepper
1 *salam* leaf, whole
1 stem lemongrass, bruised

Place shallots, garlic, galangal, coriander seeds, turmeric, chilies, *kencur* and dried shrimp paste in food processor and purée lightly, or grind coarsely using a mortar and pestle.

Heat oil in wok or heavy saucepan. Add the paste and remaining ingredients, and sauté for 2 minutes or until the mixture changes color. Leave to cool before using.

Sambal Tomat
Tomato Sambal

This spicy *sambal* which includes the tang of fresh lime juice makes an ideal accompaniment to grilled fish.

4 tablespoons oil
15 shallots, peeled and sliced
10 cloves garlic, peeled and sliced
14 large red chilies, seeded and
    sliced
2 medium-sized tomatoes,
    quartered
2 teaspoons roasted dried shrimp
    paste
2 teaspoons freshly squeezed lime
    juice
Salt to taste

Heat oil in a heavy saucepan or wok. Add shallots and garlic and sauté 5 minutes over low heat. Add chilies and sauté another 5 minutes, then add tomatoes and shrimp paste and simmer for another 10 minutes.

Add lime juice. Put all ingredients in a food processor and purée coarsely. Season to taste with salt. Cool before using. This *sambal* can be frozen.

Tomato Sambal

Sambal Sere Tabia
Fried Bird's-Eye Chilies

25 bird's-eye chilies
1/4 cup oil
1 1/2 teaspoons dried shrimp paste
1/4 teaspoon salt

Clean and discard the stems of the chilies. Heat oil in a wok or saucepan until smoking. Crumble dried shrimp paste and combine with salt.

Add chilies, shrimp paste and salt to the oil, stir over heat for 1 minute and then remove from heat and allow to cool. Store chilies and cooking oil in an airtight container for up to 1 week in a refrigerator.

Base Kacang
Peanut Sauce

1 pound raw peanuts, deep-fried for 2 minutes
4 cloves garlic, peeled
3 inches *kencur*, peeled and coarsely chopped
10–15 bird's-eye chilies, sliced
1/2 cup sweet soy sauce (*kecap manis*)

3 lime leaves
2 teaspoons salt
6 cups water
1 tablespoon freshly squeezed lime juice
2 tablespoons Fried Shallots (page 81)

Combine peanuts, garlic, *kencur* and chilies and process or grind until coarse. Put in a heavy pan with all other ingredients except lime juice and shallots and simmer over very low heat for 1 hour, stirring to prevent sticking, stir in lime juice and shallots just before serving.

Kuah Siap
Chicken Stock

11 pounds chicken bones, chopped in 1-inch pieces
1 1/2 cups Spice Paste for Chicken (page 80)
1 stem lemongrass, lightly bruised
3 lime leaves
2 *salam* leaves
1 teaspoon black peppercorns, coarsely crushed
1 teaspoon salt

Rinse bones until water is clear, put in large saucepan with cold water to cover and bring to boil.

Drain water, wash bones again under running water. Return bones to the pan, cover with fresh water and return to a boil. Reduce heat and remove foam with a ladle. Add all seasoning ingredients and simmer stock gently for 3–3 1/2 hours, skimming as necessary. Do not cover the pan during cooking as it will make the stock cloudy. Strain stock, cool and store in small containers in the freezer. Makes 3 quarts.

Sambal Matah
Shallot & Lemongrass Sambal

15 shallots
4 cloves garlic, sliced finely
10–15 bird's eye chilies, sliced
5 fragrant lime leaves, cut in hair-like shreds
1 teaspoon roasted dried shrimp paste
4 stalks lemongrass, tender part only, very finely sliced
1 teaspoon salt
1/4 teaspoon black peppercorns, finely crushed
2 tablespoons fresh lime juice
1/3 cup oil

Peel shallots and slice in half lengthwise, then cut in fine crosswise slices. Combine with all other ingredients and mix thoroughly for a couple of minutes before serving with fish or chicken.

Bawang Goreng
Fried Shallots

1/4 cup oil
10–15 shallots, peeled and thinly sliced

Heat oil until moderately hot. Add shallots and fry until golden brown.

Remove and drain thoroughly on paper towels before storing in an airtight jar.

Palm Sugar Syrup

Combine equal amounts of chopped palm sugar and water, adding a pandan leaf if available. Bring to a boil, simmer for 10 minutes, strain and store in the refrigerator.

"Japanese cuisine today is a symbiosis of culinary influences imported from the outside world, refined and adapted to reflect local preferences in taste and presentation."

JAPAN

From the land of endless ingenuity has come a cuisine designed for the eyes as well as the palate.

Left: Everyone enjoys a box lunch, from school children and salary men to Buddhist monks.

Right: The serene beauty of Kyoto's Golden Pavilion temple is emblematic of traditional Japanese culture.

More than any other cuisine in the world, Japanese food is a complete aesthetic experience for the eyes, the nose and the palate. The presentation of food is as important as the food itself, with great care given to detail, color, form and balance. In Japan, cuisine is culture, and culture cuisine; food is meant to create order out of chaos, complement nature from whence it came and still be presentational. It is a cuisine developed out of austerity and a sense of restraint.

The Land and its People

Japan's position north-east on the Southeast Asian monsoonal belt means the islands generally experience a temperate oceanic climate. Surrounded by sea, the Japanese have made its bounty—seaweed, fish and shellfish—a vital part of their diet. There is a Japanese saying that a meal should always include "something from the mountain and something from the sea," hence vegetables and rice.

Poultry and meat are also eaten, although they are less important than the humble soybean, which appears as nutritionally rich bean curd (*tofu*); as *miso*, fermented soybean paste used for soups and seasoning; and as soy sauce.

Over 43 percent of the nation's 124 million people is crammed into the three major coastal metropolises of Tokyo, Osaka and Nagoya. Fully two-thirds of the land is mountainous or forested; just over 14 percent is agricultural, and a little over four percent is used for housing.

Japan is composed of four main islands— Hokkaido, Honshu, Shikoku and Kyushu—and several thousand smaller islands stretching 1,900 miles from Hokkaido.

Hokkaido is a land of wide expanses, dairy farms, ranches and meadows, reminiscent of the American Midwest, and home to the Ainu, the indigenous people of Japan, a small Caucasoid minority. They were once hunters and fishermen who are thought to have roamed large areas of northern Honshu.

Each season has its special foods. Restaurants and private homes change their serving dishes to suit the season, as in this autumnal spread.

cuisine. *Shojin ryori* (vegetarian Buddhist temple fare), heavily influenced by Chinese Buddhist temple cooking, features small portions of a wide variety of vegetarian foods prepared in one of five standard cooking methods. *Shojin ryori* guidelines place emphasis on food of five colors (green, red, yellow, white and black-purple) and six flavors (bitter, sour, sweet, hot, salty and delicate). It was an extremely important culinary influence and the tradition lives on today. *Shojin ryori* also led to the development of *cha kaiseki*, food served before the tea ceremony, in the mid–16th century.

Japan's trade with the outside world from the 14th to 16th centuries brought many new influences. Kabocha, the green-skinned winter squash, was introduced by the Portuguese in the 16th century. The Portuguese are also credited with introducing *tempura* (batter-fried foods) as well as the popular cake *kasutera* (*castilla*). A century later, the Dutch brought corn, potatoes and sweet potatoes. European cooking created some interest and developed into what came to be known in Japan as "the cooking of the Southern Barbarians" or *Nanban ryori*.

During the Edo Period (1603–1857), Japan underwent almost three centuries of self-imposed seclusion from the outside world, which led to the development of a highly refined and distinctive Japanese culture. The Meiji Period (1868–1912) marked the return of contact and trade, and the early 20th century renewed interest in things foreign.

Japanese cuisine today is a symbiosis of culinary influences imported from the outside world, refined and adapted to reflect local preferences in taste and presentation. The desire to adapt outside influences to local tastes has produced unique blendings of East and West, including green-tea ice-cream and seaweed-flavored potato chips, even cod-roe spaghetti!

The Chinese influence is discernible: It was from China that Japan learned the art of making bean curd and how to use chopsticks. China was also the origin of soy sauce, although today's Japanese-style soy sauce is a product of the 15th century. Tea was first introduced from China in the 9th century, but gradually faded from use only to be reintroduced by a Zen priest in the late 12th century. Rice cultivation began in Japan around 300 b.c., and is still the cornerstone of a Japanese meal.

Central Japan encompasses the Sea of Japan coastal areas, where fishing villages can still be found, and the Japan Alps region centred in Nagano Prefecture, sometimes called the Roof of Japan. Three major mountain ranges traverse Nagano, and from the Koumi train line that runs through central Nagano, it is possible to enjoy views of the Japan Alps, the still-active volcano Mount Asama and Mount Fuji, at 12, 300 feet, Japan's highest mountain and a sacred symbol of the nation.

Kyushu, the third largest of Japan's islands, is renowned for its Imari and Arita pottery, hot springs resorts and active volcanoes. Nagasaki in western Kyushu was traditionally the center of trade with China and Holland and Japan's door to the outside world. Shikoku is Japan's fourth largest island.

The Ryukyu archipelago includes the southernmost province of Okinawa, comprising 160 islands, and stretches towards Taiwan.

The Making of a Cuisine

Japan's distinctive style of cuisine began to develop during the Heian Period (794–1185). The capital was moved from Nara to Kyoto, and the thriving aristocracy indulged its interests in art, literature, poetry, fine cuisine and elaborate games and pastimes. Elegant dining became an important part of the lifestyle and the aristocracy were not only gourmets, but gourmands who supplemented their regular two meals a day with numerous between-meal snacks. Today, *Kyo ryori*, the cuisine of Kyoto, represents the ultimate in Japanese dining and features an assortment of carefully prepared and exquisitely presented delicacies.

In 1185, the government moved to Kamakura, where the more austere samurai lifestyle and Zen Buddhism fostered a more simple

The Food of the People

The drastic extremes in Japan's climate—from the very cold northern island of Hokkaido to the subtropical southern islands of Okinawa—have led to the creation of regional cuisines.

In Hokkaido, which is not conducive to rice cultivation, the people have acquired a taste for potatoes, corn, dairy products, barbecued meats and salmon. Their version of Chinese noodles, called *Sapporo ramen*, is often served with a dab of butter. Seafood *o-nabe* (one-pot stew) featuring crab, scallops and salmon is also a specialty of the region.

There are differences in the food preferences of the residents of the Kanto region (centered around Tokyo and Yokohama) and the Kansai region (Kyoto, Osaka and environs). In the Kansai area, fermented *miso* is almost white compared with the darker brown and red *miso* favored in the Kanto region. Eastern and Western Japan are also divided by differing tastes in *sushi*, sweets and pickles. The Kyoto area is identified with the light, delicately flavored cuisine of the ancient court, true *haute cuisine*.

Located halfway between Tokyo and Kyoto is Nagoya, known for its flat *udon* noodles and *uiro*, a sweet rice jelly. The island's famous Sanuki *udon* noodles, fresh sardines and mandarins are popular with pilgrims visiting the Buddhist temples on Shikoku. Kyushu is known for its tea, fruits and seafood, and for the Chinese and Western culinary influences that developed because of Nagasaki's role as a center of trade with the outside world.

On the islands of Okinawa, dishes featuring pork are favored. Sweets made with raw sugar, pineapple and papaya are also popular, as are several powerful local drinks: *awamori*, made from sweet potatoes, and *habu* sake, complete with a deadly *habu* snake coiled inside the bottle.

The *o-bento* or box lunch is a microcosm of Japanese cuisine, consisting of white rice and an assortment of tiny helpings of meat, fish, vegetables, egg, fruit and a sour plum (*umeboshi*), all arranged in a small rectangular box. Since only small portions of each dish are included and a well-balanced variety of foods is necessary, preparing a proper *o-bento* can be a time-consuming ritual. As with almost all Japanese dishes, attention to detail and attractive presentation are paramount. The most famous of the commercially made *o-bento* are the *ekiben*, the box lunches available at most of the nation's train stations. These vary greatly from one area of the country to another and are considered to be an important way of promoting regional delicacies, customs and crafts.

The Four Seasons

One of the most striking aspects of Japanese cuisine is the emphasis on seasonal cuisine. Every food has its appropriate season, which not only ensures that Japanese tastes are in harmony with nature but that the cooks use the freshest possible ingredients.

By far the most important of seasonal dining specialties is *osechi ryori*, the special foods that are served during the first week of the new year. Dozens of items are decoratively arranged in tiered lacquer boxes which are brought out again and again over the first few days of the new year. Customs vary from home to home and region to region, but the typical New Year foods usually include *kamaboko* fish sausages bearing auspicious bamboo, plum and pine designs, *konbu* seaweed rolls tied into bows with dried gourd strips, chestnuts in a sticky sweet-potato paste, herring roe, shredded carrot and white radish in a sweet vinegared dressing and pickled lotus root. Vegetables such as *shiitake* mushrooms, radishes, lotus root, carrots and burdock are boiled in a soy sauce and *dashi* broth. The savory steamed egg custard *chawan-mushi* is also often eaten.

The staple accompaniment for these dishes is *o-mochi*, rice cakes that can be grilled or boiled in a soup called *o-zoni*. *Mochigome*, a special type of glutinous rice, is prepared and molded into a ball while still hot and placed in a large round wooden mortar where it is pounded rhythmically. The final product is rolled out flat and cut into rectangular cakes.

Cherry blossom-viewing parties are a seasonal must for the majority of Japanese to signal the coming of spring. Top restaurants may serve a cup of cherry blossom tea with sev-

eral delicate blossoms floating in the clear, slightly salty beverage to signal the auspicious event. Other spring delicacies include bamboo sprouts, *bonito* and rape blossoms.

Summer is the time for grilled eel, which is believed to supply the energy needed to survive the sticky, humid weather. It is also the time for octopus, abalone and fresh fruits and vegetables, especially the summer favorite, *edamame*—fresh soybeans boiled in the pod and dusted with salt—the perfect accompaniment for beer on a hot summer's night. Another summer treat is cold noodles served with a *dashi* and soy sauce dip.

Strings of persimmons drying can be seen dangling from the eaves of many a farmhouse in the countryside in autumn. This is also the season for roasted chestnuts, *soba* noodles and mushrooms. *Matsutake*, highly prized mushrooms savored for their distinctive fragrance, appear now and are used in soups and rice dishes. Late autumn is the time for preserving the year's vegetable harvest for winter. A large variety of pickling methods are popular in Japan, the most common using *miso*, salt, vinegar or rice bran as preservatives.

Winter brings *fugu sashimi*, strips of raw blowfish which can be a deadly delicacy if the fish is not handled properly by a licensed chef. Mandarins and *o-nabe*, warming one-pot stews, are also enjoyed. On the final day of the year, it is customary to eat *soba* to guarantee health and longevity in the new year.

Few things are as quintessentially Japanese as the ritual tea ceremony which encapsulates all the refinement, discipline and mystique of Japanese culture. *Cha-noyu*, the Way of Tea, began in the 15th century, and in its early form placed much emphasis on displaying and admiring imported Chinese art objects. The Way of Tea gave rise to two of the more interesting aspects of Japanese cuisine: *cha kaiseki*, Japanese haute cuisine designed to be served as a light meal before a tea ceremony, and *wagashi*, traditional Japanese sweets which became an important accessory to the tea ceremony from the mid–16th century.

The Japanese Kitchen and Table

Don't be misled into thinking that because the individual portions of food that make a Japanese meal are small, you'll finish a Japanese meal hungry. With the variety of tastes, textures and flavors, you're certain to feel satisfied—physically and mentally—at the end of a meal.

A Japanese meal can be divided into a beginning, a middle and an end. The beginning includes appetizers, clear soups and raw fish (*sashimi*). The middle of the meal is made up of a number of seafood, meat, poultry and vegetable dishes prepared by either grilling, steaming, simmering, deep-frying or serving as a vinegared "salad." To ensure variety, each style of preparation would be used only once for the foods making up the middle of the meal. For example, if the fish was deep-fried, the vegetables might be simmered in seasoned stock, the meat grilled and a mixture of egg and savory tidbits steamed. Alternatively, this variety of "middle" dishes might be replaced by a hot-pot (*nabe*), a one-dish combination of vegetables, seafood, meat, bean curd and noodles. The meal concludes with rice, *miso* soup and pickles, green tea and fresh fruit—the basis of every main meal in Japan.

Accompanying dishes are varied according to availability, season, how much time you have for preparation of the meal and so on. The Japanese do not categorize their food by the basic ingredient (for example, vegetables, beef or fish), but by the method with which it is prepared. Food is thus classified as grilled, steamed, simmered, deep-fried or vinegared.

The two extremes of Japanese cuisine are a full *kaiseki ryori*, an array of a dozen or more tiny portions of food, and the basic meal consisting of boiled rice, miso soup and pickles. If you are new to Japanese cuisine, keep the menu simple. You might like to prepare an appetizer and a couple of other dishes using fish, meat, poultry or vegetables around the basic rice, soup and pickles. You might even limit the meal to one simple appetizer and a one-pot dish such as *sukiyaki*, followed by

This beautifully presented meal shows the imaginative use of ceramics, lacquer-ware, porcelain and basketware that is typically Japanese.

the rice, soup and pickles. It is better to serve three carefully cooked, beautifully presented dishes than six less-than-perfect ones.

In private homes and many restaurants, all the dishes making up the meal are presented at the same time. At a formal meal, the appetizers arrive first, followed by the "middle" dishes, each served in the order dictated by their method of preparation.

The presentation of Japanese food is an art that encourages the cook's imagination and creativity. Even the choice of tableware is influenced by the season and the type of food being served. Generally speaking, foods which are round, such as pieces of rolled meat or slices of lotus root, are presented on rectangular or square plates, while square-shaped foods are likely to be served on round plates for contrast. Such imagination is shown in Japan, however, that plates and bowls are not just square, rectangular or round; they might be hexagonal, semicircular, fan-shaped or resemble a leaf or shell. And, it has been said in Japan that "a person cannot go out naked in public, neither can food." In most cases, garnishes are edible.

The secret to preparing Japanese cuisine at home is an understanding of the basic ingredients and of how a meal is composed; the culinary methods used are actually very simple. But the most important requirement of all is simply a love of good food, prepared and presented with a sense of harmony.

The formal tea ceremony, with its bitter powdered green tea, led to the creation of delicate *wagashi* sweets during the 16th century.

SUGGESTED MENUS

A family meal (1)

With Japanese meals many small dishes are served, and often there is no "main" attraction—they all are! But you do not necessarily have to follow this practice.

For a family meal, you may like to serve the following:
• Rolled Sushi (page 92);
• Miso-Topped Bean Curd (page 94) and a small side dish of Green Beans with Sesame (page 94) with rice;
• Jellied Plums (page 100) are a simple dessert to make but look dramatic.

A family meal (2)

Another great menu for a family dinner.
• Begin with individual bowls of Savory Custard (page 89);
• Miso Soup with Mushrooms (page 90) and Shrimp with Sake (page 96);
• Green Tea Ice Cream is always a favourite with which to finish (page 100).

A dinner party

For a dinner party that will delight your guests, you can't go wrong with dishes such as:
• Shrimp-Stuffed Mushrooms (page 88), served with small side dishes of Spinach with Sesame Dressing (page 88) and Tempura Whitebait in Soup (page 90);
• Sukiyaki (page 98) or Shabu-Shabu (page 98) that diners can cook as they eat;
• the beautiful Lily Bulb Dumplings (page 100) for dessert are a refreshing and unusual finish.

A melting pot menu

If you prefer a mix-and-match menu, put together a meal that features the following:
• Salmon Bean Curd Balls (page 88) from Japan;
• Saffron Chicken (page 55) with Naan (page 49) from India and a dish of Spicy Kang-kung (page 118) from Malaysia/Singapore;
• Round off the meal with some homely but delicious Pineapple Tartlets (page 156) from Vietnam, served with sliced fresh fruit.

THE ESSENTIAL FLAVORS OF JAPANESE COOKING

Dried bonito and **konbu seaweed** are essential for making the clear *dashi* that is used in much of Japanese cooking. Flavorful **miso**, with **bean curd** and **wakame** or **nori seaweed**, makes a quick and easy soup. Popular flavorings are **ginger**, **sake** and **soy sauce**. **Mirin** and **rice vinegar** are added to rice for **sushi**. **Sesame paste** is used in dipping sauces.

Spinach with Sesame Dressing.

Japanese appetizers are usually served in small portions on patterned lacquer or ceramic ware. Many of the dishes here would make ideal first courses at a formal dinner or as canapés with drinks.

Horenso Goma Ae
Spinach with Sesame Dressing

This is a very elegant dish. Serve at room temperature at the start of a meal.

- 10 ounces spinach, washed but left whole
- 5 tablespoons white sesame seeds
- 5 teaspoons light soy sauce
- 2 teaspoons sugar
- 4 teaspoons Basic *Dashi* Stock (page 101)
- 1 tablespoon very finely shredded *nori*

Bring a large pan of water to a boil, add the spinach leaves and cook until the leaves soften and darken in color. Pour the spinach into a colander or sieve and cool under running water. Drain, pressing on the spinach with the back of a wooden spoon to extract the water. Put the spinach in a bamboo rolling mat and roll up tightly to squeeze out all the moisture and shape into a roll.

Toast the sesame seeds in a dry pan until golden brown, then crush in a mortar or small blender until coarsely blended. Add the soy sauce, sugar and *dashi* to form a soft paste.

Just before serving, cut the rolled spinach into 1 inch pieces and divide among 4 small plates. Top each with a little of the sesame paste and sprinkle with the shredded *nori*.

Urajiro Shiitake
Shrimp-Stuffed Mushrooms

- 12 ounces fresh shrimp, peeled
- 16 fresh *shiitake* mushrooms, stems discarded
- 3 tablespoons cornstarch
- Oil for deep-frying
- 4 sprigs watercress or parsley
- 1/2 cup *Tempura* Batter (page 101)
- 2 tablespoons giant white radish, very finely grated and mixed with cayenne to taste

Dipping Sauce
- 1 cup Basic *Dashi* Stock (page 101)
- 4 tablespoons sugar
- 4 tablespoons dark soy sauce

Chop or process the shrimp to make a smooth paste. Press a little of the shrimp paste into each mushroom, dusting the top with a little cornstarch. Deep-fry the mushrooms, a few at a time, in hot oil for 2 minutes. Drain and divide among 4 serving plates. Dip each sprig of watercress or parsley in *tempura* batter and deep-fry until the batter is gold-en brown. Remove, drain and put beside the mushrooms. Garnish each serving with 1/2 tablespoon of the radish.

To prepare the dipping sauce, combine the *dashi*, sugar and soy sauce, mixing well, and divide among 4 bowls.

Sake No Tsumire-Age
Salmon Beancurd Balls

This combination of delicately seasoned salmon and bean curd makes a light and palate-pleasing dish.

- 8 ounces salmon fillet, coarsely chopped
- 9-ounce block bean curd
- A handful of *mitsuba* leaves or parsley with stalks attached
- 2 fresh *shiitake* mushrooms, stems discarded and caps very finely shredded
- 1 1/4 inches carrot, cut in matchsticks
- 1 cloud-ear fungus, soaked until swollen and very finely shredded
- 1 egg, lightly beaten
- 1/2 teaspoon salt
- 2 teaspoons light soy sauce
- 1 teaspoon sugar
- 5 teaspoons cornstarch
- Oil for deep-frying

Accompaniments
- 4 tablespoons light soy sauce
- 2 teaspoons Japanese mustard paste

Put the chopped salmon in a bowl. Soak the bean curd in water for 1–2 minutes, drain in a cloth-lined sieve, then squeeze out excess moisture by wrapping the bean-curd in the cloth and twisting tightly. Add this to the salmon.

Separate the stalks from the *mitsuba* or parsley and chop finely, keeping the whole leaves aside. Add 1–2 teaspoons of the chopped stems to the salmon and bean curd, then add all other ingredients except oil and accompaniments. Mix well and shape into small balls.

Deep-fry in hot oil, turning frequently, until golden brown and cooked. Drain and put in individual serving baskets. Spray the *mitsuba* or parsley leaves with a little water, then dip in additional cornstarch. Deep-fry in hot oil for a few seconds until the coating sets. Garnish the salmon balls with the fried leaves. Place 1 tablespoon soy sauce and 1/2 teaspoon mustard in individual dipping bowls and serve.

HELPFUL HINT
The effect will be different, but firm-fleshed fish also works well with this dish.

Shrimp-Stuffed Mushrooms (left) and Salmon Bean Curd Balls (right).

Gyuniku No Tataki
Seared Beef

- 1 pound beef sirloin or rump, in one piece
- 1 teaspoon salt
- 2 medium onions
- 3-inch piece of giant white radish, shredded
- 4 *ohba* leaves or sprigs of watercress
- 4 teaspoons finely grated giant white radish mixed with cayenne to taste
- 1 tablespoon finely sliced scallion
- 1/4 cup *Ponzu* Sauce (page 101)

Sprinkle the beef with salt and sear in a very hot pan for a few seconds on each side, just until the color changes. Remove from heat, plunge in ice water for a few seconds to cool. Dry with a cloth and cut in 1/4-inch slices.

Peel the onions, halve lengthwise, then cut in thin crosswise slices. Break up the slices with your fingers and put in ice water. Rinse, drain and dry the onion.

To serve, arrange the white radish in the center of a plate and surround with the beef. Arrange the *ohba* or watercress in the center, top with the onion, garnish with scallion and surround with tiny balls of the grated radish. Serve with tiny dishes of ponzu sauce as a dip.

Tori No Matsukaze
Chicken Loaf

Tiny poppy seeds scattered over the top of this seasoned chicken loaf are supposedly reminiscent of sand on a beach, which is perhaps why the dish is known as "Wind in the Pines."

- 13 ounces ground chicken
- 2 eggs, lightly beaten
- 3/4 inch ginger, very finely chopped
- 2 tablespoons red *miso*
- 2 teaspoons *sake*
- 2 teaspoons dark soy sauce
- 2 tablespoons sugar
- 2 teaspoons white flour
- 1 tablespoon white poppy seeds

Preheat the oven to 350° F. Blend the chicken in a food processor to make a paste. Add all other ingredients except poppy seeds and process until well mixed, or mix with a wooden spoon.

Grease an 8-inch square baking pan and line with parchment paper or oiled foil. Put in the chicken mixture, spreading evenly, then sprinkle with the poppy seeds. Set the pan in a pan half-filled with water and bake for about 30 minutes. Remove from oven and lift out the parchment paper or foil. Cut the loaf into rectangles or fan shapes. Serve at room temperature.

Chawan-Mushi
Savory Custard

Baked eel can be purchased in vacuum packs from Japanese food stores.

- 2 ounces chicken breast, in bite-sized pieces
- 2 teaspoons light soy sauce
- 1 1/2 ounces baked eel, cut in 4 pieces
- 2/3 ounce lily root, cleaned and cut in 4 pieces (optional)
- 4 fresh *shiitake* mushrooms, stems discarded
- 4 large shrimp, peeled and intestinal veins removed
- 1 tablespoon 1 1/4 inch lengths of *mitsuba* or parsley stalks
- 8 gingko nuts, peeled, blanched and thin skins removed
- 2 large eggs
- 1 1/2 cups Basic *Dashi* Stock (page 101)
- 3 teaspoons light soy sauce
- A little shredded *yuzu* orange or lemon peel to garnish

Sprinkle the chicken with soy sauce. Assemble the eel, lily root, mushrooms, shrimp, *mitsuba* or parsley stalks and gingko nuts.

Break the eggs into a bowl and mix gently with chopsticks to avoid making bubbles. Add the *dashi* stock and soy sauce. Mix well and strain.

Divide all the assembled ingredients among 4 individual china bowls or cups with lids and pour in the egg mixture. Steam for 10 minutes over medium heat. Serve garnished with *yuzu* orange or lemon peel.

Chicken Loaf.

Tamago Dofu
Cold Savory Custard

This chilled custard makes a refreshing summer appetizer.

- 3 eggs
- 14 tablespoons Basic *Dashi* Stock (page 101)
- 2 tablespoons light soy sauce
- 1 teaspoon *mirin*
- 4 large shrimp, about 3 ounces each, cooked, peeled, tails on
- 2/3 cup *Soba Dashi* (2) (page 101)
- A little grated yuzu orange or lime or lemon peel
- 4 sprigs shiso flower

Combine the eggs, basic *dashi* stock, soy sauce and *mirin*. Pour through a strainer into a small dish about 4 inches square. Put this into a steamer and steam over boiling water for about 25 minutes, until it sets. Cool, then refrigerate.

Just before serving, cut the savory custard into 4 squares and place each in a small glass or china bowl. Place a shrimp on top of each serving, pour in a little of the *soba dashi* and top each serving with grated peel and a *shiso* flower sprig.

Seared Beef and Cold Savory Custard.

Soups in Japan are quite different than Western-style soups, and are usually lighter and clean-tasting—rather like consommé. Use the freshest ingredients you can get your hands on and watch them shine!

Wakatake Sui
Clear Bamboo Shoot Soup

- 4 large shrimps, about 3 ounces each, peeled and halved lengthwise
- 2 teaspoons cornstarch
- 3 cups Clear Soup (page 101)
- 1 ounce simmered bamboo shoots, sliced (1/4 cup)
- 2 1/2 ounces *wakame* seaweed, sprigs of *kinome*, watercress or parsley

Shake the shrimp and cornstarch in a plastic bag, then put shrimp in a sieve and shake to dislodge excess cornstarch. Blanch shrimp in boiling water for about 20 seconds, until the cornstarch sets. Remove immediately, plunge in iced water for a few seconds, then reserve.

Pour the clear soup in a pan, add the bamboo shoots, bring to a boil, then add shrimp and *wakame*. Bring back to a boil and immediately remove from the heat. Divide the bamboo shoots, *wakame* and shrimp among 4 lacquer bowls and pour over the soup. Garnish with the *kinome*, watercress or parsley and serve at the beginning of a meal.

Shirauo Fubuki Jitate
Tempura Whitebait in Soup

The slight crunch of the *tempura* whitebait gives added contrast to the clear, clean soup.

- 1 egg yolk
- 2 tablespoons *Tempura* Batter (page 101)
- 1 1/2 ounces fresh whitebait
- 2 tablespoons white flour
- Oil for deep-frying
- 1 pound giant white radish
- 3 cups Clear Soup (page 101)
- Salt
- Sprigs of *mitsuba* or parsley
- A little grated *yuzu* orange or lime or lemon peel

Mix the egg yolk with the *tempura* batter. Shake the white fish and flour together in a plastic bag, then dip into the batter. Heat oil in a wok or deep-fryer and fry until crisp and golden. Peel and grate the white radish, place in a towel and squeeze out all the moisture.

Bring the clear soup to a boil and add the radish. Season with salt to taste and add the *mitsuba* or parsley. Divide among 4 lacquer soup bowls and add the fried fish just before serving. Top with a little grated peel.

Tempura Whitebait in Soup.

Tofu To Nameko No Miso Shiru
Miso Soup with Mushrooms

Nameko mushrooms, attractive reddish-brown little fungi with a slippery texture, are excellent fresh, although the bottled or canned variety could be used in this soup if fresh *nameko* are not available.

- 3 cups Basic *Dashi* Stock (page 101)
- 1/4 cup *inaka miso*
- 1 ounce *nameko* mushrooms, rinsed
- 5 ounces silken bean curd, finely diced
- 4 teaspoons very finely sliced scallions

Put the *dashi* into a saucepan and bring to a boil. Add the *miso*, stirring to dissolve. Put in the mushrooms and bean curd and heat, but do not allow to boil. Pour the soup into 4 lacquer soup bowls and sprinkle each portion with a teaspoon of scallions.

Tempura Soba
Buckwheat Noodles with Tempura

- 12 cups water
- 1 teaspoon salt
- 9 ounces buckwheat (*soba*) noodles
- 4 cups *soba dashi* (1) (page 101)
- 4 teaspoons finely sliced scallions
- Seven-spice powder (*shichimi*) to taste

Tempura
- 8 medium-sized shrimp
- 1 heaped tablespoon flour
- 4 fresh *shiitake* mushrooms, stems discarded and caps cross cut
- 4 shiso leaves
- 1 1/4 cups *Tempura* Batter (page 101)
- Oil for deep-frying

Bring the water and salt to a boil and add the noodles. Boil uncovered for 4–5 minutes, until the noodles are cooked. Drain, chill in iced water and drain again.

Put the *soba dashi* into a saucepan and bring to a boil. Keep warm while preparing the *tempura*.

For the *tempura*, peel the shrimp, discarding the head but leaving on the tail. Split open down the back, remove intestinal tract and press the shrimp open gently with your hand to make a butterfly shape. Dip into flour, shake, dip into the batter and deep-fry until golden brown and cooked. Drain. Dip the *shiitake* mushrooms and *shiso* leaves in batter and deep-fry. Drain.

Put the cooked noodles back into the *soba dashi* and reheat. Divide the noodles among 4 bowls. Taste the *soba dashi* and season with salt if needed, then pour over the noodles. Top each portion of noodles with 2 shrimp, 1 mushroom and 1 *shiso* leaf and garnish each with 1 teaspoon of scallion and a little seven-spice powder.

Clear Bamboo Shoot Soup.

Cold Buckwheat Noodles with Assorted Toppings.

Banshu-Mushi

Fish with Noodles

8 ounces red snapper fillet

1/2 teaspoon salt

4 ounces dried fine wheat
noodles (*somen*)

4 ounces *shimeji*
mushrooms

1 heaped tablespoon very finely
grated giant white radish, mixed
with cayenne to taste

1 1/2 inches scallion,
very finely shredded lengthwise

Stock

1 cup Basic *Dashi* Stock
(page 101)

2 1/2 tablespoons *mirin*

2 1/2 tablespoons light soy sauce

Sprinkle the fish with salt, cut
into 4 pieces and put on a plate.
Set a steamer over boiling water
and cook for 5–6 minutes.
Remove and set aside.
Heat all the stock ingredients
together in a saucepan and
reserve.

Divide the noodles into 4
bundles and tie one end of each
bundle with cotton thread to
prevent the noodles from separating during cooking. Cook the
noodles in plenty of boiling
water until just cooked, rinse
under cold water and drain, leav-

ing the thread still in position.
Place each bundle of noodles in
a serving bowl, leaving half of
the bundle hanging out. Top
each bundle of noodles with a
piece of fish and fold back the
noodles so as to enclose the fish.
Cut off the end of the noodles
tied with the thread and discard.
Add mushrooms to the bowl
and return to the steamer. Cook
over rapidly boiling water for 5
minutes.

Remove the fish from the
steamer and pour over the
hot stock. Garnish each
portion with 1/2 table-
spoon of grated radish
shaped into a ball and
sprinkle over a little scallion.

HELPFUL HINT

Tempura: For crispy but not
oily dried food, make sure
your oil is very hot—before
adding food, otherwise it will
absorb oil and give a soggy finish. Drain on paper towels
before serving.

Wanko Soba

*Cold Buckwheat Noodles with
Assorted Toppings*

Mushrooms

4 dried *shiitake* mushrooms

2 cups water

1 1/2 teaspoons sugar

1 1/2 teaspoons dark soy sauce

12 ounces dried buckwheat
(*soba*) noodles

2 cups *Soba Dashi* Stock (2)
(page 101)

Toppings

4 teaspoons wasabi paste

4 heaped tablespoons finely
shredded *nori*

2 eggs, lightly beaten, fried as an
omelet and shredded

8 *shiso* leaves, shredded

2 scallions, white part only,
finely shredded lengthwise

1 1/4 ounces salmon or tuna, flaked

2 tablespoons Japanese pickles

Tempura Fritters

2 ounces burdock, peeled and cut
in matchsticks 1 1/4 inches long

1/3 cup sliced onion

1 tablespoon finely chopped
mitsuba or parsley leaves

1/4 cup *Tempura* Batter
(page 101)

Oil for deep-frying

Prepare the mushrooms: Soak
mushrooms in water until soft.
Drain and put the soaking water
into a saucepan and bring to a
boil. Add the mushrooms and
sugar, return to a boil, skim the
surface and reduce the heat.
Cover and simmer gently for 40
minutes. Add the soy sauce and
simmer for another 40 minutes.
Cool, then shred the mushrooms finely.

Boil the noodles in plenty of
lightly salted water for 4–5
minutes, drain and chill in cold
water. Drain the noodles again
and refrigerate.

To make the *tempura* fritters,
combine all ingredients and
deep-fry, a spoonful at a time, in
hot oil until golden brown.
Drain and keep aside.

When serving, arrange
small handfuls of the noodles in
lacquer bowls. Put the remaining noodles in a basket or dish
and keep on the table.

Pour a little of the cold *soba
dashi* over the bowl of noodles
and add topping to taste. It is
customary to add more noodles
and *dashi* to the bowl, and continue with a different topping
until the noodles are used up.

Buckwheat Noodles with Tempura.

Sushi and sashimi, both of which feature the best the seas and oceans have to offer, are now very popular in many countries. For these dishes, it is imperative that you buy the freshest fish possible, nothing less will do.

Hosomaki
Rolled Sushi

Three different fillings are used in these *nori*-wrapped rolls of vinegared rice: tuna, cucumber and pickled giant white radish, the last available in jars in Japanese stores.

- 6 ounces fresh tuna
- 3 8-inch x 7-inch sheets *nori*
- 6 ounces cucumber
- 3 cups Vinegared Rice (page 101)
- 1 teaspoon mixed Japanese wasabi paste
- 6 ounces pickled giant white radish strips
- 2 tablespoons pickled ginger slices

Cut the raw tuna into 4 strips of the same length as the *nori*. Cut the cucumber in quarters lengthwise, remove the seeds and cut into sticks.

Cut the *nori* in half. Place the half *nori* sheet on a bamboo rolling mat, shiny side down. Top with 1/2 cup rice, spread evenly on the sheet, leaving a border of 1/2 inch free on the inside of the sheet.

Take a little wasabi paste with your finger and spread it across the centre of the rice. Place the tuna across the center of the horseradish and start to roll using the bamboo mat,

making sure the *nori* sheet end goes under the rice. Roll the mat up firmly and squeeze gently. Remove the rolled sushi from the mat, cut in half and then into three pieces with a wet knife.

Repeat the process with a filling of cucumber and again with pickled radish. Serve with pickled ginger.

Chirashi-Zushi
Sushi Rice with Topping

The tiny dried fish called for are sold in packets; they are actually dried and cooked silver fish. Grilled eel is available canned or in vacuum packs from Japanese food stores.

- 5 cups cooked Vinegared Rice (page 101)
- 1 tablespoon tiny dried fish
- 4 tablespoons finely shredded *nori*
- 4 eggs, lightly beaten and fried as an omelet and shredded
- 4 medium-sized cooked shrimp, halved and open butterfly style
- 3 ounces raw tuna, cut in strips
- 2 ounces squid, blanched and cut in strips
- 2/3 ounce grilled eel
- 1/3 cup shrimp flakes (page 93)
- 4 tablespoons pickled ginger slices
- 4 teaspoons light soy sauce
- 4 teaspoons mixed Japanese wasabi paste

Mixed Rolled Sushi.

Mix sushi rice with dried fish if using. Put the mixture into 4 lacquer bowls or wooden boxes and level the surface. Scatter with seaweed and omelet and place all other ingredients decoratively on top.

HELPFUL HINT
The trick to making sushi rolls is to have all the ingredients cut up and ready to go. These can be prepared ahead of time and refrigerated in airtight containers.

Battera Sushi
Vinegared Rice with Kelp

Shiraita konbu, very fine golden-colored kelp, is used to cover this sushi. The sushi can be pressed into a rectangular container if you like.

Place the skin on the bottom and layer it with rice, fish, sesame seeds and golden kelp. Cover and put on a weight to compress the sushi.

Leave to stand for 15 minutes before cutting.

- 10 ounces mackerel fillets
- 3/4 cup salt
- 1 large sheet or 2 small sheets golden kelp (*shiraita konbu*)
- 14 tablespoons rice vinegar
- 1 1/2 vinegared rice (page 101)
- 1 teaspoon white sesame seeds
- 4 tablespoons light soy sauce
- 4 tablespoons pickled ginger slices

Sprinkle the mackerel fillets lightly with salt and refrigerate for 1 1/2 hours. Rinse and pat dry.

Soak the golden kelp in water to cover until soft and transparent. Remove any small bones from the mackerel. Place vinegar in a glass or ceramic dish, add the mackerel fillets and refrigerate for 40 minutes. Cut the skin from fish.

Wet a cotton cloth, wring it dry, then place it on a bamboo rolling mat. Put the skin across the cloth and spread the rice evenly over the skin. Top with a fillet of fish, sprinkle with sesame seeds and cover the top with the golden kelp.

Roll up, shaping the contents as you go into a smooth, even roll.

Unroll, cut into 3/4-inch slices and serve with soy sauce and pickled ginger.

Rolled Sushi.

Norimaki
Mixed Rolled Sushi

Shrimp Flakes
5 ounces small shrimp, peeled and deveined
1 egg yolk
2 1/2 tablespoons sugar
1/4 teaspoon salt
A little red food coloring

1 1/4 ounces grilled eel
2 ounces cooked shrimp, peeled
1/4 English cucumber
1/4 cup shrimp flakes (see below)
2 eggs, beaten and fried as an omelet
2 sheets of toasted *nori*
2 cups Vinegared Rice (page 101)
4 tablespoons pickled ginger slices
4 tablespoons light soy sauce

To make the shrimp flakes rinse the shrimp in lightly salted water. Drain and simmer in a little salted water until they change color. Drain, cool and blend in a food processor to make a purée. Tie the shrimp in cheesecloth and leave to soak in water for 1–2 minutes to remove any smell. Drain the shrimp and knead the cheesecloth gently to extract all moisture.

Put the shrimp in a bowl and add egg yolk, sugar and salt, mixing well. Add just a touch of food coloring diluted in water to make the shrimp a pale pink. Put the shrimp into a nonstick pan and cook over low heat, stirring from time to time, for about 30 minutes or until almost dry. (This can be kept refrigerated for up to 1 week.)

Vinegared Rice with Kelp.

Cut the eel, shrimp, cucumber and omelet into sticks of the same length. Place *nori* on a bamboo rolling mat and spread half the sushi rice on the *nori*, leaving a 1/2-inch border free at the top and bottom. Sprinkle the rice with half the shrimp flakes. Arrange half the ingredients side by side in a row on the rice. Start to roll using the bamboo mat, making sure the *nori* sheet end goes under the rice. Roll the mat up firmly and squeeze gently. Remove the rolled sushi from the mat, cut in half and then into 3/4-inch slices with a wet knife. Repeat with the remaining filling.

Serve with pickled ginger and soy sauce for dipping.

HELPFUL HINT
Packets or jars of prepared prawn or shrimp flakes are often available in Japanese grocery stores.

Tsukuri Moriawase
Assorted Sashimi

A wide variety of seafood is enjoyed raw as sashimi, cut in different ways depending upon the texture of each particular ingredient. Sashimi is served with a variety of garnishes, condiments and dipping sauces, some sauces being considered more appropriate to certain types of seafood than others.

4 jumbo shrimp
4 ounces scallops

1/2 teaspoon oil
5 ounces halfbeak fillet or tuna
10 ounces snapper fillet
1/2 cup shredded giant white radish
4 *shiso* leaves
4 teaspoons wasabi paste
4 tablespoons *Tosa* Soy Sauce (page 101)

Peel the shrimp, remove the dark intestinal vein but leave on the head and tail for a more attractive appearance. Clean and dry the scallops. Heat the oil in a nonstick pan until moderately hot and sear the scallops for 30 seconds on each side. Remove and set aside.

Scale both fish and remove any small bones. Cut the halfbeak fillet on the diagonal into strips about 1/2-inch wide and 1 1/4-inches long. If using tuna, cut into 3/4-inch cubes. The snapper can either be sliced paper thin or cut to resemble a leaf.

Arrange shrimp, scallops and fish decoratively on a plate, a rectangular one looks best. Garnish with giant white radish, *shiso* leaf and wasabi, and serve with bowls of *tosa* soy sauce for dipping.

HELPFUL HINT
You may decide to serve just one or two types of fish, or a range of several, but whatever variety you choose, be absolutely certain that the fish is spanking fresh.

Onigiri
Rice Balls

These hearty triangular rice balls make ideal snacks or a light lunch, and the choice of the filling is up to you. Leave the *nori* off until you are ready to serve. The amounts given here should make 12–13 rice balls.

5 1/3 cups short-grain rice
Salt to taste
3–4 sheets toasted *nori*, cut into 5-inch x 2-inch strips

Filling
Umeboshi (pickled plums)
1/2 teaspoon per rice ball
Salted salmon, 1 teaspoon per rice ball
Dried *bonito* flakes mixed with a

Assorted Sashimi.

little light soy sauce, 1 heaped teaspoon per rice ball
Strips of salted dried kelp (*shio-kobu*), 1 heaped teaspoon per rice ball

Wash the rice gently under running water until the water runs clear. Leave to drain for 1 hour, then put into a saucepan with the water and bring to a boil over high heat. Reduce the heat and simmer gently for 15–20 minutes until the rice is cooked and the water absorbed. Remove from the heat, cover the rice with a towel to absorb any moisture and put back the lid. Stand for 20 minutes.

To make the rice balls, sprinkle a little salt onto the palm of one hand and take a handful (about 1/2 cup) of rice. Flatten it to make a depression in the center and put in a little of your chosen filling. Mold the rice to enclose the filling and shape into a triangle. Wrap with a piece of *nori* and moisten the end to seal. Set aside while preparing the remaining rice balls. Serve at room temperature.

Seared Bonito with Tangy Dressing.

Katsuo Tataki
Seared Bonito with Tangy Dressing

Tangy and light, this refreshing chilled dish is perfect for a hot summer's day.

- 12 ounces *bonito* fillet, skin on
- 1/3 cup scallion, very finely shredded lengthwise
- 4-inch piece ginger, very finely shredded lengthwise
- 1–2 cloves garlic, very finely chopped
- 1/2 lemon, thinly sliced
- 1/3 cup Ponzu Sauce (page 101)
- 1/4 cup shredded giant white radish
- 1 heaped tablespoon finely grated white radish, mixed with seven-spice or cayenne to taste

Heat a lightly greased non-stick frying pan. Put in the *bonito* fillet, skin side up, and sear until the outside of the fish turns white. Turn and sear the other side, then soak in ice water for 10–15 seconds to chill.

Wipe away any moisture and marinate the whole fillet with half of the scallion, ginger, garlic, lemon and *ponzu* sauce, patting the fish with the side of a knife to let the sauce penetrate. Chill in the refrigerator for a minimum of 10 minutes. Cut the marinated *bonito* into 1/2-inch slices.

Arrange the *bonito* on a bed of radish strips garnished with the remaining sliced scallion, ginger and garlic on a platter. Arrange the remaining lemon slices and and seasoned grated radish on the side and serve either at room temperature or chilled.

Ingen Goma-Ae
Green Beans with Sesame

Green beans marry beautifully with the flavor of sesame, although spinach can be substituted if preferred.

- 2 cups green beans
- 1/2 cup sesame paste
- 1/2 cup Basic *Dashi* Stock (page 101)
- 4 teaspoons light soy sauce
- 5 teaspoons sugar
- 4 tablespoons finely shredded toasted nori

Boil the beans in lightly salted water until just tender. (Can also be steamed.)

Drain and cool under cold running water. Cut into 1 1/2 inch lengths, on the diagonal if liked.

Mix the sesame paste, *dashi*, light soy sauce and sugar. Put the beans into 4 serving bowls, top each with a spoonful of the sesame dressing and garnish with 1 tablespoon of shredded *nori*.

Tofu Dengaku
Miso-Topped Bean Curd

A striking-looking dish of grilled bean curd served with three different colored toppings.

- 2 blocks bean curd (16–18 ounces)
- 6 tablespoons Red *Dengaku Miso* (page 101)
- 3/4 White *Dengaku Miso* (page 101)
- 1 teaspoon very finely grated *yuzu* orange or lemon peel
- 1/3 cup *kinome*, watercress, parsley leaves or spinach leaves

To remove excess moisture from the bean curd, wrap in a clean towel, place between 2 cutting boards and let stand for 20 minutes. Cut the bean curd into pieces measuring 3/4 inch thick, 2 inches long and 3/4 inch wide.

To make the red *miso* topping, put the red *dengaku miso* in a bowl; it needs no further addition.

To make the yellow topping, mix 6 tablespoons of the white *dengaku miso* with the *yuzu* peel and set aside.

To make the green topping, purée the *kinome*, watercress or parsley leaves to obtain a juice and mix with the remaining white *dengaku miso*. For a stronger green color, use spinach leaves.

Grill beancurd until lightly colored on both sides. Spread each piece with one of the three colored toppings and return to the grill until they take color. Carefully insert a skewer into each bean curd and serve hot.

Butaniku Shoga-Yaki
Pork with Ginger

This pork dish is enlivened with the addition of fresh ginger juice and *sake*.

- 1 pound pork loin, sliced
- 4 teaspoons Ginger Juice (page 101)
- 3 tablespoons light soy sauce
- 3 tablespoons *sake*
- 8 ounces cabbage
- 1 green bell pepper
- 2 medium onions
- 2 teaspoons vegetable oil

Cut pork slices into 1 1/2-inch cubes and set aside.

Mix ginger juice, soy sauce and *sake* and keep aside. Cut cabbage leaves and pepper into 1 1/2-inch squares. Cut onions in half lengthwise and then cut crosswise into 1 1/2-inch slices.

Heat the oil in a frying pan or wok and stir-fry the pork until it changes colour. Add the cabbage, pepper and onion and continue stir-frying until the vegetables and pork are cooked. Pour in the seasoning, mix well and serve hot.

Miso-topped Bean Curd.

Katsudon
Pork Cutlets on Rice

This unusual recipe, a Japanese variation of a traditional European dish, incorporates Western ingredients with the essentials of the Japanese kitchen: rice, *dashi* and soy.

Pork Cutlets
1 pound pork loin
A sprinkle of salt and pepper
2 tablespoons white flour
1 egg, lightly beaten
2 cups breadcrumbs
Oil for deep frying

6–8 cups hot cooked rice
2 onions, sliced
1 cup Basic *Dashi* Stock
   (page 101)
1/3 cup *mirin*
1/3 cup thick soy sauce
4 teaspoons sugar
4 sprigs *mitsuba* or parsley with
   long stems
4 eggs

To make the pork cutlets, cut the pork loin into 4 steaks, making incisions along the fatty edge to prevent it from curling during frying. Season the meat lightly with salt and pepper, dust with flour on both sides, dip in beaten egg and press firmly into the bread crumbs.

Heat oil and deep-fry the crumbed pork until golden brown and cooked. Drain on paper towels and set aside.

Divide the rice among 4 large bowls.

Put the onions, *dashi*, *mirin*, soy sauce and sugar in a pan and simmer until the onions are tender. Put one-quarter of this onion mixture into a small pan, place one cooked pork cutlet on top, add one-quarter of the *mitsuba* or parsley and pour the beaten egg over the top. Simmer until the eggs are just cooked but still runny; they must not be over cooked or they will be firm and dry.

Top one portion of rice with this mixture. Repeat with the remaining pork cutlets and serve with a side dish of pickles.

Chikuzen-ni
Vegetables Simmered in Soy Sauce

Any combination of vegetables can be used for this recipe, so take advantage of the best of the season. The amount of stock used is sufficient for about 1 pound of vegetables.

3 ounces each of
   bamboo shoots, carrot,
   burdock, lotus root, Japanese
   sato-imo or new potatoes, devil's
   tongue jelly (*konnyaku*)
4 fresh *shiitake* mushrooms
12 sugar peas or snow peas
3 ounces chicken
2 teaspoons oil

Stock
3 cups Basic *Dashi* Stock
   (page 101)
6 tablespoons dark soy sauce
2 tablespoons sugar
1/4 cup *sake*

Peel and cut all vegetables and chicken into dice. Separate the devil's tongue jelly with a spoon. Boil the vegetables and devil's tongue jelly, one at a time, in lightly salted water for 5 minutes. Blanch the chicken in boiling water for 20 seconds, then drain, chill in iced water and drain again.

Heat the oil and stir-fry the vegetables for 2 minutes. Set the vegetables aside.

To make the stock, put the *dashi* into a pan and add the stir-fried vegetables. Skim the surface to remove any foam and add all other stock ingredients and chicken. Bring to a boil and simmer gently with the pan covered for 20–30 minutes.

Arrange the vegetables and chicken in bowls, add a little of the cooking liquid and serve.

Kobocha No Nimono
Winter Squash

Pumpkin is a very popular vegetable, not only for its sweet taste but its beautiful color. This simple but delicious recipe makes a good sidedish as part of a Western meal

Vegetables Simmered in Soy Sauce

1 pound wintersquash
3 cups Basic *Dashi* Stock
   (page 101)
7 tablespoons sugar
1/4 cup light soy sauce

Remove the seeds from the squash and scoop out any fibers with a spoon. Cut into 2-inch square pieces, and peel off the skin on the edges of each piece, so that the squash holds its shape during cooking. Cut the squash into decorative shapes as desired.

Put the *dashi* and sugar into a pan and bring to a boil. Add the squash and simmer gently for 7–8 minutes. Turn the squash

pieces over, add soy sauce and continue cooking until the squash is tender.

Serve warm or at room temperature, and pour a little of the cooking liquid into each bowl.

HELPFUL HINT
The best winter squash to use for this recipe is butternut variety, although any other dense-fleshed winter squash may be used.

Simmered Winter Squash (left) and Green Beans with Sesame (right).

Yosenabe

*Seafood, Chicken, Vegetable
and Noodle Hotpot*

Yosenabe literally means a mixture of anything, so the ingredients included in this hotpot can be adjusted to suit your taste and availability.

- 5 ounces seabream fillet
- 5 ounces salmon fillet
- 5 ounces Spanish mackerel
  fillet
- 5 ounces chicken
- 5 ounces oysters
- 7-inch piece giant white radish
- 5 ounces clams
- 5 ounces shrimp, peeled, tails
  left on and intestinal vein
  removed
- 1 pound Chinese Napa cabbage
- 4 ounces edible chrysanthemum
  leaves, hard stems removed
- 4 fresh *shiitake* mushrooms, stems
  discarded and caps cross cut
- 4 ounces golden *(enokitake)*
  mushrooms, hard ends of stems
  removed
- 1 large carrot, peeled and sliced
- 1 cup scallions, cut in 1¹/₂-inch
  lengths
- 8 ounces bean curd, cut in large
  dice
- 4 ounces cellophane noodles,
  soaked until transparent
- Sprigs of *kinome* or watercress to
  garnish

Stock
- 7 cups Basic *Dashi* Stock
  (page 101)
- ¹/₂ cup light soy sauce
- 2 tablespoons *mirin*

Cut the fish fillets and chicken into 1¹/₄-inch squares. Blanch each separately in boiling water until they change color, drain and set aside.

Remove the oysters from their shells and place oysters in a colander. Grate half of the white radish and mix gently by hand with the oysters to remove any dirt. Clean by shaking the

colander in salted water. Drain and set the oysters aside. Put the clams, still in their shells, and peeled shrimp to one side.

Boil the cabbage for 2 minutes, drain and spread on a bamboo rolling mat. Roll up and squeeze tightly to remove excess moisture. Unroll and cut the cabbage roll into slices ³/₄-inch thick. Cut the chrysanthemum leaves into 2–3 inch lengths. Slice the remaining giant white radish.

Arrange all ingredients attractively on a large platter. Prepare the stock by putting all ingredients into a large pan and bringing to a boil. Pour the stock into a heatproof casserole and set on a fire in the center of the table, with the platter of raw ingredients nearby. To cook, put the chicken and clams into the stock, followed by the fish, shrimp, oysters, noodles, and vegetables. Wait until the ingredients are cooked before adding the next batch of ingredients.

Ebi-ni

Shrimp with Sake

- 12 fresh shrimp (weighing
  8–10 ounces)
- 1 cup Basic *Dashi* Stock
  (page 101)
- ¹/₂ cup *sake*
- 2 tablespoons sugar
- 2 tablespoons light soy sauce
- ³/₄ inch ginger, sliced
- 8 snow peas, blanched in lightly
  salted water and chilled

Trim the whiskers and legs of each shrimp but do not peel. Use a toothpick to remove the intestinal vein at the back of the head. Place the shrimp in a pan with the *dashi*, *sake*, sugar, soy sauce and ginger. Simmer for

Prawns with Sake (left) and Prawns with Noodles (right).

3–4 minutes over high heat. Add the snow peas at the last moment. Drain the shrimp and peel, leaving on the head and tail. Arrange on a plate with the snow peas and serve at once.

Ebi Amondo-Age

*Deep-Fried Shrimp
with Almonds*

A modern Japanese dish that uses almonds rather than the more traditional broken noodles for a crunchy exterior. If desired, 12 ounces of shredded sweet potato, tossed in 2 tablespoons of white flour, can be substituted for the almonds. Dust the shrimp with a little cornstarch, then dip in lightly beaten egg white rather than *tempura* batter before pressing into the sweet potato.

- 12 fresh shrimp (about 8
  ounces)
- 2 tablespoons white flour
- ¹/₂ cup *Tempura* Batter
  (page 101)
- 2¹/₂ cups flaked
  almonds
- Oil for deep-frying
- 4 fresh *shiitake* mushrooms, stalks
  discarded and caps cross cut
- 8 small Japanese green peppers,

- or 1 green bell pepper cut in
  strips
- ¹/₂ cup *Tempura Dashi* (page 101)
- 4 tablespoons finely grated
  white radish
- Seven-spice powder *(shichimi)*,
  to taste

Trim the whiskers and legs of the shrimp with scissors. Peel the body section, but leave on the head and the tail. Remove the dark intestinal vein with a toothpick. Make two or three incisions on the underside of each shrimp to prevent it from curling. Pat dry and dust with flour. Dip each shrimp into the *tempura* batter and then press into the almonds to coat well.

Deep-fry the shrimp in hot oil until golden brown. Drain and set aside.

Dust the *shiitake* mushrooms and green peppers in flour, dip in *tempura* batter and deep-fry.

Arrange the fried shrimp, mushrooms and green peppers on 4 plates.

Serve with small bowls of *tempura dashi* for dipping and grated white radish. Each diner sprinkles his portion with seven-spice powder to taste.

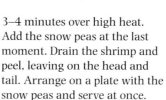

*Seafood, Chicken, Vegetable
and Noodle Hotpot.*

Shirauo Kara-Age
Deep-Fried Whitebait

- 1 pound fresh whitebait
- 4 tablespoons cornstarch
- Oil for deep-frying
- Salt to taste
- 1 lemon, cut in wedges

Wash and dry the whitebait. Toss in cornstarch and shake in a colander or sieve to remove excess flour. Heat oil in a wok or deep-fryer until very hot and deep-fry a handful of whitebait at a time until crisp, and golden brown in color.

Drain and sprinkle with salt just before serving. Garnish with lemon wedges.

Karei Shio-yaki
Flat Fish with Salt

- Sweet Vinegar
- 2 cups water
- $1^{1}/8$ cups rice vinegar
- $^{2}/3$ cup sugar
- 2 teaspoons salt

- Lotus Root Garnish
- 2 ounces fresh lotus root, peeled and thinly sliced
- 3 tablespoons Sweet Vinegar
- 1 red chili, seeds discarded
- $^{1}/3$ cup *Ponzu* Sauce (page 101)

- $1^{1}/3$ pounds flat fish, such as flounder, sole or pomfret

- 2 tablespoons salt
- Lemon wedge to garnish
- 10-inch piece giant white radish, very finely grated and squeezed to extract moisture

Prepare lotus root garnish several hours before it is required.For the sweet vinegar, bring water and vinegar to the boil in a saucepan, then add sugar and salt and stir until dissolved. Remove from heat.

Boil the sliced lotus root in water for 30 seconds, drain and put it in the sweet vinegar. Heat the chilli in a dry pan for a few seconds, then add to the vinegar and *ponzu* sauce.Refrigerate.

Clean and scale the fish. Dry with a paper towel and make two deep crosswise incisions on each side. Put a skewer through the tail end of the fish, making it come out in the centre and continuing to the head so that the fish has a wave shape. Sprinkle both sides of the fish lightly with salt, then press a liberal amount of salt onto the tail and fins.

Cook the fish over a moderately hot charcoal fire or under a grill, turning it with the skewer to avoid damaging the skin, until the fish is golden on both sides and cooked through. Serve on a plate garnished with lemon, grated radish and lotus root.

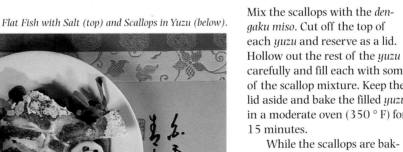

Deep-Fried Shrimp with Almonds (top right) and Deep-Fried Whitebait (left).

Flat Fish with Salt (top) and Scallops in Yuzu (below).

Hotate Uuzu Kama-Yaki
Scallops In Yuzu

Fresh scallops are lightly baked with *miso* in *yuzu* shells for an exotic presentation. If *yuzus* are not available, mandarins are an acceptable substitute.

- 6 ounces fresh scallops, quartered
- $^{1}/2$ cup red Dengaku *Miso*
- 4 *yuzu* oranges or mandarins
- 4 white *hime* radishes, or 4-inch piece of giant white radish, quartered
- 4 teaspoons mor *miso* or red *miso*

Mix the scallops with the *dengaku miso*. Cut off the top of each *yuzu* and reserve as a lid. Hollow out the rest of the *yuzu* carefully and fill each with some of the scallop mixture. Keep the lid aside and bake the filled *yuzu* in a moderate oven (350 ° F) for 15 minutes.

While the scallops are baking, peel the radish and boil in lightly salted water until soft. Drain, cool the radish in iced water and reserve.

Place a *yuzu* and its lid on each serving dish and garnish with the radish and 1 teaspoon of miso.

> ### HELPFUL HINT
> Shrimp can be substituted for scallops. Shell and devein the shrimp before combining with the *miso.*

Nuta
Tuna, Seaweed and Cucumber

- 8 ounces fresh tuna
- $1^{1}/2$ heaped tablespoons dried *wakame* seaweed
- 1 teaspoon salt

- 4 ounces Japanese cucumbers
- $^{1}/3$ cup white *miso*
- $1^{1}/2$ teaspoons sesame paste or smooth peanut butter
- $2^{1}/2$ tablespoons rice vinegar
- 4 teaspoons sugar
- 2 teaspoons light soy sauce
- 2 teaspoons Japanese mustard
- 2 *mioga* buds, cut in fine lengthwise strips (optional)

Plunge the tuna in boiling water for 5–10 seconds until the outside starts to turn pinkish white. Remove from the water, chill in iced water for a few seconds, drain again and cut into 2-inch x $^{3}/4$-inch pieces about $^{1}/2$ inch thick.

Soak the dried *wakame* in hot water until expanded and tender. Drain and set aside. Rub the salt into the outside of the cucumber with your fingers, then slice paper thin. Sprinkle with a generous pinch of salt. Rinse off salt and squeeze out the moisture.

Mix the *miso* with the sesame paste, vinegar, sugar, soy sauce and mustard.

Arrange the tuna, *wakame* and cucumber in a bowl. Garnish with a little of the *miso* mixture and top with some shredded *mioga*, if available.

Sukiyaki
Beef with Vegetables

Sukiyaki only became known in Japan around the turn of the century, when the Japanese began eating beef (previously proscribed by Buddhist law). There are two styles of cooking this mixture of meat, vegetables, bean curd and noodles: the Osaka style involves cooking the sauce in the pan at the table with each new addition of ingredients. The Tokyo style requires the sauce to be prepared in advance.

- 1¼ pounds prime sirloin beef, sliced
- 3 small onions, cut crosswise in ¼-inch slices
- 5 cups scallions, diagonally sliced in ³/₄-inch pieces
- 2 cups chrysanthemum leaves, cut in 3-inch pieces
- 2 ounces fresh *shiitake* mushrooms, stems discarded and caps cross cut
- 4 ounces golden (*enokitake*) mushrooms, hard part of stems discarded
- 4 ounces burdock, shaved thinly, (optional)
- 12 ounces *shirataki konnyaku* or wheat noodles (*udon*), boiled until just cooked, then drained
- 1 piece grilled bean curd (*yakidofu*), cut in small pieces
- 8 small baked gluten cakes (*fu*) or 1 cake cotton bean curd, cubed
- 4 tablespoons beef fat (suet)
- 4 eggs

Sauce
- ³/₄ cup light soy sauce
- ²/₃ cup *mirin*
- ²/₃ cup *sake*
- ½ sugar

Arrange the beef, vegetables, noodles and both types of bean curd on a platter. Keep the beef fat on a small dish to use for greasing the cooking pan. Put the eggs into individual dipping bowls.

Prepare the sauce by putting all ingredients into a pan. Bring to a boil, remove from heat and pour the sauce into a jug.

When it is time to eat the *sukiyaki*, put the beef fat in a heavy-bottomed frying pan and heat gently so that is melts and spreads over the whole surface of the pan. Discard the fat.

Beef with Vegetables.

Add a little of the sliced beef and vegetables, pour on a little of the prepared sauce and simmer. When the ingredients are cooked through, diners can help themselves to whatever they fancy, dipping each morsel in the egg (lightly stirred with the chopsticks) before eating.

Add more ingredients to the pan as needed.

Shabu-Shabu
Japanese One-Pot

An assortment of beef slices, vegetables and cellophane noodles are cooked at the table in a type of fondue generally known as a steamboat or Mongolian hotpot.

- 1¼ pounds prime sirloin beef, sliced paper-thin
- 1 pound long white Chinese Napa cabbage
- 10 ounces chrysanthemum leaves, hard part of stems discarded
- 8 fresh *shiitake* mushrooms, stems discarded and caps cross cut
- 8 ounces golden (*enokitake*) mushrooms, hard end of stems removed
- 2 cups scallions, diagonally sliced in ³/₄-inch pieces
- 4 ounces cellophane noodles, soaked in water until transparent

- 6 ounces silken bean curd, cubed

Accompaniments
- 1 cup sesame sauce for dipping
- 1 cup *Ponzu* Sauce (page 101)
- 4 tablespoons finely sliced scallions
- 4 tablespoons finely grated giant white radish mixed with cayenne to taste

Stock
- Twelve 5-inch x 3-inch pieces dried kelp (*konbu*)
- 8 cups water
- 2 teaspoons salt

Arrange the beef slices on a plate. Cut the cabbage into 1¹/₂-inch squares. Cut out the hard part of the stalk and slice thinly. Arrange the cabbage and all other ingredients on a platter.

For the accompaniments, put the sesame sauce into 4 separate bowls. Do the same for the *ponzu* sauce. Put 1 tablespoon each of the scallions and grated radish onto 4 separate dishes. Give each diner a bowl of sesame dressing, a bowl of *ponzu* and a dish of scallions with radish.

To make the stock, wipe the kelp lightly with a damp cloth to clean. Slash in a few places with kitchen scissors to a knife to release the flavor. Put water and kelp into a saucepan and bring to a boil. Remove the kelp immediately when the stock reaches boiling point. Reduce heat and simmer for 2–3 minutes. Add the salt.

Pour stock into the steamboat and bring to a boil. Each person selects a morsel of food and swishes it in the stock until cooked. The food is dipped into one of the sauces, with a little of the scallion added to the sesame

Japanese One-Pot.

sauce, and the onion or radish added to the *ponzu*.

Skim the stock of any foam that arises during cooking. When all the ingredients have been eaten, serve the remaining stock (which will have become a rich soup) in bowls with a little scallion on top if liked.

Tebasaki To Sato-Imo
Braised Chicken Wings

1 pound chicken wings
4 teaspoons *sake*
1 tablespoon oil
3/4 inch ginger, sliced
12 scallions, cut in 2-inch lengths
12 ounces *sato-imo* or new potatoes, peeled
2 teaspoons sugar
3 tablespoons plus 1 teaspoon dark soy sauce
12 snow peas, blanched in lightly salted water
4 strips orange or lemon peel

Marinate chicken wings in *sake* for 30 minutes. Heat the oil and stir-fry the chicken wings until they change color. Add ginger, scallions and just enough water to just cover the chicken. Cover the pan and simmer for 10–15 minutes, then add the potatoes, sugar and soy sauce. Simmer for about 30 minutes until the

potatoes are soft.

Divide the chicken wings and potatoes among 4 bowls and garnish each portion with 3 snow peas and a strip of orange or lemon peel.

Teriyaki Suteki
Sirloin Steak Teriyaki

Tender cubes of steak are brushed with Teriyaki Sauce and grilled with vegetables.

Teriyaki Sauce
1 cup dark soy sauce
1 cup *sake*
1 1/4 cups *mirin*
2 1/2 tablespoons sugar

1 1/3 pounds sirloin steak, cut in 1 1/4-inch cubes
8 small Japanese green peppers or 1 large green bell pepper), cut in 8 strips
1 teaspoon oil
2 cups bean sprouts
1 cup oyster mushrooms, cut in 1/4-inch slices

To make the *teriyaki* sauce, combine all the ingredients in a saucepan and bring to a boil over medium heat. Simmer until the sauce is reduced to just over 1 cup of liquid.

Thread the steak on skewers and grill until about half-cooked. Brush with the sauce and return to the grill for another 30 seconds or so. Brush again, cook a little longer, then give the steak a final brushing with the sauce and cook for another 30 seconds or so.

If using Japanese peppers, make a small slit in the side of each. Thread the Japanese peppers or bell pepper strips on to skewers and grill until done.

Heat the oil and stir-fry the bean sprouts and mushrooms until just cooked. Serve the vegetables as a garnish for the steak, which should be removed from the skewers before serving.

Renkon Hasami Age
Lotus Root, Pork and Eggplant Slices

Lotus Root, Pork and Aubergine Slices (left) and Sirloin Steak Teriyaki (right).

This is rather like a sandwich with a filling of seasoned ground pork between slices of lotus root or eggplant. The "sandwich" is then

dipped in a *tempura* batter and deep-fried. The pork filling can be prepared in advance.

Filling
8 ounces ground pork
1/4 cup finely chopped onion
2 teaspoons cornstarch
1 egg, lightly beaten
1 teaspoon dark soy sauce

10 ounces lotus root, peeled and cut in 1/2-inch slices and kept in water
2 tablespoons white flour
8 ounces eggplants, cut in 1/2-inch slices
Oil for deep-frying
Salt and pepper to taste
2 teaspoons Japanese mustard paste

Tempura Batter
2 egg yolks
1 cup water
1 3/4 cups white flour

To make the filling, combine all ingredients and mix well.

Just before the dish is required, dry the sliced lotus root and dust both sides with a little flour. Place some filling on the lotus root and top with another slice of root. Repeat with the eggplant.

To make the batter, mix the eggs and water, then stir in the flour. Do this quickly and do not overmix—leave some lumps in the batter if necessary.

Dip the pork-filled vegetable slices in the batter and deep-fry in hot oil until golden brown. Sprinkle with a little salt and pepper to taste and serve with Japanese mustard.

HELPFUL HINT

Japanese One-Pot: To obtain paper-thin slices of beef, place the beef in the freezer until half-frozen. Remove and slice with a very sharp knife.

Sakura Mochi
Cherry Blossom Dumplings

Wrapped in cherry leaves, these dumplings filled with red-bean jam are inevitably associated with spring time or *sakura*. If you can't find edible cherry leaves packed in brine, the dumplings can be served without them.

1 cup white flour
2 teaspoons sugar
$^1/_2$ cup water
1/2 egg white, beaten until fluffy and white
Pinch of salt
Oil to grease pan
$3^1/_2$ ounces red-bean jam
8 cherry blossom leaves (soaked in water for 2 hours if using brine-soaked leaves)

Lily Bulb Dumplings (left) and Cherry Blossom Dumplings (right).

Sift flour into a bowl and add sugar. Add water a little at a time. Fold in the egg white and salt.

Lightly grease a nonstick frying pan and put over low heat. Spread in some of the batter into an oval shape. Cook until the top of the dumpling becomes dry and turn over. Cook on the second side but do not allow the dumpling to take color. Remove the dumpling, spread with red-bean jam. Fold over and wrap with a cherry blossom leaf.

Matcha Aisukuriimu
Green Tea Ice Cream

A popular summertime dessert in Japanese restaurants, this might be termed a "modern classic." Finely powdered green tea gives a uniquely Japanese flavour to this delightfully rich ice cream.

$1^1/_2$ ounces green tea powder (about 6 tablespoons)
$^1/_2$ cup cognac or brandy
5 cups fresh milk
1 cup fresh cream
$1^1/_3$ cups instant non fat milk powder
$1^3/_4$ cups sugar

Put the green tea powder into a bowl, add the cognac and mix well. Put the milk, cream, sugar and milk powder into another bowl and mix well. Transfer to a saucepan and bring to a boil over moderate heat. Remove from the heat and allow to cool until lukewarm, then add the green tea paste, mixing well.

Chill immediately in the freezer until ice crystals start to form around the edges of the container. Put the mixture into a blender or food processor and blend for a few seconds to break up the crystals. Return to the fridge and leave until set. Alternatively, freeze in an ice-cream maker according to the manufacturer's instructions.

Chakin-Shibori
Lily Bulb Dumplings

The sweet, nutty flavor and floury texture of lily bulbs, which are readily available in Japan during the winter months, go well with a red-bean filling.

12 ounces lily bulb or sweet potato
$^1/_4$ cup sugar
$2^1/_2$ ounces red-bean jam, sieved
2 tablespoons finely grated yuzu orange or lemon peel

Separate the lily bulb, which looks somewhat like a head of garlic, into petals. Put the petals onto a plate and steam for about 3 minutes or until soft. Drain.

Alternatively, steam the unpeeled sweet potatoes whole, then drain and peel.

Mash the steamed vegetable, then mix with sugar and knead well.

Shape about 2 tablespoons of the purée into a dumpling and fill with 1 teaspoon red-bean jam. Shape into a dumpling by putting the ball into a cloth and squeezing gently at the top. Remove from the cloth and sprinkle with grated peel. Repeat until all the purée is used up, then serve.

Kingyoku-Kan
Jellied Plums

A simple but decorative dessert, with large grapes or plums set in jellied plum wine (*umeshu*). If plum wine is not available, substitute any fruit wine such as peach or raspberry.

8 large black or white grapes or small plums
$2^1/_2$ envelopes unflavored gelatin
$^1/_4$ cup warm water
$2^1/_2$ cups plum wine (*umeshu*) or peach or raspberry wine
$2^1/_2$ tablespoons sugar
1 teaspoon cognac or brandy

Blanch the grapes or plums in hot water for about 10 seconds, drain and put in cold water to chill for a few seconds. Peel the fruit and set aside.

Sprinkle the gelatin over the warm water and leave until it softens.

Heat the wine in a nonreactive saucepan and add sugar and gelatin. Stir until dissolved, then remove from the heat. Add the cognac and pour into 8 tiny containers (such as ramekins or small porcelain soup bowls). Put 1 grape or plum into each bowl of still-liquid jelly, then chill until the jelly is firm. Unmold and serve chilled.

Green Tea Ice Cream.

Katsuo Dashi
Basic Dashi Stock

Instant *dashi* granules make a quick alternative but it is preferable to make your own *dashi*.

- 2¹/₂-inch x 1¹/₂-inch piece dried kelp (*konbu*)
- 7 cups water
- 1¹/₂ ounces dried *bonito* flakes (about 4 cups)

Wipe the kelp with a damp cloth, put it in a saucepan with the water and bring to a boil uncovered. Just before the water comes to a boil, remove and discard the kelp. Sprinkle in the *bonito* flakes and remove the saucepan from the heat. As soon as the *bonito* flakes start to sink, strain the stock and discard the *bonito* flakes. This stock can be kept refrigerated for up to 3 days.

Soba Dashi (1)
Stock for Hot Soba Noodles

- ³/₄ cup Basic *Dashi* Stock (see above)
- 2 teaspoons light soy sauce
- ¹/₂ teaspoon *mirin*

Put all ingredients into a saucepan, bring to a boil and remove from the heat immediately. Serve with hot *soba* noodles. Keeps refrigerated for 2 days.

Soba Dashi (2)
Stock for Cold Soba Noodles

- 2 cups) Basic *Dashi* Stock (see above)
- 7 tablespoons dark soy sauce
- 7 tablespoons *mirin*

Put all ingredients into a saucepan, bring to a boil and remove from heat immediately. Skim the surface and allow to cool. Serve with cold *soba* noodles. Keeps refrigerated for up to 4 days.

Suiji
Clear Soup

A variety of ingredients can be added to this soup such as diced vegetables etc.

- 2¹/₂ cups Basic *Dashi* Stock (left)
- 1 teaspoon light soy sauce
- 1 teaspoon salt
- ¹/₂ teaspoon *sake*

Put the stock, soy sauce and salt into a saucepan and heat until it comes almost to a boil.
Remove from the heat immediately and add the *sake*.

Tempura Dashi
Tempura Dipping Sauce

- 14 tablespoons Basic *Dashi* Stock (left)
- 2¹/₂ tablespoons light soy sauce
- 2¹/₂ tablespoons *mirin*

Put the basic *dashi* stock in a saucepan, bring to a boil and add soy sauce and *mirin*.
Remove from the heat immediately and serve hot as a dipping sauce for *tempura*.

Tosa Shoyu
Tosa Soy Sauce

If red *sake* is not available, use 3 tablespoons of regular *sake*.

- 1¹/₂ tablespoons red *sake*
- 1¹/₂ tablespoons regular *sake*
- 1¹/₃ cups dark soy sauce
- ¹/₃ cup *tamari* soy sauce
- ¹/₂ ounce dried *bonito* flakes
- 5-inch x 2-inch piece dried kelp (*konbu*)

Put both types of *sake* in a small saucepan and bring to a boil to remove the alcohol. Allow to cool, then combine with all other ingredients and store for 1 week before straining. Can be stored for up to 1 year.

Dengaku Miso

- 1 pound red or white *miso* (1³/₄ cups)
- ¹/₃ cup *sake*
- ¹/₃ *mirin*
- 3 tablespoons sugar

Put all ingredients into a saucepan and heat slowly, stirring from time to time. When it has come to a boil, reduce heat to a minimum and cook, stirring from time to time, for 20 minutes. Cool and refrigerate for up to 1 month.

Hoba Miso

- 2¹/₂ tablespoons *sake*
- ¹/₂ cup red *Dengaku Miso*
- 2 tablespoons *inaka miso*

Heat *sake* in a saucepan and simmer for a few seconds to remove the alcohol. Add both types of *miso*, mix and refrigerate for up to 1 month. Can be used to brush on scallops or fish before grilling.

Tempura Ko
Tempura Batter

- 2 egg yolks
- 1¹/₈ cups iced water
- 1³/₄ cups white flour, sifted

Put the egg yolks in a bowl and mix in the water gradually. Add the flour all at once and stir briefly, leaving in any lumps. Do not mix the batter to a smooth paste; a tempura batter should contain lumps of dry flour. The mixture can be refrigerated until required, although it is best made just before it is needed.

Sushi-Meshi
Vinegared Rice

- 4 cups short-grain rice
- 5 cups water
- 1¹/₄-inch square dried kelp (*konbu*)
- ¹/₂ cup rice vinegar
- 3 tablespoons sugar
- 5 teaspoons salt

Wash the rice gently under running water until the water runs clear. Leave the rice to drain in a colander for about 1 hour. Put in a saucepan with the water and kelp and bring to a boil over high heat. Reduce to medium heat and simmer for about 15 minutes, until the rice is cooked and the water has been absorbed. Turn off the heat. Remove the lid and cover the top of the pan with a towel to absorb any condensation. Put back the lid and leave the covered saucepan to one side for 20 minutes.
While the rice is cooking, mix rice vinegar, sugar and salt in a small bowl, stirring until the sugar has dissolved. Set

---

aside. Put the cooked rice in a wide wooden tub or plastic bowl. Stir gently in a circular motion with a rice paddle or wooden spoon, sprinkling in the dressing little by little, until it has been absorbed. Ideally, the rice mixture should be fanned to help cool it while the dressing is being stirred in.
Cover the bowl containing the vinegared rice with a damp cloth until it is needed. Keep at room temperature, not in the fridge, and use within 12 hours.

Gari
Pickled Ginger

- 8 ounces young ginger
- 6 tablespoons rice vinegar
- 2 tablespoons *mirin*
- 2 tablespoons *sake*
- 5 teaspoons sugar

Brush the ginger under running water, then blanch in boiling water for 1 minute. Drain.
Put the vinegar, mirin, sake and sugar in a small saucepan and bring to a boil, stirring until the sugar dissolves. Allow to cool.
Put the ginger into a sterilized jar and pour over the cooled vinegar. Cover and keep 3–4 days before using. Will keep refrigerated for up to 1 month.

Ponzu Sauce
Citrus Sauce

- 3-inch x 2¹/₂-inch piece dried kelp (*konbu*)
- 1³/₄ cups musk lime (*ponzu* or calamansi) juice, or lemon juice
- 1³/₄ cups dark soy sauce
- ¹/₃ cup *mirin*
- ¹/₄ cup *tamari* soy sauce
- 1¹/₂ ounces dried *bonito* flakes (about 4 cups)

Heat the dried kelp over a gas flame or under a broiler, then put into a bowl with all the other ingredients. Refrigerate for 3 days, then strain. Can be stored for up to 1 year.

"Malaysians and Singaporeans of all ethnic backgrounds view eating as a communal activity—as a quick visit to any hawker stall will show you."

MALAYSIA & SINGAPORE

Culinary exchange between the Chinese, the Indians and the Malays has made the peninsula a true melting pot.

Left: Malay food served outside a restaurant in the historic Emerald Hill area in Singapore.

Right: Rice is the staple food in both countries and comes in many varieties.

It is not possible to live cheek by jowl with people of another ethnic community without picking up ideas on food. Over the centuries, the Malay peninsula saw sailing ships arriving from the west from Arabia, India and, much later on, from Europe. From the east came Chinese junks, Siamese vessels and the inter-island sailing craft of the Buginese and Javanese people of the Indonesian archipelago. This has resulted in a melting pot culture, where the delicacy of Chinese cooking, the exuberance of Indian spices and the fragrance of Malay herbs coexist.

The original people of the peninsula—known collectively as *orang asli*—consist of about twenty different tribes belonging to two distinct linguistic groups. Later arrivals to the area, who spread south from Yunnan in southern China and began settling in Malaysia around 4000 years ago, are the ancestors of today's dominant ethnic group, the Malays.

The ethnic and social structures of the Muslim Malaccan sultanate were to change irrevocably from the 16th century: Since then it has witnessed the settlement of the Portuguese, the Dutch and, in the 19th century, the British. With the British came large numbers of Chinese and Indian workers, which changed the face of the country forever.

In 1963, the Federation of Malaysia was formed, consisting of the states of the peninsula; Singapore, the island at the tip of the peninsula, and the former British colonies of Sabah and Sarawak. Singapore broke away in 1965, and has since come into its own as an important entrepôt. Today Singapore is one of Asia's most dynamic and modern cities.

The Land and its People

Their location near the equator means that Malaysia and Singapore are humid and steamy all year-round. Tropical rains frequently bring freshness during the afternoons, and in contrast with

During the Feast of the Hungry Ghosts, offerings of food and incense are made to the spirits.

the usually hot days, nights are balmy and the early mornings fresh and cool.

The postcard-pretty tropical landscape—rice paddies, beaches fringed by groves of coconut palms—exists along the coasts, and much of the lush alluvial plains of the peninsula's west coast is planted with palm oil and rubber. Orchards proliferate here and luscious tropical fruits such as the highly prized durian, furry rambutan, mangosteen, starfruit and langsat can be found. To the far north of the peninsula, the climate is often dry and the landscape of endless paddy fields relieved by abrupt limestone hills.

The temperate climate on the main mountain range that runs north-south along the peninsula, the Banjaran Titiwangsa, makes getaways such as Cameron Highlands perfect not only for holiday makers but for the tea plantations and market gardens that provide much of the fresh produce for the peninsula's markets.

The generally muddy coastal waters of the Malacca Straits on the west coast are ideal for crabs and shellfish. The small *kampungs* (villages) along the east coast are ideal fishing grounds and make their livelihood from the South China Sea.

Over on the Borneo peninsula, Sabah has a mountain range that culminates in Southeast Asia's tallest peak, Mount Kinabalu (13,455 feet). Much of the terrain of Sarawak is low-lying.

Singapore is for the most part low-lying, and urban development has accelerated swamp reclamation and deforestation. Dense equatorial rain forests and a few low hills which once shaped the landscape

have given way to a dense cover of high-rise office blocks, shopping complexes, condominiums and public housing. Singapore has grown almost none of its food for decades; much of its scarce land is devoted to industry and housing its population.

Located as they are in the middle of the world, and with produce coming in from all over, few foods are ever out of season in Singapore and Malaysia.

The Making of a Cuisine

Perhaps the contemporary food of Malaysia and Singapore is best represented by the open-air eating stalls. Here, you might start dinner with some *popiah* (spring roll), move on to a fish-head curry and spicy *kangkung* with rice, and take home a packet of *hokkien mee* for supper. Almost any self-respecting Malaysian or Singaporean cook can whip up a tasty Malay-style chicken or fish curry, *roti canai* or *murtabak*, or a very fine Chinese stir-fry.

When Chinese merchants sailed their junks across the South China Sea, they set in train a process that was to have a profound influence on the region. A few of these Chinese traders stayed on in the Malay peninsula, often marrying local women and forming the beginnings of Nonya or Straits-Chinese culture. The British encouraged Chinese migration to supply labor for the tin mines. Thousands of Chinese workers poured in to Singapore and the Malay peninsula. Others headed straight for the gold mines and coal fields of Sarawak to try their luck, or moved to British North Borneo (now Sabah) to work on the land.

The Chinese brought with them the cooking styles of their homeland, mostly the southern provinces of Guangdong and Fukien, and introduced to the indigenous people of the Malay peninsula and northern Borneo a range of ingredients now used by every ethnic group in Malaysia and Singapore today: noodles, bean sprouts, bean curd and soy sauce. In turn, the Chinese developed a penchant for spices and chilies.

Like their Chinese counterparts, Indian traders have been recorded in the region for more than a thousand years, but it was in the 19th century that they came to Malaya in large numbers as contract laborers.

Malay cuisine is the link between Indonesia to the west and south, and Thailand to the north. Although the results are rather different, there is overlap, especially with the food of nearby Sumatra and, in the northern states of Malaysia, with Thailand. Although Malay food is not as prominent in Singapore as Chinese, familiar favorites such as the *korma*, *rendang*, chicken curry and various sambals are very much part of a mainstream diet.

While the Malays, Chinese and Indians continue to create their traditional foods, cross-cultural borrowing in the kitchen has led to a number of uniquely "Malaysian" and "Singaporean" dishes, such as the *mee goreng* and *rojak*.

The Food of the People

Despite regional differences, Malay food can be described as spicy and flavorful, although this does not necessarily mean chili-hot. But you can rest assured that even if the main dishes are not hot, there'll be a chili-based *sambal* on hand.

Over the centuries, traditional Southeast Asian spices have been joined by Indian, Middle Eastern and Chinese spices, so the partnership of coriander and cumin (the basis of many Malay "curries") is enhanced by pepper, cardamom, star anise, and fenugreek.

The Malaysian northern states of Kedah, Perlis and Kelantan, all of which border Thailand and Trengganu, show distinct Thai influences. (So, too, does Penang.) Fiery hot chilies, so much a part of Thai food, are popular in the northern states. In addition to Malaysian herbs such as lemongrass, pandan leaf, the fragrant leaf of the kaffir lime and the pungent *polygonum* or *daun kesum*, *daun kemangia*, a basil popular in Thailand, leaves of a number of rhizomes such as turmeric and zedoary (known locally as *cekur*) and the wonderfully fragrant wild ginger bud are used. Tamarind, sour carambola and limes give food a tangy and fragrant sourness.

Food without seasoning is unthinkable—even a piece of fish is rubbed with turmeric powder and salt before cooking. Many of the seasonings that enhance Malay food are not dried spices but rhizomes such as fresh turmeric and *lengkuas* (galangal), and other "wet" ingredients such as chilies, onions and garlic. Fresh seasonings and dried spices are pounded to a fine paste and cooked gen-

tly in oil before liquid—either creamy coconut milk or a sour broth—is added, together with the vegetables, meat or fish.

Produce from the sea is an important part of the Malay diet. Tiny dried anchovies (*ikan bilis*) and dried shrimp are popular flavorings, and dried shrimp paste (*belacan*) is used to give an inimitable finish to many dishes.

The *kenduri* or feast is one time when Malay cuisine comes into its own. All the women of the family or village take out their giant cooking pots and work through the night, scraping and squeezing coconuts for milk, pounding shallots, garlic, chilies and spices, cutting and chopping, simmering and stirring, until they have created an impressive array of fish curries, *gulai* (curries) of vegetables bathed in coconut milk and seasoned perhaps with fresh shrimp; coconut-rich *rendang* of beef or chicken, tingling hot shrimp *sambals*, and a colorful array of desserts. With their innate courtesy and hospitality, the Malays consider it an honor to be able to invite any fortunate passer-by to join in the *kenduri*.

Nonya—the Food of Love

The so-called Straits-born Chinese, descendants of early settlers in Penang and Malacca, combine elements of both Chinese and Malay culture, quite unlike the mass of Chinese migrants who arrived around the turn of this century and up until the 1930s. These pioneering Chinese traders took Malay wives, although as time went on, children of these early mixed marriages generally married pure

A selection of pickles to be served with the main meal.

Above: **A spread of Nonya food, which is often time consuming to prepare but well worth the effort.** *Below right:* **The owner of a hawker stall in Singapore entices customers with his fresh produce.**

were all transformed in the kitchen, added to and blended with aromatics such as the kaffir lime leaf, polygonum or *laksa* leaf, zedoary, fresh turmeric leaves and pandan.

One of the most popular Nonya dishes among Malaysians of any background is *laksa*, a rice-noodle soup that marries Malay seasonings with Chinese noodles. Nonya cakes are renowned for their richness and variety. Most are based on Malay recipes, using freshly grated tapioca root, sweet potato, agar-agar, glutinous rice, palm sugar and coconut milk

The Kitchen and Table

Whatever the ethnic community in Malaysia and Singapore, eating is a communal activity, whether at home or in a restaurant. The assortment of dishes appear all at once, diners get individual servings of rice and then help themselves to the dishes using a serving spoon. One exception to this is the Chinese banquet, a formal eight or ten-course dinner, where the dishes appear sequentially.

"Don't use your fingers" is not an admonishment you will hear often in Malaysia and Singapore. Indians, Malays and Straits Chinese will tell you that curry and rice taste best when you can literally feel the food with your fingers. Eating with your hand has its own etiquette too. Only the right hand is used, and just the tips of the fingers; the palm is kept perfectly clean. Washing the hands before eating is not only polite but more hygienic. In the finer Indian and Malay restaurants, a waiter will bring a bowl of warm water before and after a meal. In the more pedestrian curry shops or "banana leaf" restaurants, there will be a row of wash basins and soap for customers to clean up. Even with clean hands, diners should touch only the food on their plate, never that in the communal dishes, and the left hand is used to hold the serving spoon to keep it clean.

Chinese food is more likely to be eaten with chopsticks, although at some Chinese food stalls and in many Chinese homes, forks, spoons and plates are used. However, at a ten-course Chinese meal, chopsticks are *de rigueur*. Sucking or licking the tips of the chopsticks is impolite and contact between mouth and the tips is kept to a minimum. Spoons are set out for larger mouthfuls. Often before and always at the end of the meal, hot towels are handed round for cleaning the face and hands.

Although Chinese tea is the traditional drink with Chinese food, there is nothing quite like beer to take the heat off your tongue and to cool you down when you eat spicy food on a steamy evening.

Most urban kitchens in Malaysia and Singapore these days are a curious blend of old and new: the microwave next to the mortar and pestle; the food processor next to a well-seasoned wok.

Chinese or the children of other Straits Chinese. The women, known as *Nonyas*, and the men, *Babas*, generally spoke a mixture of Malay and Chinese, dressed in modified Malay style, and combined the best of both cuisines in the kitchen.

Typical Chinese ingredients (such as bean curd, soy sauce, preserved soybeans, black shrimp paste, sesame seeds, dried mushrooms and dried lily buds) were blended with Malay herbs, spices and fragrant roots. Being non-Muslim, the Straits Chinese cooked pork dishes in the Malay style, and added distinctive local ingredients (coconut milk, spices and sour tamarind juice) to basic Chinese recipes.

Distinct differences evolved between the cuisine of the Penang Nonyas and that of Malacca. In Penang, which is geographically much closer to Thailand, the Nonyas developed a passion for sour food (using lots of lime and tamarind juice), fiery hot chilies, fragrant herbs and pungent black shrimp paste. Malacca Nonyas prepare food that is generally rich in coconut milk and Malay spices (such as coriander and cumin), and usually use more sugar than their northern counterparts.

Many fruits and vegetables were prepared in imaginative ways by the Nonyas. Unripe jackfruit, the heart of the banana bud, sweet potato leaves and tiny sour carambola

SUGGESTED MENUS

A family meal

For a family dinner, serve the following with rice:
- Chicken with Lime Leaf (page 118), a little bit of Shrimp Sambal (page 117) and Snake Gourd (page 119);
- Sago with Honeydew (page 120) is a popular sweet treat with both the young and old.

Snacks

Curry Puffs (page 108) are great as a mid-morning or afternoon snack, as are the Stuffed Deep-Fried Yam Dumplings (page 109). The Nonya Pancakes (page 120) and Mango Jellies (page 120) would normally be eaten in-between meals as fillers in Malaysia and Singapore.

A light lunch

The recipes in this chapter are particularly well suited to smorgasbords. For a light lunch:
- Popiah (page 108) make a delightful start;
- Shrimp Noodle Soup (page 111) or Indian Fried Noodles (page 113);
- finish with some sliced fresh fruit.

Other great lunch dishes include Claypot Rice or Chicken Rice (page 114).

A dinner party

For a formal dinner, impress your guests with these dishes:
- Oyster Omelets (page 109), cooked in individual servings, and small portions of Tea-Smoked Seabass (page 118);
- Duck in Fragrant Soy Sauce (page 114) or the Chili Crab (page 117), which is a sure-fire hit;
- cooling Almond Jelly (page 120) is a good way to round off the meal.

A melting pot menu

You could start your Asia-wide menu with
- Noodles in Spicy Coconut-Milk (page 112);
- Pork Cutlets on Rice (page 95) from Japan are an interesting blend of East and West, serve with Vietnamese Pan-fried Water Spinach with Yellow Bean Sauce (page 151);
- finish with the wonderful Mixed Ice from Indonesia (page 78).

THE ESSENTIAL FLAVORS OF MALAYSIAN AND SINGAPOREAN COOKING

The aromatic curry pastes need **chilies**, **garlic**, **ginger**, **limes**, **lemongrass** and **shallots**, but these ingredients are also used by themselves. **Coconut milk** and **palm sugar** are frequently added to soften the heat of curries and, in desserts, the fragrant **pandan leaf** is used. **Rice** and **soy sauce** are must-haves.

Popiah.

The recipes given in this section are not usually eaten as appetizers as such during a meal, but as snacks or in-between meals. However, they make excellent nibbles to be served with drinks at the start of a meal.

Popiah

This Nonya version of a popular Chinese snack is ideal for lunch. *Popiah* wrappers are similar to the fresh wrappers used for Filipino *lumpia*. If neither are available, use egg roll wrappers.

$1/4$ cup oil
3 eggs

Filling
8 shallots
8 cloves garlic
2 tablespoons salted soybean paste
$1/4$ cup oil
1 pound jicama, shredded
2 pieces hard bean curd, fried and shredded
1 teaspoon black soy sauce
4 ounces peeled shrimp
1 cup shredded cabbage,
1 cup shredded green beans
4 tablespoons sugar
2 teaspoons salt

To serve
20 large fresh *popiah* skins
Sweet black sauce to taste
10 cloves garlic, blended to make a paste
6 red chilies, blended to a paste
Long-leafed lettuce
1 cup bean sprouts, blanched
$1/3$ cup dry roasted peanuts, skinned and coarsely ground
3 tablespoons Fried Shallots (page 121)

Grease an omelet pan with $1/2$ teaspoon oil and make 3 very thin omelets. When cooked, shred finely and set aside.

To make the filling, crush the shallots and garlic together with the soybean paste.

Heat oil and fry the paste until fragrant. Spoon out 3 teaspoons of this mixture and add jicama to the remaining paste in the pan. Cook for 5 minutes until softened, then add the bean curd and cook until very soft. Season with black soy sauce.

Curry Puffs.

Put 1 teaspoon of the reserved seasoning in a separate pan and fry shrimp until cooked. Repeat with the cabbage, then the beans. Mix into the cooked jicama and add sugar and salt.

To serve, put all prepared ingredients on the table. Place a *popiah* skin on a flat surface and spread with a little sweet black sauce, garlic paste and chili paste. Place a lettuce leaf on top, a spoonful of the cooked filling, a few shrimp, some cabbage, beans, bean sprouts, peanuts and shallots. Fold in the sides, roll up and serve immediately

Curry Puffs

A perennial favorite originally created by Indian cooks.

Filling
5 tablespoons oil
1 medium red or yellow onion, finely chopped
$1 1/2$ teaspoons *kurma* powder or chicken curry powder
2 teaspoons meat or chicken curry powder
1 teaspoon cayenne
$1/2$ teaspoon turmeric powder
2 cups finely diced cooked chicken
2 large potatoes, boiled and finely diced
$1 1/2$ teaspoons sugar
$1/2$ teaspoon black pepper
$1/2$ teaspoon salt

Pastry
4 cups white flour
10 tablespoons butter or margarine
14 tablespoons water
$1/2$ teaspoon salt
Oil for deep-frying

To make the filling, heat oil and fry onion gently until golden brown. Add the curry powders, cayenne, turmeric and fry gently. Add the chicken, potatoes, sugar, pepper and salt and cook for 5 minutes. Mix well and leave aside to cool.

To make the pastry, mix flour with butter or margarine, water and salt and knead well. Rest for 30 minutes. Cut the dough into circles 3 inches in diameter. Take a tablespoon of filling and place in center. Fold pastry over to make a half-circle and crimp the edges. Heat oil in wok and deep-fry until golden. Note: Not all margarines are suitable for pastry, due to their high moisture content. The Malaysian brand Planta is recommended, as is Crisco, a solid vegetable shortening.

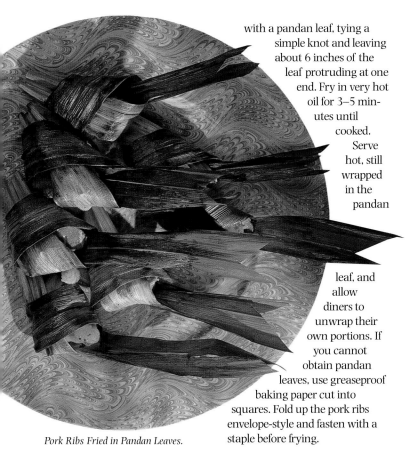

Pork Ribs Fried in Pandan Leaves.

with a pandan leaf, tying a simple knot and leaving about 6 inches of the leaf protruding at one end. Fry in very hot oil for 3–5 minutes until cooked. Serve hot, still wrapped in the pandan leaf, and allow diners to unwrap their own portions. If you cannot obtain pandan leaves, use greaseproof baking paper cut into squares. Fold up the pork ribs envelope-style and fasten with a staple before frying.

Pork Ribs Fried in Pandan Leaves

The fragrance of pandan(screwpine) leaves enriches a number of savory rice, meat and chicken dishes of Malay or Nonya origin. The use of pandan leaves to wrap food before deep-frying is a Thai influence. This Singapore adaptation uses pork ribs.

- 2 pounds pork ribs, cut into 1^1/$_2$-inch pieces
- 8 cloves garlic
- 8 shallots
- 6 tablespoons honey
- 2 tablespoons red sweet sauce
- 1 tablespoons five-spice powder
- 3 tablespoons Lea & Perrins or Worcestershire sauce
- 1 tablespoon HP sauce or steak sauce
- 2 tablespoons plum sauce
- 4 tablespoons oil
- 1 teaspoon sesame oil
- 24 pandan leaves
- Oil for deep-frying

Choose meaty pork ribs and have them cut to the correct length. Pound or blend together the garlic and shallots, then mix with all other ingredients except pandan leaves and oil for deep-frying. Leave to marinate for about 2 hours.

Wrap each of the pork ribs

Wu Kok

Stuffed Deep-Fried Yam Dumplings

A Teochew delicacy filled with red-roasted pork (*char siew*). *Char siew* is readily available from Chinese barbecue stores.

Filling
- 8 ounces red roasted pork (*char siew*), diced (page 121)
- 1/3 cup green peas
- 1 small onion, finely diced
- 1 small carrot, diced
- 1/2 cup oyster sauce
- 1/2 teaspoon five-spice powder
- 1/2 teaspoon sesame oil
- 1/2 teaspoon sugar
- 2 tablespoons light soy sauce
- 1 tablespoon cornstarch

- 1 yam, about 1 1/4 pounds
- 9 tablespoons tapioca starch
- 1/2 cup pork oil or vegetable shortening, such as Crisco
- 1 tablespoon five-spice powder
- 1 teaspoon sesame oil
- 1 teaspoon salt
- 1 tablespoon sugar
- 1/2 teaspoon ground white pepper
- Oil for deep-frying

To make the filling, combine all ingredients in a bowl and mix well. Chill in the refrigerator.

Peel yam and cut into pieces.

Steam for about 30 minutes over boiling water until soft. Mash the yam and set aside.

Mix tapioca starch with enough boiling water to form a stiff paste and knead into a dough. Add pork oil, five-spice powder, sesame oil, salt, sugar and pepper and the mashed yam. Mix thoroughly and divide into 10–12 portions. Flatten each portion into a round shape.

Divide the filling into 10–12 portions and put one in the middle of each piece of flattened yam dough. Squeeze together to enclose the filling and make into a dumpling.

Heat oil in a wok or deep-fryer and deep-fry the dumplings until golden brown. Drain and serve hot.

Note: To make pork oil, chop hard (back) pork fat into a fine dice and cook over low heat with about 2 tablespoons water until the water evaporates and all the oil runs out.

Oyster Omelet

Fresh oysters are cooked in a light omelet flavored with soy sauce and Chinese wine.

- 8–10 large fresh oysters
- 2 tablespoons tapioca starch
- 1 tablespoon rice flour
- 8 tablespoons water
- 1 tablespoon oil
- 3 eggs, beaten
- 2 cloves garlic, finely chopped
- 1 tablespoon light soy sauce
- 1 tablespoon Chinese rice wine
- Ground white pepper
- Cilantro sprigs to garnish

Wash oysters and drain well. Mix tapioca starch and rice with the water to make a very thin batter.

Heat a large heavy frying pan until very hot and add oil. Pour in the batter and cook for about 15 seconds. Add the eggs. When the eggs are almost set, make a hole in the center, pour in a little oil and fry the garlic for a few seconds. Mix, then season with soy sauce, rice wine and pepper. Add oysters and heat through.

Sprinkle with fresh cilantro and serve with a *sambal* (page 121).

HELPFUL HINT

Oyster omelets make elegant dinner-party appetizers. The omelets can be made in two-oyster batches for individual servings.

Stuffed Deep-Fried Yam Dumplings.

The Chinese principle of the "restorative" dish meets the spicy and hot in the selection of soups here. Once again, one-bowl or one-plate noodle dishes proliferate—a testament to their popularity in Malaysia and Singapore.

Bak Kut Teh
Spiced Pork Bone Soup

A popular hawker stall snack, eaten as a late-night or early morning pick-me-up. The Chinese herbs should be available from any Chinese medicine shop. They can be omitted, although the flavor will be less rich and the soup presumably less of a restorative.

1 pound pork ribs, cut into
    2-inch lengths
8 ounces lean pork, in one piece
12 cups water
Salt and pepper to taste

Seasoning
4 *gan cao*
1 *luo han guo*
1$^1/_2$ ounces *dang xin*
1 ounces *chuan kong*
1 ounce *dang guei*
$^1/_2$ ounce) *sheng di*
5 whole star anise
1 cinnamon stick, about 3 inches
    long
10 cloves
1 piece dried mandarin peel
$^1/_2$ cup light soy sauce
$^1/_4$ cup black soy sauce
2 tablespoons sugar

Put pork ribs, meat and water in a large pan.

Wrap all seasoning ingredients except soy sauces and sugar in a piece of clean cheesecloth and add to the pan. Add both soys and sugar and bring to a boil. Simmer gently, uncovered, for 1$^1/_2$ to 2 hours until the meat is almost falling off the bone. Season to taste with salt (if needed) and ground white pepper .

When serving, cut the lean pork meat into small pieces. Put in a bowl together with the pork ribs and top with the stock.

Superior Won Ton Soup

Stuffed ravioli-like dumplings or *won ton* in soup are found in Chinese restaurants throughout the world, usually served with thin egg noodles for a quick meal. This is a luxurious version.

15 *won ton* skins
6 cups basic stock (see below)
1$^1/_2$ cups snow peas, blanched for
    a few seconds
6 dried black mushrooms, soaked,
    boiled until soft, thinly sliced
Salt and pepper

Basic Stock
3 dried scallops
10 ounces boneless chicken
$^1/_2$ cup very fine dried Chinese
    anchovies
12 cups water
2 cloves garlic, smashed
$^1/_2$ inch ginger, sliced
$^1/_2$ teaspoon white peppercorns
3 carrots
7 ribs celery

Filling
8 ounces shrimp, peeled and
    deveined
5 ounces boneless chicken or
    pork
4 ounces water chestnuts, peeled
1$^1/_2$ ounces dried black fungus
    or 2 dried mushrooms, soaked
1 tablespoon oyster sauce
$^1/_2$ teaspoon salt
A dash of sesame oil
2 tablespoons sugar
A dash of Chinese rice wine

1 egg, beaten
2 tablespoons cornstarch
1 tablespoon light soy sauce

To make the stock, put all the ingredients in a pot and bring to a boil. Remove the foam from the surface, lower heat and simmer, covered, for 2 hours. Strain thoroughly before using.

Superior Won Ton Soup.

To make the filling, chop the shrimp, chicken, water chestnuts and fungus together until fine. Mix in all other filling ingredients.

Put a small spoonful of the filling in the center of a wrapper and squeeze the edges together in the center. Repeat until all the filling is used up. Bring stock to a boil, add the *won tons* and simmer for 3–5 minutes or until they float to the top. Add the snow peas and mushrooms, and season with salt and pepper. Serve immediately.

If you are unable to find dried scallops (which are very expensive), use 1 pound pork bones to make the stock.

HELPFUL HINT

Don't bother making small batches of *won tons*: they freeze really well and are very handy for deep-fried pre-dinner nibbles or to be added to noodle soups, so make heaps!

Spiced Pork Bone Soup.

Yen's Brown Noodles

This version of a Cantonese-style dish is named after the chef who created it. Packets of *yee mien* noodles should be available from any Chinese food shop. The distinctive flavour of this type of noodle makes this simple dish well worth sampling.

- 5 ounces dry brown noodles (*yee mien*)
- 3 cups mustard greens or spinach
- Oil for frying
- 1 clove garlic, finely chopped
- 5 ounces peeled shrimp
- 5 ounces chicken or pork, shredded
- 3 cups water
- 2 tablespoons oyster sauce
- 2 tablespoons light soy sauce
- 1/2 teaspoon black soy sauce
- 1/2 teaspoon sesame oil
- 1/2 teaspoon ground white pepper
- 1 heaped tablespoon cornstarch, blended with 3 tablespoons water
- 2 eggs, lightly beaten

Put the noodles in a colander, sprinkle with a little cold water and leave aside to soften.

Discard hard ends of the greens and cut into 1 1/2-inch lengths. Heat about 2 inches oil in a wok and fry the noodles, a handful at a time, turning over until crisp and golden (about 1 minute). Drain and set aside. Repeat with remaining noodles. Arrange noodles in a large wide bowl or deep serving platter.

Leave about 1 tablespoon of oil in the wok and fry the garlic for a few seconds, then add shrimp and chicken or pork. Stir-fry until they are cooked, then add water and seasoning. Bring to the boil, add vegetables and simmer for a minute. Add the cornstarch mixture and stir until the sauce thickens. Stir in the egg and pour over the noodles. Serve immediately.

The noodles should have a firm texture, although not crisp and crunchy, after cooking.

Har Mee
Shrimp Noodle Soup

The flavor of this relatively simple noodle dish depends on the stock, so take the care (and time!) and you will be amply rewarded.

- 8–12 large shrimp
- 100 g (3 1/2 oz) hard back pork fat or salt pork, cut in 1/4-inch dice (optional)
- 5 ounces fresh egg noodles
- 1/2 cup bean sprouts or a few leafy greens, blanched
- 1 scallion, finely sliced
- Ground white pepper

Stock
- 1 tablespoon oil
- 4 ounces small fresh shrimp
- 3 tablespoons dried shrimp
- 1 dried chili (optional)
- 5 shallots, very finely chopped
- 5 cloves garlic, very finely chopped
- 5 whole white peppercorns, coarsely ground and gently fried until fragrant
- 8 ounces pork or chicken bones
- 8 cups water
- 1 tablespoon sugar

Peel the shrimp, saving the heads and shells for the stock but leaving the tails on. Put the shrimp in the refrigerator.

To make the stock, heat oil and fry the reserved shrimp heads and shells with the fresh and dried shrimp, and dried chili. Cook over low heat, stirring, for about 5 minutes. Crush shells firmly with the back of a wooden spoon against the side of the pan, then add all other stock ingredients except the sugar. Simmer gently, uncovered, until the liquid is reduced by about half.

Heat the sugar in a small pan with an equal amount of water and cook until it turns a dark caramel color. Add to the stock. Sieve the stock, pressing firmly on the ingredients to extract all the liquid. Season to taste with salt. Keep this hot if using immediately.

While the stock is cooking, put the pork dice in a pan and cook gently until the oil runs out and the pork fat turns golden and crisp. Drain and set the pork fat aside.

Plunge the noodles in boiling water for about 1 minute to heat through, then divide among 4 bowls. Add bean sprouts or leafy greens, top with hot stock and add 2–3 shrimp to each bowl.

Sprinkle with pork fat, scallions and a liberal dash of white pepper. Serve immediately accompanied by a dipping-sauce bowl of soy sauce and sliced red chilies, or else a *sambal* of your choice.

Prawn Noodle Soup.

Yen's Brown Noodles

Laksa Lemak
Noodles in Spicy Coconut-Milk

This Nonya version of *laksa* comes from Melaka. If you are a *laksa aficionado*, double the quantities of spice paste and store in the refrigerator. (Use within two weeks.) This recipe serves six.

Spice Paste
8 red chilies, chopped
10 shallots, chopped
1 stem lemongrass, chopped
$3/4$ inch galangal, chopped
$1/4$ inch fresh turmeric, chopped
$1/2$ teaspoon dried shrimp paste

$1/2$ cup oil
6 sprigs polygonum (*daun kesum*)
2 wild ginger buds, finely sliced
6 cups water
$1^1/2$ cups thick coconut milk
1 heaped tablespoon sugar
Salt to taste
1 pound thin fresh yellow
   noodles, or dried noodles,
   cooked and drained
1 chicken breast, steamed and
   shredded
$1^1/2$ cups bean sprouts, blanched
4 ounces peeled shrimp, steamed

Garnish
3 sprigs polygonum (*daun kesum*),
   sliced
1 wild ginger bud, finely sliced
1 cucumber, cut into matchstick
   shreds
3 eggs, made into thin omelets
   and shredded
2 red chilies, sliced

Noodles in Spicy Coconut Milk.

2 scallions, finely sliced
6 tablespoons *Sambal Belacan*
   (page 121)
6 small round limes or lemon wedges

To make the spice paste, blend all ingredients finely, adding a little of the oil if necessary to keep the blades turning.

Heat remaining oil and gently fry the blended ingredients for 10 minutes, stirring from time to time. Add the polygonum, ginger buds and water and bring to a boil. Add thick coconut milk, sugar and salt. Reduce heat and simmer very

gently, uncovered, for 10–15 minutes.

To serve, plunge noodles in boiling water for a few seconds to heat through. Divide the noodles, chicken, bean sprouts and shrimp among 6 bowls and top with the shredded polygonum and ginger bud. Pour over the sauce and add a little cucumber, omelet, chilies and scallions. Serve with side dishes of *sambal belacan* and cut limes.

> **HELPFUL HINT**
>
> Dried rice vermicelli (*meehoon*) or any dried Chinese wheat-flour noodles can also be used for this dish.

Asam Laksa Penang
Sour Penang Noodle Soup

This version of *laksa lemak* is from Penang, the island off the west coast of Malaysia. It is more sour and boasts the addition of fish. Try both and see which appeals more.

$1^1/4$ pounds small Chubb
   mackerel (*ikan kembong*), cleaned
6 cups water
5 tablespoons tamarind pulp,
   soaked and squeezed for juice
2 wild ginger buds, sliced
3 sprigs polygonum (*daun kesum*),
   sliced

$1/2$–1 tablespoon sugar, to taste
$1^1/4$ pounds fresh coarse rice
   noodles (*laksa* noodles)

Spice Paste
5 shallots
2 stems lemongrass
1 inch fresh turmeric
3 dried red chilies, soaked in
   warm water
6 fresh red chilies
1 teaspoon dried shrimp paste

Garnish
1 cucumber, peeled and shredded
6 sprigs polygonum (*daun kesum*),
   sliced
A few sprigs of mint, torn
3 large red onions, sliced
3 red chilies, sliced
$1/2$ fresh pineapple, shredded
Small bowl of black shrimp paste,
   diluted in a little warm water

Simmer the whole fish in water until cooked. Remove fish, cool, and remove the flesh from the bones. Break up the flesh. Strain the stock carefully and return to a large pan with the fish, tamarind juice, ginger buds, polygonum and sugar.

Blend the spice paste ingredients finely and then add to the fish stock. Simmer the stock for 20–30 minutes.

To serve, blanch the noodles in boiling water, drain and divide among 6 bowls. Pour over the stock and add garnish. Allow diners to add the black shrimp paste themselves, as the

Sour Penang Noodle Soup.

Indian Mutton Soup.

taste is rather pungent. If Chubb mackerel is not available, choose another well-flavored fish to ensure the soup has its characteristic fishy taste.

Indian Mee Goreng
Indian Fried Noodles

Although noodles were brought to Malaysia by the Chinese, all other ethnic groups have enthusiastically adapted them to suit their tastes. This version is a dish you certainly wouldn't find in India.

10 dried chilies, soaked in hot water
1/2 cup oil
1 teaspoon dried shrimp paste
3 cloves garlic, finely chopped
5 ounces shrimp, peeled and deveined
5 ounces boneless chicken, shredded
12 ounces fresh yellow noodles
2 cups mustard greens
1 cup bean sprouts
2 pieces hard bean curd, deep-fried and sliced
3 tablespoons light soy sauce
1 teaspoon salt
1 red chili, sliced
1 green chili, sliced
1 sprig cilantro, roughly chopped
1 sprig Chinese celery, roughly chopped
2 scallions, sliced
2 tablespoons Fried Shallots, (page 121)
6 small fresh limes, halved

Blend softened chilies to a paste, adding a little oil if necessary. Set aside 2 tablespoons of oil and heat the remainder over medium heat. Add dried shrimp paste and fry for 1 minute. Add chili paste, reduce heat to low and cook, stirring from time to time, for 30 minutes. Remove from pan.

Heat the 2 tablespoons of oil in a wok. Add garlic, cooked chili paste, prawns and chicken and fry for 3 minutes. Add noodles and fry over medium heat for 3 minutes. Add mustard greens and bean sprouts. Fry for 2 minutes, then add bean curd and stir–fry for 3 minutes. Lastly, add soy sauce and salt. Stir-fry for 1 minute.

Garnish with fresh chilies, cilantro, celery, scallions, fried shallots and fresh lime and serve immediately.

> **HELPFUL HINT**
> Cabbage or spinach can be used instead of mustard greens if preferred.

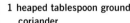
Indian Fried Noodles.

Sop Kambing
Indian Mutton Soup

Also known as *Sop Tulang* or Bone Soup, this robust dish is one of the more popular stall foods in Singapore. It makes a great late-night supper or luncheon, especially if served with crusty French bread.

2 inches ginger
6 cloves garlic
1 pound meaty mutton or lamb ribs
1 heaped tablespoon ground coriander
1 teaspoon ground fennel powder
1/2 teaspoon ground cumin powder
1 teaspoon salt
8–12 cups water
2 tablespoons oil
2 leeks, sliced (white part only)
1 cinnamon stick, 3 inches long
4 whole star anise
5 cardamom pods, bruised
1 tomato, quartered chopped
Fried shallots (page 121)
Chinese celery or cilantro leaves to garnish

Pound or blend the ginger and garlic together, then put in a pot with the mutton or lamb ribs, coriander, fennel, cumin and salt. Add 12 cups of water if using mutton, but only 8 cups if using lamb, which will cook more quickly. Simmer, uncovered, until the meat is soft.

Heat the oil in a small pan and sauté the leeks, cinnamon, star anise and cardamom until the leeks are quite tender. Add to the mutton soup and simmer for another couple of minutes.

Add tomato, then taste and add more salt if necessary. To serve, sprinkle with fried shallots and Chinese celery leaves, and accompany the soup with crusty French bread.

Chicken Rice.

Sprinkle with the sliced scallion and serve.

HELPFUL HINT

Claypot Rice. If you do not have a clay or earthenware pot, a saucepan with a heavy bottom or rice cooker will do at a pinch.

Duck in Fragrant Soy Sauce

A Teochew favourite sometimes made with goose, this is a simple but very tasty way of simmering duck in soy sauce flavored with 'black' spices (cinnamon, star anise and cloves). The addition of fresh turmeric and lemongrass, which are Southeast Asian rather than Chinese seasonings, are a Singaporean touch. *Jin kok* is a dried Chinese root, available from Chinese medicine or provision shops.

One 4-pound duck
1 tablespoon five-spice powder
7 cinnamon sticks, about 3 inches long
15 star anise
20 cloves
10 shallots, lightly bruised
10 cloves garlic, lightly bruised
3 tablespoons *jin kok* (optional)
4 cups light soy sauce
3 tablespoons black soy sauce
2 tablespoons sugar
1 stem lemongrass, bruised
1/2 inch fresh turmeric, bruised, or
   2 teaspoons ground turmeric
24 cups water

Clean the duck and rub the inside with five-spice powder. Leave in the refrigerator overnight.

Rinse the duck inside and out with water and put in a large wide pan with all the seasonings and water. Bring to the boil and simmer gently, uncovered, until the duck is very tender. Serve with steamed rice.

Nasi Ayam

Chicken Rice

This is another popular coffee-shop and hawker staple in Malaysia and Singapore. Prepare the chicken in advance.

Roast Chicken
1/2 fresh chicken
3 cloves garlic
4 shallots
2 inches ginger
3 tablespoons oyster sauce
1 tablespoon black soy sauce
2 tablespoons light soy sauce
1 tablespoon tomato sauce
1 tablespoon chili sauce
1 teaspoon cayenne
1 teaspoon salt

Rice
2 cups rice, washed thoroughly
1 inch ginger
3 cloves garlic
4 tablespoons butter
2 pandan leaves
A pinch of salt
3 tablespoons Fried Shallots
   (page 121)

Chili Sauce
5 red chillies
4 cloves garlic
1 inch ginger
3 tablespoons lime juice
1 teaspoon sesame oil
Salt and sugar to taste

Garnish
1 cucumber, sliced

Prick the chicken with a fork to allow seasonings to penetrate. Blend or pound garlic, shallots and ginger, then mix with all other ingredients and rub into chicken. Marinate 4 hours or overnight if possible. Roast chicken in a 425°F oven for about 20 minutes. Cut into pieces and put on a platter. Garnish with sliced cucumber.

Wash the rice, drain and put in a saucepan or rice cooker. Pound the ginger and garlic together and add to rice with butter, pandan leaves, salt and sufficient water to cook the rice. When the rice is cooked, fluff up with a fork, put it in a serving bowl and then decorate with fried shallots.

To make the chili sauce, blend the ingredients together until fine.

Serve the rice with the chicken, cucumber and chili sauce. A bowl of clear chicken soup is the usual accompaniment to Chicken Rice.

Claypot Rice

This Cantonese one-pot dish is very popular in the food stalls of Singapore and Malaysia. The Chinese believe that a claypot is essential to ensure the correct flavor and fragrance of this dish, though any other type of covered earthenware container could be used.

2 cups long-grain rice, washed
3 cups chicken stock (page 121)
1/2 fresh chicken, about 11/2 pounds, cut into small cubes
1 Chinese sausage, sliced
6 dried black mushrooms, soaked until soft and quartered
11/2 inches ginger, thinly sliced
1 scallion, thinly sliced

Marinade
2 tablespoons oil
3 tablespoons oyster sauce
1 tablespoon soy sauce
1 tablespoon Chinese rice wine
1/2 teaspoon sesame oil
1 teaspoon black soy sauce
1 teaspoon sugar
1/2 teaspoon ground white pepper
1 tablespoon cornstarch

Put the rice in a claypot with stock, cover and cook over low heat for about 20 minutes.

While the rice is cooking, mix the marinade ingredients together and pour over the chicken, mixing well. When the rice has cooked for 20 minutes, place the marinated chicken, sausage, mushrooms and sliced ginger on top. Cover and cook for another 10 minutes.

Devil Chicken Curry

Devil by name . . . this is quite a hot dish, tempered with lemongrass and galangal, so serve with lots of steamed rice.

Spice Paste
30 shallots, chopped
30 dried chilies, chopped, soaked and seeded
1¼ inches fresh turmeric, chopped
1 inch galangal, chopped
2 stems lemongrass, chopped
1 teaspoon brown mustard seeds, soaked in water for 5 minutes

¼ cup oil
2 onions, quartered
2 inches ginger, shredded
5 cloves garlic, sliced
2 red chilies, halved lengthwise
1 teaspoon salt
1 teaspoon light soy sauce
4 tablespoons sugar
4 potatoes, peeled and quartered
½ chicken, cut into serving pieces
½ cup distilled white vinegar
3–4 cups water

To make the spice paste, blend all ingredients with a little of the oil until fine. Set aside.

Heat remaining oil and fry the onions, ginger, garlic and chilies for 2 minutes. Drain off the oil and set mixture aside.

Fry the blended ingredients with 4 tablespoons oil for 10 minutes, then add the salt and soy sauce.

Rich Coconut Beef.

Add sugar, stir well, then put in the potatoes, chicken, vinegar and water. Simmer, uncovered, until the chicken is cooked. Taste and adjust seasonings. Add the fried ingredients, stir well and serve.

Note: Cut the chilies into pieces before soaking, and discard the seeds—which will fall to the bottom of the bowl—to reduce the heat of the dish.

Rendang Daging
Rich Coconut Beef

No festive occasion is complete without this rich Malay dish where beef is cooked to melting tenderness in a fragrant, coconut sauce. To prepare the *kerisik*, roast 3¾ cups grated fresh coconut in a slow oven until brown. Alternatively, cook in a dry wok, stirring constantly. Cool, then grind finely until the oil comes out.

Spice Paste
2 shallots, chopped
¾ inch galangal, chopped
3 stems lemon grass, chopped
2 cloves garlic, chopped
¾ inch ginger, chopped
10 dried chilies, soaked in hot water

½ cup oil
1¼ inch cinnamon stick

2 cloves
4 star anise
2 cardamom pods
1 pound top round beef, cubed
1 cup thick coconut milk
1 slice *asam gelugur* or 2 teaspoons dried tamarind pulp soaked in warm water for juice
2 fragrant lime leaves, very finely sliced
1 turmeric leaf, very finely sliced
2 tablespoons *kerisik*
1½ teaspoons sugar
Salt to taste

To make the spice paste, purée all ingredients in a blender until fine. Heat the oil, add the spice paste, cinnamon, cloves, star anise and cardamom, and fry for 5 minutes. Add the beef, coconut milk and *asam gelugur* or tamarind juice. Simmer, uncovered, stirring frequently, until the meat is almost cooked. Add the lime and turmeric leaves, *kerisik*, sugar and salt. Lower the heat and simmer until the meat is really tender and the sauce has dried up (about 1 to 1½ hours). Serve with rice and a stir-fried vegetable.

Buntut Asam Pedas
Sour Hot Oxtail Stew

The rich flavor of the oxtail is enhanced when it is cooked Malay/Indonesian style.

1 whole oxtail, 4 pounds, cut into 1½-inch pieces
10 shallots, chopped
8 cloves garlic, chopped
25 red chilies, seeded and chopped
10 bird's eye chilies, chopped
1 inch turmeric, chopped, or 1 teaspoon ground turmeric
3 tablespoons concentrated tomato paste
⅔ cup tamarind pulp, soaked in 2 cups of water, squeezed and strained for juice
2 tablespoons sugar
5 fragrant lime leaves
2 stems lemongrass, bruised
1½ inches galangal, sliced
12 cups water
Salt and pepper to taste
Fried shallots (page 121)

Trim oxtail of all fat.

Pound or blend the shallots, garlic, chilies and turmeric, adding a little water if necessary to keep the blades turning. Combine the mixture with all other ingredients except water, seasoning and fried shallots. Mix well with the oxtail and marinate for 2 hours.

Bring the water to a boil in a large pot and add the oxtail. Simmer, uncovered, over low heat until the oxtail is tender and the liquid is reduced by about half. Season to taste with salt and pepper, garnish with fried shallots and serve with steamed rice.

Devil Chicken Curry.

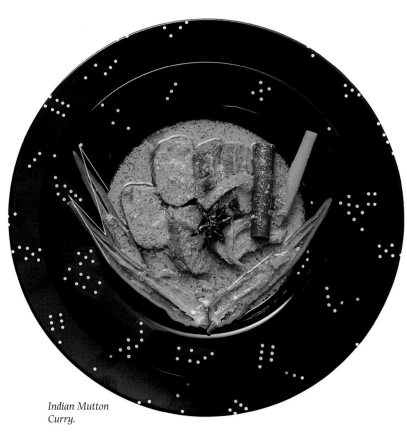

Indian Mutton Curry.

Kambing Korma
Indian Mutton Curry

A mixture of dried ground spices, whole spices and the usual trinity of shallots, garlic and ginger provide the basic flavorings for this rich mutton curry. The Singapore touch is evident in the use of candlenuts (not found in India) to enrich and thicken the sauce.

2 pounds mutton or lamb, cubed
8 cups water
10 shallots, chopped
10 cloves garlic, chopped
2 inches ginger, chopped
10 green chilies, chopped
3 tablespoons oil
1 large onion, sliced
6 cardamom pods, bruised
5 whole star anise
2 sticks cinnamon about 3 inches
    long
4 tablespoons meat curry powder
20 curry leaves
3 potatoes, quartered
1 cup plain yogurt
1 teaspoon salt
10 candlenuts, pounded or
    blended
2 slices *asam gelugur* or
    1 tablespoon tamarind pulp,
    soaked in 4 tablespoons water,
    squeezed and strained for juice
4–6 green chilies, halved
    lengthwise
6 tomatoes, quartered

Put the mutton in a large pan with water.
   Blend the shallots, garlic, ginger and green chilies with a little water. Add to the mutton and bring to a boil. Simmer, uncovered, until the meat has become just tender.
   Heat oil and gently sauté the onion, cardamom, star anise, cinnamon, curry powder and curry leaves. When fragrant, add to the meat together with the potatoes, yogurt, salt, candlenuts and tamarind. Continue simmering until the meat is soft. Add the green chilies and tomatoes just before serving.

Borneo Marinated Fish

This no-cook dish is a favourite among Sarawak's Melanau people, who call their version *umai*. Sabah's Kadazans call it *hinava*. Use only the very freshest fish for this recipe, as it is "cooked" only with lime juice.

1 pound white-fleshed fish,
    preferably Spanish mackerel
1/3 cup freshly squeezed
    lime or lemon juice
2–3 red chilies
1 teaspoon salt
6–8 shallots, thinly sliced
2 inches ginger, very finely
    shredded

2 sprigs fresh cilantro leaves,
    roughly chopped
2 sprigs Chinese celery, roughly
    chopped

Remove all skin and bone from the fish and slice thinly. Set aside 2 tablespoons of lime juice and soak the fish in the remaining juice for at least 30 minutes, stirring once or twice, until the fish turns opaque. Drain and discard the lime juice. While the fish is marinating, pound the chilies with salt until fine. When fish is ready, mix it with the chilies, shallots, ginger, fresh herbs and reserved lime juice. Taste and add more salt if desired. Serve immediately as part of a rice-based meal.

Ikan Asam Pedas
Hot and Sour Fish Curry

Fragrant and spicy, this curry is enriched by a touch of coconut milk.

Spice Paste
15 dried chilies, soaked in hot
    water and chopped
2 candlenuts
4 cloves garlic, chopped
10 shallots, chopped
1/2 teaspoon ground turmeric
1 cup water

1/3 cup oil
1/2 inch galangal, smashed
2 slices *asam gelugur* or 1 heaped
    tablespoon tamarind pulp,

soaked in water for juice
2 1/2 cups water
6 thick fish fillets or cutlets
4 sprigs polygonum (*daun kesum*),
    chopped
Salt to taste
1 teaspoon sugar
3 tablespoons thick coconut milk

To make the spice paste, blend all ingredients finely.
   Heat oil in a saucepan, then fry the galangal and paste for 5 minutes. Add the *asam* or tamarind pulp. Add 1/2 cup water and cook for another 5 minutes. Add the rest of the water and bring to a boil.
   Add the fish, polygonum, salt, sugar and coconut milk and simmer, uncovered, for another 5 minutes.

Teochew Steamed Fish

A very delicious dish that demands the freshest of fish to shine. Salted plums are available in jars from Asian food stores.

2-pound whole pomfret
1/4 cup salted Chinese cabbage
    (*kiam chye*), chopped
1 tomato, cut in wedges
3 inches ginger, finely sliced
2 red chilies, sliced
6 salted plums
1 scallion, cut into 2 inch lengths
3 dried black mushrooms, soaked
    to soften, then sliced
2 ounces shredded pork (optional)

Teochew Steamed Fish (left) and Oyster Omelet (right), recipe on page 109.

Chili Crab

Seasoning
4 tablespoons Garlic Oil (page 121)
4 tablespoons oyster sauce
1 teaspoon sesame oil
2 tablespoons light soy sauce
1 tablespoon sugar
2 tablespoons Chinese rice wine
1/2 cup Chicken Stock (page 121)

Clean and dry the pomfret thoroughly. Place all other ingredients into a bowl.

Combine all seasoning ingredients and mix well. Stir into the other ingredients and mix well. Place the pomfret on a plate which will fit into a steamer or on a tray inside a wok and spread the mixture on top of the pomfret. Cover and steam over rapidly boiling water for 15–20 minutes, until the fish is cooked. Do not overcook or the texture will be spoiled.

Sambal Udang
Shrimp Sambal

Spice Paste
10 red chilies, chopped
3 medium red onions, chopped
2.5 cm (1 in) galangal, chopped
10 cloves garlic, chopped
3 candlenuts

1/2 cup oil
2 tablespoons brown sugar
1 teaspoon salt
3 tablespoons thick coconut milk
4 tablespoons lime juice
1 pound medium-sized shrimp, peeled and deveined

To make the spice paste, blend all ingredients until fine, adding a little of the oil if necessary to keep the blades turning. Heat oil in a saucepan and fry the blended ingredients for about 10 minutes until fragrant. Add brown sugar, salt and coconut milk and bring to a boil. Add lime juice and shrimp and simmer for 5 minutes or until the shrimp are just cooked.

Butter Shrimp

A relatively recent Malaysian creation, this combines traditionally Malay, Chinese, Indian and Western ingredients.

1 1/4 pounds large shrimp
Oil for deep-frying
2–3 tablespoons butter
15 bird's-eye chilies, roughly chopped
10–15 sprigs curry leaves
2 cloves garlic, finely chopped
1/2 teaspoon salt
2 tablespoons sugar
1/2 teaspoon light soy sauce
1/2 teaspoon Chinese rice wine
1/2 grated coconut, dry-fried until golden

Remove heads from the shrimp but leave the shells. Slit down the back to remove intestinal tract, trim feelers and legs, and dry thoroughly. Heat the oil and deep-fry the shrimp.

Drain and reserve. Melt the butter, add chilies, curry leaves, garlic and salt and fry for 2 minutes. Add shrimp, sugar, soy sauce, wine and grated coconut. Cook over high heat for 1–2 minutes, stirring frequently. Serve immediately.

Chili Crab

This is virtually Singapore's national dish. Provide finger bowls of warm water (in Asia they use tea) for diners to use—this dish is more delicious eaten with the fingers!

2 pounds fresh crabs, cleaned and halved
Oil for deep-frying
4 cloves garlic, finely chopped
2 inches young ginger, roughly chopped
3 red chilies, finely chopped
1/4 cup chili sauce
1/4 cup tomato sauce
1 tablespoon sugar
1 tablespoon light soy sauce
1 teaspoon sesame oil
Salt and pepper to taste
1 cup Chicken Stock (page 121)
1 tablespoon cornflour, mixed with 3 tablespoons water
1 egg, lightly beaten
1 scallion, sliced

Deep-fry the crabs in hot oil just until bright red. Remove and set aside. Pour out the oil and put 1/4 cup fresh oil into the wok. Heat and add garlic, ginger and chilies. Stir until fragrant, then add chili sauce, tomato sauce, sugar, soy sauce and sesame oil. Simmer for 1 minute, then season to taste with salt and pepper. Add the fried crab and stir to coat well with sauce. Add chicken stock and cook over high heat for 3 minutes. Stir thoroughly and thicken with cornstarch and egg. Season to taste with salt and pepper and sprinkle with scallions.

Shrimp Sambal.

Ayam Limau Purut
Chicken with Lime Leaf

The charm of this Nonya curry comes from its aromatic fresh herbs and seasonings.

Spice Paste
2 medium red or yellow onions, chopped
8 red chilies, chopped
3 cloves garlic, chopped
1 stem lemon grass, chopped
1 1/4 inches galangal, chopped
1 teaspoon ground turmeric

1/2 cup oil
1/2 chicken, cut in serving pieces
1 slice *asam gelugur* or lime juice to taste
1/2 cup water
1 cup thick coconut milk
4 fragrant lime leaves
Salt to taste
Lime juice to taste (optional)

To make the spice paste, blend the ingredients, adding a little of the oil if necessary to keep the blades turning. Heat oil and fry the paste for about 5 minutes until fragrant.

Add the chicken, *asam gelugur* and water and simmer until the chicken is half cooked.

Add the coconut milk and lime leaves and simmer, uncovered, until the chicken is tender. Add salt and, if using, lime juice.

Salted Fish and Pineapple Curry.

Salted Fish and Pineapple Curry

Salted fish is popular in Malaysia, and not just as a standby for times when fresh fish may be unavailable owing to monsoon storms. This Eurasian curry uses good quality dried fish cut in 1/2-inch-thick slices.

1 just-ripe pineapple
4 ounces salted fish, cut into large cubes
1/4 cup oil
1/2 cup water
1 1/2 cups thick coconut milk
Salt to taste

Spice Paste
6 shallots, chopped
3 red chilies, chopped
1 inch fresh turmeric, chopped
1 inch galangal, chopped
2 stems lemongrass, chopped
1/2 teaspoon dried shrimp paste
1/2 teaspoon salt

Peel the pineapple, clean and quarter, remove core, wash and cut into triangular pieces. Blend half the pineapple with about 1/4 cup water to make a purée and set aside.

Soak the fish in water for about 10 minutes, then drain and dry well.

Blend spice paste ingredients until fine. Heat oil in a saucepan, add the paste and stir-fry gently for 5 minutes.

Add pineapple pieces and stir-fry until well coated with spices. Put in salted fish, the pineapple purée, water and coconut milk. Reduce heat and simmer curry gently for about 10–15 minutes until pineapple is tender. Add salt to taste.

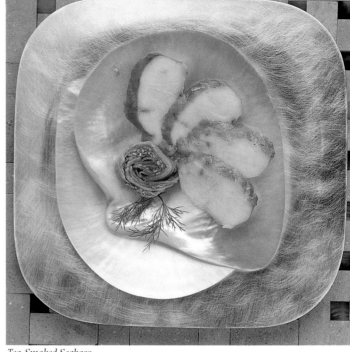

Tea-Smoked Seabass.

Tea-Smoked Seabass

Smoking food—especially duck—over a mixture of tea leaves is a popular method of preparing food in Yunnan and Sichuan provinces in China.

Make sure the exhaust fan is turned on and the room well ventilated (windows open) before you start smoking, or you'll be smoked out.

Marinade
2 cups iced water
5 tablespoons soy sauce
1 tablespoon sugar
1/2 cup Ginger Juice (page 121)
1 tablespoon salt

1 whole 1–1 1/4-pound seabass fillet or other firm white fish fillet such as snapper or garoupa
5 tablespoons Chinese black tea leaves
5 star anise
3 cinnamon sticks, about 3 inches long
20 cloves
5 tablespoons raw rice
5 cloves garlic, crushed

Combine all marinade ingredients and pour over the fish.

Leave for about 3 hours. Remove the seabass from the marinade, drain, dry with paper towels and set aside.

Heat a wok over a low flame and put in the remaining ingredients. Put the fish on a wire grill or round bamboo rack inside the wok at least 2 inches above the smoking ingredients. Cover the wok and smoke over a low flame for 10–15 minutes, until the fish has turned brown and is cooked through.

Slice and serve hot or cold.

Spicy Kangkung

Kangkung (water spinach) is a very popular vegetable in Southeast Asia. You do need lots, as they cook down to virtually nothing.

2 pounds *kangkung* (water spinach)
3 tablespoons dried shrimp, soaked to soften
6 cloves garlic
6 shallots
5 red chilies
1 inch ginger
2 teaspoons dried shrimp paste
3–4 tablespoons oil
2 tablespoons sugar
1 teaspoon sesame oil
1 tablespoon light soy sauce
Salt and pepper to taste
1 red chili, finely sliced

Chicken with Lime Leaf (left) and Vegetables in Coconut Milk (right).

Snake Gourd

Colors and textures contrast beautifully in this southern Indian dish.

- 1 cup yellow lentils
- 1/2 teaspoon ground turmeric
- 2 cups water
- 1 snake gourd
- 4 shallots, sliced
- 1 clove garlic, sliced
- 2 tablespoons oil
- 1 tablespoon brown mustard seeds
- 1 teaspoon salt
- 1 sprig curry leaves
- 2 red chilies, seeds removed, sliced

Wash lentils thoroughly, combine with turmeric and water, and simmer until soft.

While the lentils are cooking, prepare the gourd. For a more decorative appearance, scrape the skin deeply lengthwise with a fork and cut in half lengthwise. Remove the pulpy center and cut across into 1/2-inch slices. Alternatively, peel the gourd, remove the center and cut in circles 1/2-inch thick.

Fry the shallots and garlic in oil until soft. Add mustard seeds and cook until they begin to pop. Add lentils, gourd and salt, and cook until tender. Just before removing from the heat, add curry leaves and chilies. Toss through and serve.

HELPFUL HINT

If snake gourd is not available, substitute 1 pound long beans or sliced zucchini or summer squash.

Use only the tender tips and leaves of the *kangkung*, discarding any tough stems.

Pound or blend the dried shrimp until fine. Set aside.

Blend garlic, shallots, chilies and ginger until fine. using a little of the oil if necessary to keep the blades turning. Add the shrimp paste and blend for another few seconds.

Heat the remaining oil in a wok or heavy pan. Add the paste and dried shrimp. Cook over low heat, stirring frequently, for about 5 minutes, until fragrant.

Add sugar, sesame oil and soy sauce, stirring until well mixed, then add *kangkung* and stir well. Cook with the lid on until the *kangkung* is tender. Season to taste with salt and pepper, and sprinkle with sliced chili.

for 5 minutes in warm water
- 3 tablespoons oil
- 1 1/2 cups water
- 1 1/2 cups thick coconut milk
- 1 carrot, cut into 1 1/2 inch match sticks
- 1 small eggplant, cut into 1 1/2-inch matchsticks
- 3 long beans, cut into 1 1/2-inch lengths
- 1/4 cabbage, coarsely shredded
- 1 piece hard bean curd, deep-fried and quartered
- Salt to taste

To make the spice paste, blend all ingredients finely, adding a little oil if necessary to keep the blades turning. Heat the oil and fry the paste for 5 minutes, then add water and coconut milk. Bring slowly to a boil.

Add the vegetables, bean curd and salt and simmer, uncovered, until the vegetables are just cooked.

- 2 sprigs curry leaves
- 1 tablespoon fish or chicken curry powder
- 2-3 teaspoons cayenne
- 1/2 teaspoon ground turmeric
- 2 cups water
- 1 teaspoon salt
- Sugar to taste

Prepare the pumpkin and set aside. Heat the oil and fry the onion until golden, then add mustard seed and curry leaves and fry until mustard seeds pop. Add the spice powders and fry for 30 seconds, then put in pumpkin and stir for a minute or two, until well coated with spices. Slowly add the water, stirring, then add salt and sugar to taste. Simmer, uncovered, until tender and dry.

Sayur Lemak

Vegetables in Coconut Milk

A Nonya adaptation of Malay-style vegetables simmered in coconut milk.

- Spice Paste
- 2 red chilies, chopped
- 3 candlenuts, in small pieces
- 5 shallots, chopped
- 1/2 teaspoon ground turmeric
- 1/2 teaspoon dried shrimp paste
- 1 teaspoon dried shrimp, soaked

Spicy Pumpkin

Gourds are very popular among Malaysians of Southern Indian origin, especially sweet-tasting pumpkin, which goes well with spices.

- 1 1/2 pound pumpkin, peeled and cut in 1-inch pieces
- 3 tablespoons oil
- 1 large onion, finely chopped
- 1 tablespoon brown mustard seeds

Snake Gourd (left) and Spicy Pumpkin (right).

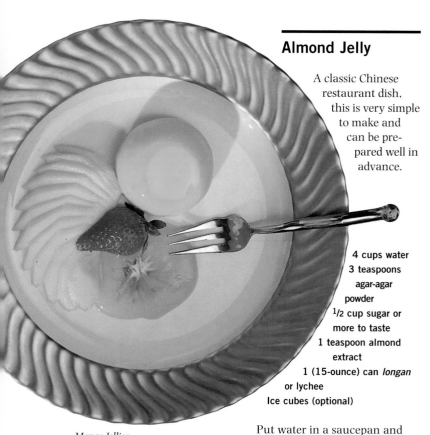

Mango Jellies.

In Malaysian and Singaporean homes, desserts are not commonly served at the end of a meal, although elaborate restaurant meals often finish with some of the dishes featured here.

Mango Jellies

- 4 cups water
- 1 cup sugar
- 2 tablespoons unflavored gelatin, softened in warm water
- 1 cup coconut milk
- 1/2 cup evaporated milk
- 2 eggs, beaten
- 1 medium mango (1 1/2 cups), puréed
- 1 large mango, very finely diced

Combine water and sugar in a pan and stir over low heat until sugar is dissolved. Add soaked gelatin and continue heating until thoroughly dissolved. Remove from heat and add all ingredients except the diced mango. Mix until well blended then add the diced mango.

Pour into individual molds and refrigerate until set. Garnish with fresh fruit and a little mango purée if you like.

Almond Jelly

A classic Chinese restaurant dish, this is very simple to make and can be prepared well in advance.

- 4 cups water
- 3 teaspoons agar-agar powder
- 1/2 cup sugar or more to taste
- 1 teaspoon almond extract
- 1 (15-ounce) can *longan* or lychee
- Ice cubes (optional)

Put water in a saucepan and sprinkle with agar-agar powder. Bring gently to a boil, stirring, then add the sugar and almond extract. Simmer for a minute, then pour into a dish about 15 6 inches square. Leave to set, then refrigerate until required.

Refrigerate the *longans* or lychees.

Just before serving, put the chilled *longans* or lychees in a large bowl. Cut the almond jelly into squares and add to the fruit. Add a few ice cubes if using and serve immediately.

Sago with Honeydew

- 3/4 cup pearl sago
- 7 cups water
- 1 cup coconut milk
- 1 cup sugar
- 1/2 cup water
- 1/2 honeydew melon

Soak sago in 2 cups water for 30 minutes. Drain. Bring the remaining 5 cups water to a boil and add sago. Cook until transparent. Drain in a sieve and wash under cold running water. Leave sago aside until cool.

Boil sugar and 1/2 cup water together to make a syrup.

Peel the melon, cut in half and discard seeds. Blend half the honeydew to make juice and cut the other half into small cubes, or make small balls with a melon baller. Mix the sago, coconut milk, honeydew juice, honeydew cubes and sugar syrup to taste. Serve chilled.

Nonya Pancake

A Nonya version of the Malay stuffed pancake, *kuih dadar*, is served with a coconut sauce as a tea-time treat or snack, rather than as a dessert, in Malaysia.

Batter
- 10 pandan leaves
- 1 cup water
- 1 cup white flour
- 1 egg
- Scant 1/3 cup fresh milk
- 1/4 teaspoon salt
- 2 teaspoons melted butter

Filling
- 2 cups grated coconut
- 1 1/2 cups water
- 3 pandan leaves
- 1/4 teaspoon salt
- 3/4 palm sugar, chopped

Coconut Sauce
- 1/2 cup thick coconut milk
- 1/2 cup water
- 3 pandan leaves
- 1 teaspoon sugar
- 1 teaspoon cornstarch
- A pinch of salt

To make the batter, blend the pandan leaves with water. Strain to obtain the juice. Sift the flour into a bowl and add egg, milk, salt and pandan juice. Stir until smooth, adding more water if necessary to obtain a thin consistency. Set aside.

Combine all filling ingredients in a saucepan and simmer over very low heat, stirring occasionally, for about 45 minutes, until thick and dry. Set aside to cool.

To make the coconut sauce, combine all ingredients in a saucepan and stir continuously over low heat until it thickens and clears. Sieve and serve warm or at room temperature.

To cook the pancakes, grease a nonstick pan with a little butter and pour in enough batter to make a pancake about 6–8 inches in diameter. Cook gently on both sides and reserve. Repeat until all the batter is used up.

To serve, put 2–3 tablespoonfuls of the filling in the center of a pancake. Tuck in the edges and roll up into a cigar. Serve the pancakes, warm or at room temperature, with the coconut sauce.

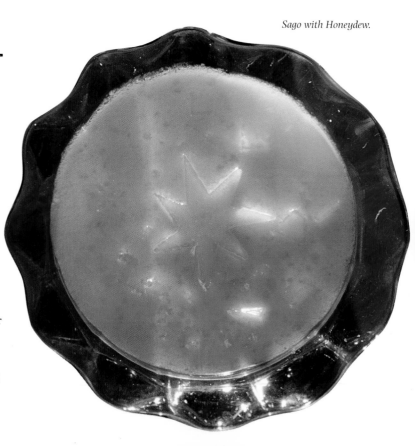

Sago with Honeydew.

Fried Shallots and Garlic Oil

1 cup oil
24 shallots or 10–15 cloves garlic, peeled and finely sliced

Heat oil and deep-fry shallots or garlic until golden brown and crisp. (Take care not to let them burn or the flavor will be bitter.) Drain and cool completely before storing.

Keep the shallot or garlic oil and use it for frying or seasoning other dishes.

Ginger Juice

Use young ginger if possible—they are much juicier.

4 ounces fresh ginger, peeled and coarsely chopped
5 tablespoons water

Blend ginger with water until very fine. Strain through a sieve, pushing down with the back of a spoon to extract all the juice. This should provide about $1/2$ cup ginger juice, which can be stored in a refrigerator for up to 1 week.

Char Siew
Red Roasted Pork

This is often used with Chinese noodle dishes, in fried rice and as a stuffing in steamed buns (*pau*).

$1/2$ cup sugar
4 tablespoons light soy sauce
2 tablespoons black soy sauce
1 tablespoon red food coloring
1 teaspoon five-spice powder
1 teaspoon sesame oil
1 teaspoon Chinese wine
$1^1/4$ pounds pork belly (part meat, part fat), or pork fillet if less fat preferred

Combine all ingredients in a bowl except pork and stir well. Add pork and marinate for about 1 hour.

Roast on a wire rack in a moderately hot oven (400 ° F) for about 30 minutes. Leave to cool and slice as needed.

Chicken Stock

2 large mature hens or chickens, quartered
20 cups water
3 inches ginger, crushed
2 leeks, sliced
1 large onion, halved
1 carrot, diced
5 stalks Chinese celery (with leaves)

Wash hens well, then blanch in boiling water for 3 minutes. Remove hens and discard water. Bring another 20 cups fresh water to a boil with the chicken and vegetables. Simmer, uncovered, over low heat for 2–3 hours. This makes 3–4 quarts stock. It freezes well.

Chili Sauce

5 red chilies, roughly chopped
10 tablespoons water
3 tablespoons sugar
10 tablespoons distilled white vinegar
1 teaspoon salt

Blend chilies with water. Add the remaining ingredients and bring to a boil. Remove from heat and allow to cool.

Popiah Wrappers

$1^1/8$ cups rice flour
3 tablespoons white flour
$1/2$ teaspoon salt
4 eggs
1 teaspoon oil
2 cups water
$1/2$ teaspoon salt

Sift both types of flour and salt into a bowl. Combine eggs, oil and water and stir into the dried ingredients, mixing until smooth. Leave in the refrigerator for at least 1 hour.

Cook in a nonstick pan, greasing it with the minimum amount of oil to stop the batter from sticking. Pour in just a little batter, swirl the pan to make a very thin pancake and cook on one side only over moderate heat until set. Put on a plate and repeat until the batter is used up. Makes about 20–25 wrappers.

Chili Peanuts with Anchovies

4 red chilies
1 shallot
1 tablespoon oil
$1/2$ teaspoon salt
1 tablespoon sugar
$3^1/4$ cup roasted peanuts, skins on
1 ounce anchovies, heads and intestinal tract removed and fried till crisp

Blend the chilies and shallot together. Heat the oil and gently fry the blended mixture with the salt and sugar for 1 minute. Add the peanuts and anchovies. Stir-fry for 3 minutes and remove from heat. Refrigerate for up to 3 weeks.

Chili Sauce.

Sambal Belacan
Shrimp Paste Sambal

12 large red chilies, roughly chopped
2 tablespoons dried shrimp paste, roasted
$2/3$ cup water
4 tablespoons lime juice

Blend the chilies and shrimp paste with the water. Season to taste with lime juice.

Dried Cucumber Acar

2 cucumbers
1 large carrot

Dressing
$3/4$ cup distilled white vinegar
3 tablespoons sugar

$1/2$ teaspoon salt
Pinch of ground turmeric
2 shallots, sliced
$1/2$ inch ginger, very finely sliced
1 clove garlic, peeled and shredded
2 tablespoons raisins

Cut the cucumbers in half lengthwise and remove the seeds. Cut into matchstick pieces $1^1/2$ inches in length. Peel the carrot and cut the same size as the cucumber. Dry the cucumbers and carrot in the hot sun for 2 hours.

Combine the vinegar, sugar, salt and turmeric and bring to a boil. Remove immediately from the heat and allow to cool. Add the shallots, ginger, garlic and raisins and mix with the cucumbers and carrot. Store in the refrigerator for 1 month.

Chili Ginger Sauce

6 red chilies, roughly chopped
$1^1/4$ inches ginger, chopped
4 cloves garlic
$2/3$ cup water
2 teaspoons salt
5 tablespoons sugar
5 tablespoons lime juice
1 teaspoon sesame oil

Blend the chilies, ginger, garlic and water. Season to taste with the salt, sugar, lime juice and sesame oil.

"The secrets of classic Thai cooking have been liked to culinary treasures."

THAILAND

From the Kingdom of Sukhothai comes a cuisine that balances the sweet and the sour with the hot and the salty.

Left: Floating markets, where everything you might need is piled onto a boat and paddled along rivers and canals.

Right: A woman winnowing wheat.

The Thais have a saying, *gan gin gan yu*—as you eat, so you are, which perfectly encapsulates their approach to food. Whether Thai cuisine comes about because of the fresh ingredients used, or the meticulous act of preparation, or the seasoning or garnishing is immaterial; Thai food has an elegance and refinement that is all its own. The only country in Southeast Asia to remain independent during the era of colonization, Thailand's blends of hot and sweet, sour and salty are different from the dishes of its neighbours, even though they may use some of the same ingredients: chilli, garlic, lemongrass, fish sauce, palm sugar and lime.

It is easy to see an analogy between the various aspects of Thai culture, including its cuisine. One of the most notable characteristics of Thai decorative art, for instance, is its passion for intricate detail, particularly apparent in complex mosaics of colored glass and porcelain that adorn so many religious buildings. From afar, these suggest a solid, seamless pattern; only on closer inspection are the separate components revealed, and the skillful way they have been put together. So, too, in Thai cuisine, a wide variety of elements has been brought together and artfully composed into something that is intrinsically quite special.

The Land and its People

A stone tablet credited to King Ramkhamhaeng of Sukhothai, the first independent Thai kingdom founded in the early 13th century, bears the couplet: "In the water there are fish, in the fields there is rice." This testifies to a natural abundance that was to sustain a series of capital cities along the length of the fertile Chao Phraya River valley and, more specifically, to the two mainstays of the Thai diet then and now. Rice culture came with the earliest settlers, long before the Thais themselves arrived on the scene, and led to a vast complex of paddy fields watered by an intricate system of canals, rivers and reservoirs. Fish were plentiful, not only in the waterways, but also in the seas.

Other ingredients were gradually added over the centuries from a wide variety of cultures: from China and India, from Persia (modern-day Iran) and Portugal. Even such a seemingly essential element as the pungent chili was, in fact, from South America. However these ingredients came, though, they were subtly modified and refined into a cuisine that is today distinctively Thai.

Like its cuisine, Thailand encompasses a wide range of topography that covers some 198,500 square miles over some 73 provinces (*changwat*). To the north is a complex system of forested mountain ranges divided by the fertile Ping, Yom, Wang and Nan river valleys. The northeast consists of a sparsely vegetated, semi-arid plateau that stretches to the Mekong River. The flat central plains, watered by the Chao Phraya River, form one of the richest rice-growing regions on earth. The colorful checkerboard of paddy fields, orchards and vegetable gardens that makes up these plains sustains the greater part of the country's agricultural and industrial growth. The mountainous southern isthmus, extending down to the border with Malaysia, is bordered on one side by the Gulf of Thailand and on the other by the Indian Ocean.

The Thais are an agricultural people. Even today, despite the growth of urban areas, the great majority of the population can be found in villages; most villagers still derive their living from agriculture. The tropical climate allows year-round cultivation of rice, fruits and vegetables. There are three distinguishable seasons: wet (June to October), cool (November to February) and hot (March to May).

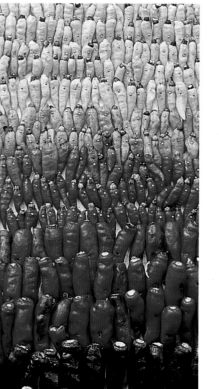

Chilies pinned out in the sun to dry.

Evidence of settlers dates back to the Paleolithic age some 500,000 years ago. The most extensive prehistoric remains come from the northeast, where a remarkable culture flourished from around 4000 b.c. to just after the start of the Christian era. Indian traders later established ports along the southern peninsula, bringing not only Buddhism but numerous cultural and culinary influences. Mon settlers arrived around the same time in the Chao Phraya valley and founded the Dvaravati kingdom, to be replaced eventually by the Khmers.

Between the 7th and 11th centuries, the ethnic Thais, originating as a minority group from the northern parts of Burma and southern China, gradually migrated southward in search of greater independence and fertile land. By the 13th century, the Thais had established themselves in such numbers that they were eventually able to overthrow their Khmer overlords and establish a kingdom of their own.

This kingdom was called Sukhothai (Sanskrit for "Dawn of Happiness"), and though its power lasted less than two centuries, its influence proved far more enduring. Under King Ramkhamhaeng, the Thai alphabet was devised, works of Buddhist art were created and a truly indigenous Thai culture emerged.

Ayuthia, the next capital, began in 1350 as a small city-state on the Chao Phraya River and over the next 400 years became one of the most cosmopolitan cities in Southeast Asia. In this period, first contact was made with Europe and an active trade established with other Asian countries. Ayuthia fell to an invading Burmese army in 1767. King Rama I founded the present Chakri Dynasty in 1782 and moved the capital across the Chao Phraya to what is now Bangkok.

Bangkok prospered and the Chinese immigrants and Western traders who were drawn in large numbers to it helped bring diversity to the new city. By the end of the 19th century, Bangkok was well on its way to becoming a modern, Western-style city—at least in appearance.

The Making of a Cuisine

Little is known about the cooking of Sukhothai, but rice and fish were no doubt major ingredients. Fruits were plentiful, as were mushrooms that grew wild in the forests and a variety of vegetables. One item not present, however, was the chili, which was either brought directly by the Portuguese, who opened relations in 1511, or came via Malacca or India. Simon de la Loubere, who came with a French diplomatic mission in 1687, was struck by the fact that the people ate sparingly. Good salt was rare, and despite its abundance, fresh fish was seldom eaten. Jesuit missionary Nicolas Gervaise noted that *kapi*, the popular fermented shrimp paste, "has such a pungent smell that it nauseates anyone not accustomed to it," and gives perhaps the first general recipe for a typical Thai condiment based on it: "salt, pepper, ginger, cinnamon, cloves, garlic, white onions, nutmeg and several strongly flavoured herbs . . . mixed in considerable quantities with this shrimp paste."

The complex seasonings that we now regard as typical of Thai cuisine, including chillies, were certainly well established by the Rattanakosin, or Bangkok, period. Sir John Bowring regarded the essential sauce *nam prik* as "one of the most appetite-exciting condiments."

Alongside the development of this individual cuisine was a more refined one that prevailed in royal and aristocratic households, "Palace cooking," which focused on subtlety and visual appeal.

The Food of the People

Thai food today may be plain or fancy: a dish can be prepared in a few minutes over a charcoal brazier or require hours of chopping, grinding and carving. It may vary considerably from region to region. Always, though, it remains a singular creation, not quite like any of the influences that have shaped it over the centuries.

In the mountainous north, where borders are shared with Burma and Laos, the cuisine is as distinctive as the handicrafts for which the region is noted. Here, the earliest Thais settled on their migration southward from China, forming first a group of small city-states and then a loose federation known as Lanna, with Chiang Mai as the principal city.

The north has retained much of its native culture: its language, crafts, customs and food. Instead of the soft-boiled rice of the central region, northerners prefer a steamed glutinous variety, rolled into small balls and dipped into liquid dishes. Curries of the region tend to be thinner, without the coconut milk widely used in central and southern cooking. There is also a distinctive local version of *nam prik ong*, a basic dipping sauce served with raw vegetables and crispy pork skin, as well as a pork sausage called *naem*, eaten plain with rice or mixed into various dishes. When it is in season, the favorite local fruit is the succulent longan, which grows in almost every compound.

The influence of neighboring Burma and Laos is apparent in many northern dishes. The former for the popular Khao Soi, a curry broth with egg noodles and chicken, pork or beef, and *gaeng hang lay*, a pork curry seasoned with ginger, tamarind and turmeric; the latter for *nam prik noom*, a sauce with a strong chili-lime flavor, and *ook gai*, a red chicken curry with lemongrass.

Northeastern Thailand was long regarded as remote from the cosmopolitan world of Bangkok—not so much because of geography as a perceptible social prejudice on the part of city dwellers. Isan, as Thais call the northeast, was the poorest of the country's four main regions; its infertile soil and devastating droughts frequently drove farmers to the capital in search of work. The people of Isan have a definite skill for transforming food in ways that show both imagination and ingenuity. Barbecued chicken (*gai yang*) is grilled with lashings of peppery sauce and garlic, while catfish is the base of a delectable curry and *laab* dip is made with raw meat and ground roasted rice. Some of the region's delicacies are unique: grubworms, grasshoppers, ant eggs, snail curry and fermented fish of exceptional pungency. Increasingly, the less challenging dishes typical of the region have won widespread admiration, and some diners are known to look upon a properly prepared *som tam* (spicy green papaya salad) or *laab* (even spicier minced pork or chicken) as being the true marks of a superior Thai cook. Perhaps because chilies add such character to the most mundane dish, northeasterners tend to use them with greater abandon than Thais of other areas.

Much northeastern cooking reflects the influence of Laos just across the Mekong River—not surprising, since many residents are ethnically Lao. Dill (*pak chee Lao* or "Laotian coriander") is widely used as a garnish, and glutinous rice is preferred. Also of Lao origin and popular on festive occasions is *khanom buang*, a crispy crêpe stuffed with dried shrimp, bean sprouts and other ingredients.

Southern Thailand, by contrast, is nurtured by rain that falls for eight months of the year. Cultivated areas tend to be vast rubber and coconut plantations rather than the rice fields and fruit orchards of the central plains. Coconuts growing plentifully everywhere provide milk for thickening soups and curries, oil for frying and grated flesh as a condiment for many dishes. Thousands of boats fish the surrounding waters from villages along the coastlines on the Gulf of Thailand and the Indian Ocean, bringing back seafood for local consumption and profitable export.

The south is home to most of Thailand's two million Muslims, its largest religious minority. In other southern places like Songkhla and the island of Phuket, the Chinese predominate. Southern food reflects the cross-pollination. Seafood may be prepared simply, grilled or steamed; or baked in a claypot with thin noodles and garlic; or included as the main component of *tom yam*, the ubiquitous Thai soup laced with lemongrass and chilies. In general, southerners like their food chili-hot, and are fond of the bitter taste of a flat, native bean called *sataw*, which other Thais tend to find less appealing. Small, juicy pineapples are a popular end to a meal.

Contributions from other cultures include *gaeng mussaman*, an Indian-style curry of chicken or beef perfumed with cardamom, cloves and cinnamon; Malay fish curries; and Indonesian satay.

The central plains is the Thai heartland. Here, you'll find the best jasmine rice, pearly white and fragrant, and mangoes, durians, mangosteens, rambutans, guavas, papayas and pomelos, even grapes. Vegetables such as cabbage, mushrooms, morning glory (water spinach), cucumber, tomatoes and pumpkins, as well as more recent introductions like asparagus and baby corn, are grown in vast quantities.

Food in the villages amid the fields tends to be plain: rice with stir-fried vegetables, fish from a nearby canal or river, perhaps some minced chicken with garlic, chilies and basil and a salad of salted eggs, chilies and scallion with a squeeze of lime.

In Bangkok, everything is available, even the most exotic regional delicacies, if you know where to look. The city streets are punctuated with the many fast foods based on Chinese noodles, prepared at a moment's notice at any sidewalk café or by vendors who push their carts along residential streets. Tasty, nourishing, occasionally even distinguished, these quick meals epitomize the busy life of Bangkok and also the Thai capacity for making something special out of simple ingredients. Such is its popularity that Thai street food has evolved into a distinctive culinary category all its own, generally characterized by speed of preparation and easy portability of equipment.

Palace Cooking

Dr Malcolm Smith, who served as physician to some members of the Thai royal family in the early years of this century, describes the innermost part of Bangkok's mile-square Grand Palace known as the "Inside," where the women of the court lived, thus: "A town complete in itself, a congested network of houses and narrow streets, with gardens, lawns, artificial lakes and shops. It had its own government, its own institutions, its own laws and law-courts. It was a town of women, controlled by women."

At its peak, during the reign of King Rama V (Chulalongkorn), the "Inside" had a population estimated at nearly 3,000, a select few of them bearing the exalted rank of Queen but the great majority ladies-in-waiting and lower attendants. The inner palace can be viewed as a kind of ultra-exclusive finishing school where the most refined aristocratic skills were perfected and passed on.

The royal women learned how to prepare various foods that were not merely more subtle in flavor than their outside versions, but highly memorable in visual appeal. The most visible of palace skills was the art of fruit and vegetable carving, garnishes and delicacies that sometimes required as long to prepare as the dishes that they adorned.

The hallmarks of so-called "palace food"—which was, in fact, to be found in most aristocratic homes as well—were painstaking hours of preparation and a highly refined style of presentation. *Foi thong*, for instance, is a blend of egg yolks and sugar transformed into a nest of silky golden threads, while *look choop* are tiny imitation fruits shaped by hand from a mixture of sweet bean paste and coconut milk, tinted to exactly match their real-life models.

When royal polygamy ended under King Rama VI, the ladies of the "Inside" and their numerous attendants gradually left their protected existence. Fortunately, palace cooking did not vanish with the hidden world but survived through the descendants of the royal women. In recent years, it has been discovered by a wider public through several restaurants that take pride in their re-creations of this unique cuisine.

The Thai Kitchen and Table

The hospitality and generosity of the shared Thai table is easily achieved in the home. In this section you will find recipes for popular Thai salads, curries, soups, steamed, deep-fried and stir-fried dishes, grilled dishes, desserts, relishes and accompaniments. When cooking, try to use only the freshest ingredients. Taste as you go along, and aim to balance the flavors and textures within the dish and between the compilation of dishes to be served.

Rice is the mainstay of Thai meals, mostly steamed long-grain jasmine rice, a nod to the traditions and ritual of its cultivation. All other dishes—salads, curries, soups—are called *gap kao*, to be served with rice; they are mere condiments. There is no set progression of dishes; all main course dishes are served at once. When cooking for a gathering of four, rather than increase the quantity of a single dish, do as the Thais do and increase the variety of dishes: perhaps a soup, a curry, a salad, a steamed dish and a selection of relishes. Diners are free to help themselves, in any order they want, mixing dishes at will and seasoning them with a wide variety of condiments to achieve the desired taste.

The ideal Thai meal is a harmonious blend of the spicy, sweet, hot, wet, mild, crisp, sour and soft, and is meant to be satisfying to the eye, nose and palate. Complex dishes are accompanied by simpler ones: the richness of this dish may be cut by the piquancy of that, the saltiness of this recipe is a perfect foil for another. As a result the palate is not overwhelmed; there is give and take. The Thais call this harmonious layering of flavor upon flavor *rot chart*—the heart and soul of true Thai cuisine.

Many Thai desserts are based on glutinous rice, coconut milk, palm sugar, pandan leaf and agar-agar, but the most common dessert is one or more of the abundant fresh fruits, usually brought out after the other dishes have been removed. On special occasions, more elaborate desserts such as *foi thong* (golden threads) or banana-leaf cups of *takaw*, a confection of tapioca starch, sugar and coconut that comes in a wide variety of forms, may be served.

Snacks are so popular in Thailand they deserve special mention. They may consist of nothing more than freshly sliced fruit sprinkled with salt, sugar, dried chilies or a combination of these seasonings. Or they may be a selection of traditional sweets. Some vendors offer noodle creations. To produce the universally popular *kwayteow*, a bowl of freshly cooked rice noodles is given a few ladles of meat stock, topped with cooked pork or chicken, and sprinkled with sugar, crushed peanuts and dried chili flakes. For *pad thai*, noodles are quickly stir-fried with garlic, scallions, salted dried shrimp and a variety of spices. Whether eaten in a restaurant, on a city sidewalk, on the open verandah of a farm house, even in the middle of a rice field at harvest time, a Thai meal is nearly always a social affair.

Kantoke, a meal taken while seated at a low round table, is a traditional way of dining in the north of Thailand.

SUGGESTED MENUS

Family meals

For a simple family meal, try serving steamed jasmine rice with
• Spicy Shrimp Soup with Lemongrass (page 130);
•Dry Beef Curry (page 135) and Kale with Crispy Pork (page 134);
• finish with Bananas in Coconut Milk (page 138);

or

• Green Papaya Salad (page 133);
• Red Chicken Curry with Bamboo Shoots (page 135) served with rice;
• fresh fruit like jackfruit, mango, or rambutan.

A dinner party

For a stylish dinner party, serve:
• Patty Shells with Minced Chicken (page 128) for an stunning canapé;
•Spicy Pomelo Salad (page 133), the elegant River Fish with Chili Sauce (page 136) and Roast Duck Curry (page 135);
• glittering Red Rubies (page 138) as a palate cleanser.

Finger food

The appetizers in this section make particularly good finger food—try the following at your next party or picnic:
• Pork and Shrimp Rolls (page 128);
• Chicken in Pandan Leaves (page 128);
• Steamed Seafood Cakes (page 128).

A melting pot menu

For a refined but simple Asian tasting menu:
• Shrimp Mousse on Sugar Cane (page 147) from Vietnam as a starter;
• Indonesian Pork in Sweet Soy Sauce (page 73) with Stir-fried Mixed Vegetables (page 34) from China combine well for a main course that is not too heavy;
• Red Bean Pancakes (page 40), also from China, are a delicious dessert with which to finish.

THE ESSENTIAL FLAVORS OF THAI COOKING

Thai cuisine uses the redolent **fish sauce** in almost everything besides desserts. The curries are built on subtle blends of **cilantro**, **lemongrass**, **galangal**, **chilies** and **kaffir lime leaf** and **rind**. Other typically Thai flavors include **Thai sweet basil** (*horapa*), **ginger**, **shrimp paste** and **tamarind**. **Coconut milk** and **palm sugar** are added to curries and sweets. Staples you will need include **jasmine** and **glutinous rice**.

Thai people love good food, and the emphasis on quality applies to both palace cuisine and street food. An array of treats is available —Thais seem to find it more satisfactory to eat a little of this and a little of that—along the *klongs* and sidewalks, and outside offices and shopping centres. The ready-to-eat delicacies may include barbecued or grilled food on or off skewers, salads, noodle soups, wrapped in dough or edible leaves, or be a sweet. Here are a few dishes that would work well as finger food.

Krathong Thong
Patty Shells with Minced Chicken

The delicate crisp shells used for this snack are made using a special brass mold. Thin shortcrust pastry shells or even *vol-au-vent* cases can be used instead. The recipe makes 20–25 cups.

Patty Shells
1/2 cup rice flour
6 tablespoons white flour
4 tablespoons thin coconut milk
2 tablespoons tapioca starch
1 egg yolk
1/4 teaspoon sugar
1/4 teaspoon salt
1/4 teaspoon baking soda
Peanut or corn oil for deep-frying

Filling
2 tablespoons peanut
  or corn oil

4 tablespoons finely diced onion
2 cups finely chopped cooked
  chicken or pork
1/4 cup corn kernels
2 tablespoons finely
  diced carrot
2 tablespoons sugar
1/4 teaspoon black soy
  sauce
1/2 teaspoon salt
1/2 teaspoon ground
  white pepper
Cilantro leaves for
  garnish
1 red chili, finely sliced

To make the patty shells, mix all ingredients except oil together in a bowl. Heat oil, dip the mould in the oil to heat. (Make sure the *krathong* mold is very hot before you plunge it into the batter; the batter must adhere to the mold as you put it back into the oil to cook.) Dip the mold into the batter and plunge back into oil. Fry for about 5 minutes until light brown, then shake to remove the cup from the mold. Drain on paper towels. Repeat until batter is all used up.

To make the filling put the oil in a hot wok and stir-fry onion and pork or chicken for 2 minutes. Add the rest of the ingredients and fry for about 3 minutes until the vegetables are fairly soft. Let cool.

Divide the filling between the cups. Garnish with cilantro and red chili.

Tong Geon Yong
Pork and Shrimp Rolls

The Chinese influence is evident in the use of dried bean curd skin. The filling can be made in advance and the rolls assembled just before frying.

4 ounces shrimp, finely chopped
4 ounces pork, finely chopped
1 tablespoon light soy sauce
1 teaspoon each of cilantro root,
  garlic and peppercorns, pounded
  together
Dried bean curd skin
Strips of scallion, blanched
Corn oil for deep-frying

Mix shrimp and pork together with soy sauce and the pounded ingredients.

Wipe sheets of dried bean curd skin with a moist cloth to soften. Cut circles about 4 1/2 inches in diameter and place a little filling in the center.

Squeeze in the sides to make a bundle and tie with a strip of scallion. Alternatively, cut bean curd skin into 4-inch x 6-inch squares. Put a spoonful of the filling in the middle and roll up like a cigar, tucking in the ends.

Deep-fry the rolls in hot oil over medium heat until golden brown. Serve with soy sauce or plum sauce.

Gai Hor Bai Toey
Chicken Fried in Pandan Leaves

If the pandan leaves are unavailable, the chicken can be stir-fried and served with steamed rice.

2 pounds chicken thighs
20 pandan leaves
Oil for deep-frying

Marinade
2 tablespoons light soy sauce
2 tablespoons oyster sauce
1 teaspoon sugar
2 teaspoons sesame oil
1 teaspoon each garlic and cilantro
  root, pounded together

Sauce
1 cup distilled white vinegar
1/2 cup sugar
2 tablespoons black soy sauce
1 teaspoon white sesame seeds,
  fried
1/4 teaspoon salt

Debone chicken and cut thighs into 4. Mix marinade and marinate chicken for 3 hours. Mix sauce ingredients together and set aside.

Wrap two or three pieces of chicken with pandan leaves and knot lightly to form a bundle (see picture).

Heat oil in wok and deep-fry until fragrant. Serve with dipping sauce and steamed rice.

Pork and Shrimp Rolls (left) and Patty Shells with Minced Chicken (right).

Chicken Fried in Pandan Leaves.

Haw Mok Thalay
Steamed Seafood Cakes

This fragrant mixture of seafood, coconut milk and seasonings is steamed in small cups made of banana leaf. It is possible to use small ramekins or any other small heatproof dishes as a substitute.

Spice Paste
5 dried chilies, soaked in water
    and seeded
3 cloves garlic
2 tablespoons finely sliced galangal
1 teaspoon grated kaffir lime rind
2 teaspoons finely sliced cilantro
    root
5 black peppercorns
1/2 teaspoon salt
1 teaspoon shrimp paste
1 teaspoon finely sliced *krachai*
    (optional)
3/4 cup coconut cream
1 teaspoon rice flour
4 ounces filleted fish,
    thinly sliced
4 ounces shrimp, peeled and
    cleaned
4 ounces squid, cleaned and cut
into 2-inch pieces
2 eggs, beaten
3 tablespoons fish sauce
1 1/4 cups coconut milk
1/2 cup basil leaves (*horapa*),
    finely chopped
2 tablespoons shredded kaffir
    lime leaves
Fresh cilantro to garnish

1 finely sliced red chili
Banana leaf cups 2-inch square, or
    individual ramekins

To make the spice paste, pound the ingredients thoroughly in a mortar or process finely in a blender.

Mix coconut cream with the rice flour and bring to a boil, stirring until thickened. Remove from the heat, cool and set aside for topping.

Mix spice paste with the fish, shrimp, squid, eggs, fish sauce and then add the remaining coconut milk, a little at a time. Add half the basil and kaffir lime leaves and mix in.

Place one of the remaining basil leaves in the bottom of each cup, top with the fish mixture, cover and steam over boiling water for 15 minutes.

Remove the cups from steamer, and top each with a little of the boiled coconut cream, cilantro leaf, kaffir lime leaf and sliced chili. Return to the steamer, cook for one more minute, then remove the cups from the steamer.

Sakuna Chomsuan
Shrimp with Sweet and Sour Sauce

A simple but always popular appetizer. The prawns can be prepared in advance and deep-fried

Shrimp with Sweet and Sour Sauce.

just before serving. Use your favorite sweet and sour sauce for dipping or the one on page 157.

1 pound fresh shrimp
2 eggs, lightly beaten
4 cups fine bread crumbs
Cooking oil for deep-frying

Peel the shrimp, discarding the head but leaving on the tails. Slit down the back of each shrimp, remove the intestinal tract and flatten the shrimp into a butterfly shape by pressing gently with the hand.

Combine the egg and bread crumbs and dip the shrimp in this mixture.

Heat oil in a wok and deep-fry the shrimp until they turn a golden colour. Drain, and serve with sweet and sour sauce.

Chor Lad Da
Dumplings with Minced Pork and Shrimp

The surprising but brilliant color of these delicate dumplings is obtained by soaking a blue flower (*anchun*), although commercial food coloring can be substituted.

Filling
1/2 cup roasted unsalted peanuts,
    chopped
1/2 teaspoon salt
2 tablespoons sugar

4 ounces ground pork
4 ounces minced shrimp
1 cup chopped salted radish
2 tablespoons cooking oil

Dumplings
1/4 cup tapioca starch
About 2 tablespoons dried *anchun*
    flowers or 1/2 teaspoon blue
    food coloring
2 cups rice flour
1/4 cup coconut milk
2 tablespoons cooking oil
1/4 cup water
1/2 cup coconut cream
Banana leaf or aluminium foil

To make the filling, stir-fry all the filling ingredients in oil until cooked. Let cool.

To make the dumplings, combine all the remaining ingredients, excluding the coconut cream, and mix well. Cook over low heat, stirring constantly, until the mixture turns into an elastic dough. Cover with plastic wrap while making the individual dumplings to prevent the dough from drying out.

Pinch off a small ball of dough and flatten into a circle about 2 1/2 inches in diameter. Place a teaspoonful of stuffing in the center of the dough and pinch edges together to enclose. Use special tongs or pinch to give the dumplings a flower shape. Place on an oiled banana leaf or aluminum foil and put about 1 teaspoon of coconut cream over the top of each dumpling to prevent it from drying out.

Set a steamer over boiling water and steam dumplings for 8 minutes until cooked. Serve warm on a bed of crisp-fried golden garlic and top with coconut cream.

HELPFUL HINT

In Thailand, a special pair of miniature tongs with serrations on the inside is used to pinch the dough to create the "petals." Failing that, use your fingers to pinch the dough into a decorative shape.

Thai soups are usually light, accentuated with fresh aromatics, and have the four main flavors—hot, sour, sweet and salty. They are drunk throughout a meal, but make a perfectly acceptable first course to a dinner party with an Asian theme.

Gaeng Som
Sour Soup with Vegetables and Shrimp

Sour but fragrant tamarind juice adds a special touch to this relatively mild soup, which is full of vegetables and flavored with pounded shrimp or fish. As with other types of *gaeng*, this has very little liquid.

12 ounces or fish fillets
3 cups water
4 ounces straw mushrooms
1 large white radish, sliced
1/2 cup sliced green papaya
1/2 cup green beans, cut into 1 inch-pieces
2/3 cauliflower, broken into florets
1 cup bok choy, cut into 1-inch pieces
4 tablespoons tamarind juice
2 tablespoons lime juice (optional)
1 tablespoon chopped palm sugar
1 teaspoon salt

Spice Paste
3 dried chilies, soaked until soft

2 teaspoons finely chopped *krachai* (optional)
2 teaspoons finely chopped garlic
2 teaspoons finely chopped shallots

Simmer the shrimp or fish in the 3 cups of water until cooked. Cool in the stock, then peel the shrimp or remove any bones from the fish. Keep all remaining stock and set aside.

Pound or process the fish or shrimp until well mashed and set aside. Pound or blend the spice paste ingredients, then put in a pan with the reserved stock, shrimp or fish and vegetables. Bring to a boil and simmer until just cooked. Add the tamarind juice, lime juice, sugar and salt to taste.

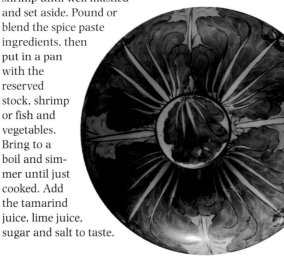

Tom Yam Goong
Spicy Shrimp Soup with Lemongrass

Tom yam goong must be one of the best known Thai dishes abroad. Be careful not to overcook the shrimp as they will become tough very easily.

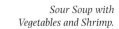

Sour Soup with Vegetables and Shrimp.

4 cups Chicken Stock (page 139)
3 stems lemongrass
2 inches galangal
3 kaffir lime leaves
8 medium to large shrimp
5 ounces straw mushrooms
3 green bird's-eye chilies
3 red bird's-eye chilies
3 tablespoons lime juice, or to taste
1/2 tablespoon fish sauce, or to taste
Handful fresh cilantro leaves

Bring stock to a boil, add lemongrass, galangal and lime leaves and simmer for 15 minutes.

Add the shrimp, mushrooms and chilies and simmer for 3 minutes. Add lime juice and fish to taste—the soup should be spicy-sour and a little salty.

Garnish the soup with fresh cilantro and serve.

Gaeng Jued Woon Sen
Clear Soup with Cellophane Noodles

10 ounces ground pork
1/2 teaspoon light soy sauce
1/4 teaspoon ground white pepper
4 cups chicken stock (page 139)
7 white peppercorns, crushed
5 cloves garlic, crushed
4 ounces cellophane noodles, soaked in water

1 teaspoon fish sauce
6 dried mushrooms soaked in cold water to soften, chopped
1/4 teaspoon sugar
3 scallions, cut into 1/2-inch pieces
2 tablespoons chopped cilantro leaves

Mix ground pork, soy sauce and white pepper together well and form into small, roughly shaped meatballs.

Heat chicken stock, add the crushed peppercorns and garlic and bring to a boil. Place the meatballs into boiling stock and add the pre-soaked cellophane noodles, fish sauce, mushrooms and sugar. Simmer until the meatballs are cooked.

Add the scallion and fresh cilantro and remove from the heat immediately. Serve with steamed rice.

Note: "Cellophane" or transparent noodles need to be soaked in warm water for about 5 minutes to soften and swell.

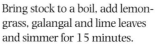

Clear Soup with Cellophane Noodles (left) and Mixed Vegetable Soup (right).

Gaeng Noppakao
Mixed Vegetable Soup

This is not so much a soup in the Western sense, but vegetables seasoned with a little pork, chicken and shrimp simmered in seasoned stock.

Seasoning
10 black peppercorns
1/2 tablespoon shrimp paste
10 shallots
1/4 cup dried shrimps

4 cups Chicken Stock (page 139)
5 cups mixed vegetables, such as summer or winter squash or straw mushrooms, baby corn or green beans, cut into bite-sized pieces
5 ounces lean pork, very thinly sliced
5 ounces chicken, very thinly sliced
5 ounces shrimp, peeled but tails left on
2 tablespoons fish sauce
1 cup lemon basil leaves

To make the seasoning, place all ingredients in a mortar or blender and pound or blend until fine. Add this mixture to the chicken stock and bring to a boil, stirring to prevent sticking. Add the vegetables, pork, chicken and shrimp and simmer until just cooked. Season to taste with fish sauce or salt, then remove from heat. Add basil and serve.

Tom Kha Gai
Spicy Chicken Soup with Coconut Milk

A delightful soup, creamy with coconut milk and redolent with the flavor of galangal, kaffir lime and lemongrass. Vary the amount of chilies according to taste. Cook gently to prevent the coconut milk from separating

1 cup Chicken stock (page 139)
2 stems lemongrass
2-inch piece galangal
3 kaffir lime leaves, torn into small pieces, cut into 1/2-inch strips
12 ounces chicken
4 ounces straw mushrooms
1 teaspoon salt
4 tablespoons lime juice
3 tablespoons fish sauce
1/2 teaspoon sugar
3 cups coconut milk
6 red bird's-eye chilies, bruised

Place the stock in a pot, add lemongrass, galangal and kaffir lime leaves. Bring to the boil over medium heat.

Add chicken, mushrooms, salt, lime juice, fish sauce and sugar to the stock. Cook slowly, uncovered, for 10 minutes, then add coconut milk and chilies. Bring almost to the boil, stirring frequently, then remove from heat and serve.

Spicy Chicken Soup with Coconut Milk.

Rice Noodles with Fish Curry Sauce.

Kanom Jeen Nam Yaa
Rice Noodles with Fish Curry Sauce

Because of their length, *kanom jeen* are commonly served at family ceremonies; they are never broken until served and signify long life.

Sauce
7 shallots, coarsely chopped
2 cloves garlic
2 slices galangal
2 tablespoons sliced lemongrass
1 cup minced *krachai* (optional)
3 dried chilies, seeds removed
1 teaspoon salt
1 teaspoon shrimp paste
1 cup water

Stock
1 (8-ounce) small, well-flavored fish
4 1/2 cups coconut milk
1/2 cup coconut cream
2–3 tablespoons fish sauce

Accompaniments
2 pounds fresh rice noodles or fresh angel-hair pasta
2 hard-boiled eggs, peeled and quartered
1/2 cup sliced cabbage
1/2 cup sliced cucumber
1/2 cup blanched bean sprouts
1 small bunch lemon basil
1 tablespoon ground dried chilies

Place all sauce ingredients in a pot and simmer over low heat until soft. Remove from heat, cool, place in a mortar or blender and pound or blend until fine.

To make the stock, wash and clean the fish, removing the head and entrails, and simmer in just enough water to cover until soft. Drain and save the water in which the fish was boiled. Remove the meat from the fish, add to the chili paste in the mortar or blender and pound to mix thoroughly.

Put the sauce into a pot and add the coconut milk. Bring to the boil, then add the fish broth and fish sauce. Simmer, stirring regularly to prevent sticking, until the sauce has thickened and the surface glistens bright red. Add the coconut cream and remove from heat.

Arrange a portion of the rice vermicelli and a little of each of the accompaniments in individual bowls. Spoon the sauce over just before serving.

HELPFUL HINT

Sour Soup with Vegetables: Any combination of vegetables can be used; suggested alternatives include any type of summer squash, eggplant, green cabbage or button mushrooms.

Most Thai salads are hot and sour, and like most of Thai cooking, call for the use of copious amounts of fresh herbs and greens. You can vary the combination of greens and spices, or perhaps combine aspects of several recipes to provide a modern twist. It is important to balance the flavors of the dressing.

Khao Yam Pak Tai
Southern-Style Rice Salad

This is a popular way of using left-over rice and makes an ideal light lunch. The seasonings added to the rice can be varied according to taste and availability.

Sauce
1 cup water
2 tablespoons chopped anchovies in brine
1 tablespoon chopped palm sugar
2 kaffir lime leaves, torn into small pieces
1/2-inch lemongrass, very finely sliced

2 cups cold cooked rice
2 cups grated coconut, browned in oven for 5–8 minutes
1 small pomelo or grapefruit, shredded
1 small green mango, shredded (optional)
1/2 cup dried shrimp, chopped
1/2 cup bean sprouts
1/2 cup finely sliced lemongrass
1/4 cup sliced green beans

1 egg, beaten, cooked into an omelet and shredded
2 dried red chilies, pounded
1 tablespoon very finely shredded kaffir lime leaf
1 tablespoon chopped fresh cilantro
4 ounces cooked shrimp for garnish (optional)
Lime wedges

To make the sauce, put all sauce ingredients into a pan, bring to the boil and simmer for 5 minutes. Remove from heat, strain and set aside.

Place the rice in small bowls, each holding about half a cup. Press down, and invert onto a large serving platter. Arrange the rest of raw ingredients around the edge of rice in separate piles.

To eat, spoon some rice onto individual plates and take a little of each ingredient to mix with the rice according to taste. Spoon the sauce over the top.

HELPFUL HINT

Canned anchovies packed in Europe make an acceptable substitute for the preserved Thai variety. If the very fine dried shrimp used in Thailand are not available, substitute with packaged fish floss.

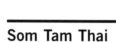

Fried Mixed Vegetables.

Southern-Style Rice Salad.

Som Tam Thai
Green Papaya Salad

Originally an Isan dish from the northeast, this salad is now prepared by roadside hawkers all over the country. *Som tam* captures the essential flavours of Thailand: chili hot, redolent with garlic and fish sauce, and sour with lime juice. If using dried shrimp, soak in warm water for 5 minutes, then chop coarsely. Prepare the salad just before eating otherwise the papaya will lose its firm texture.

10 ounces unripe green papaya, peeled and cut into very fine matchsticks
7 green bird's-eye chilies
5 cloves garlic
1/2 cup long beans, cut into 1 cm 1/2-inch pieces
2 tablespoons unsalted roasted peanuts
1 tablespoon dried shrimp
6 cherry tomatoes, quartered, or 1 large tomato, cut into wedges
3 tablespoons lime juice
1 tablespoon chopped palm sugar
1 tablespoon fish sauce

Take a little each of the papaya, chilies and garlic and pound roughly in a mortar and pestle or process very briefly in a blender. Set aside in a bowl and repeat until all the papaya, chilies and garlic are used up.

Stir in the beans, peanuts, dried shrimp and tomato, mix well and add the seasonings.

Accompany with raw vegetables such as cabbage, water spinach or morning glory, and sprigs of basil. For a complete meal, add glutinous rice and roasted chicken.

Yam Som-O
Spicy Pomelo Salad

Pomelos are eaten as a fruit as well as mixed with sour, spicy ingredients to make a salad.

1 pomelo or 2 grapefruit
2 tablespoons lime juice
1 tablespoon fish sauce
1 tablespoon sugar
5 ounces cooked shrimp
7 ounces shredded cooked chicken breast,
2 tablespoons grated fresh or dried coconut
1/2 cup coconut cream
1 tablespoon dried shrimp, finely chopped

Peel the pomelo and break up the flesh. Place the lime juice, fish sauce and sugar in a bowl and stir to mix. Add the shrimp, chicken, grated coconut and coconut cream and continue stirring until blended. Add the pomelo and toss to coat thoroughly. Transfer to a serving plate, sprinkle with dried shrimp and serve.

Pla Nuea Makreua Orn
Beef Salad with Eggplant

Although uncooked beef can be used for this salad, it works well with leftover roast or grilled beef as well.

| 3 small round green eggplants or
| 1 long thin eggplant
| 3 tablespoons oil
| 10 ounces uncooked or cooked
| beef fillet, sliced
| 1 tablespoon sliced shallots
| 5 green bird's-eye chilies,
| coarsely chopped
| 2 tablespoons lime juice
| 1 tablespoon fish sauce
| 1/4 teaspoon sugar

Cut the eggplant into 1/2-inch slices and fry until cooked. Put into a bowl.

If using uncooked beef, sauté in a frying pan in a little oil over high heat until done. Combine the beef with the eggplant and the remaining ingredients and mix together well. Serve at room temperature with steamed rice.

Pad Pak Ruam Mit
Fried Mixed Vegetables

This method of cooking vegetables can be used for individual vegetables such as kale or broccoli, or a combination, depending on availability and your preference.

| 1/2 cup snow peas
| 2 cups chopped young kale
| 2 cups sliced cabbage
| 3/4 cup chopped broccoli florets
| 3/4 cup chopped cauliflower florets
| 3/4 cup sliced mushrooms
| 1/2 cup baby corn
| 1/4 cup peanut or corn oil
| 3 tablespoons finely chopped garlic
| 1/2 cup Chicken Stock (page 139)
| 4 tablespoons oyster sauce
| 1 tablespoon light soy sauce
| 1/4 teaspoon black soy sauce
| 1/2 teaspoon white pepper powder

Mix vegetables together in a bowl. Plunge them into boiling water for a few seconds to blanch, drain and set aside.

Heat a wok until lightly smoking and add the oil. When hot, add the garlic and stir well. Add the vegetables and chicken stock all at once and stir-fry for about 3–4 minutes until just cooked—the vegetables should still be slightly crisp. Add the oyster sauce and soy sauces, then sprinkle with pepper. Mix well and cook for 1 minute more. Serve with rice.

> **HELPFUL HINT**
> Use maximum heat to stir-fry the vegetables to ensure the right texture and flavor.

Savory Stuffed Omelets.

Kai Yad Sai
Savory Stuffed Omelets

Frequently found on the menu of simple restaurants as well as at roadside stalls, this is often eaten at lunch time. The omelets can be served individually as appetizers.

| 1/4 cup oil
| 4 ground pork
| 3 tablespoons diced tomatoes
| 3 tablespoons cooked green peas
| 2 tablespoons finely diced onions
| 1/2 tablespoon sugar
| 1 tablespoon fish sauce
| 1/4 teaspoon ground white pepper
| 1/4 teaspoon black soy sauce
| 3 eggs, beaten
| 3 tablespoons chopped cilantro
| leaves (garnish)
| 1 red chili, sliced (garnish)

Heat half the oil in a wok over high heat and stir-fry the pork for 2 minutes. Add all the remaining ingredients except for the eggs, garnishes and the remaining oil. Fry until cooked then set aside.

Heat an omelet pan 6–8 inches in diameter, and add a drop of the remaining oil. Pour in enough egg to thinly cover the base. Brown the omelet lightly on both sides, flipping over half-way through cooking. Repeat until all the egg is used up. To stuff the omelets, place a spoonful of pork mixture in the center, fold two opposite sides toward the center and then fold in the remaining sides so that it resembles a square. Put onto a serving plate and repeat until all the egg and pork mixture is used up.

Garnish with cilantro leaves and finely sliced red chili. Serve with rice.

Taud Man Goong
Deep-Fried Shrimp Cakes

Hawkers in coastal towns, especially around Songkhla, Surat Thani and Phuket, offer a similar but highly seasoned snack made with fish (*Taud Man Pla*). This more delicate version is served with a savory accompaniment of pickled vegetables.

| **Accompaniment**
| 1 cup distilled white vinegar
| 1/2 cup sugar
| 1 tablespoon finely sliced
| cauliflower
| 1 tablespoon finely sliced baby corn
| 1 tablespoon sliced small cucumber
| 5 bird's-eye chilies
| 2 shallots, sliced
|
| 11/4 pounds shrimp
| 5 ounces lard
| 1 teaspoon salt
| 1/2 teaspoon sugar
| 2 cups fresh bread crumbs
| Oil for deep-frying

To make the accompaniment, bring vinegar and sugar to a boil, then leave to cool. Add all vegetables, chilies and shallots, mix and set aside.

Chop shrimp and pork fat together or process in a blender until fine. Add salt, sugar and bread crumbs, then shape into patties. Deep-fry until golden brown and fragrant.

Serve hot with the accompaniment of pickled vegetables.

> **HELPFUL HINT**
> The pickled vegetables and shrimp cakes can be prepared in advance. Fry the shrimp cakes only just before serving.

Red Pork Curry.

In Thailand main courses are usually served with rice. The dishes are served at once, and stay on the table throughout the meal. The recipes here serve four as part of a shared meal.

Kana Moo Grob
Kale with Crispy Pork

With family meals vegetables are frequently cooked with a little meat, poultry or seafood to add flavor and a contrasting texture. Kale, known in Thailand by its Chinese name, *kai lan*, is enjoyed for its firm stems. If kale is not available, try using broccoli stems.

- 2 pounds kale or 1 pound broccoli stems
- 3 tablespoons oil
- 1 tablespoon finely chopped garlic
- 10 ounces diced crispy pork
- 4 tablespoons oyster sauce
- 1/4 teaspoon salt
- 1/4 teaspoon ground white pepper
- 1 teaspoon sugar
- 1 cup Chicken Stock (page 139)

Discard the leaves and tough bottom part of the kale stems. Peel the skin off the tender stems and discard. Cut stems into 2–3 inch lengths. Heat oil in a wok. When very hot, fry the garlic until fragrant, then add the kale and crispy pork. Stir to mix well, and add all the seasonings and stock. Mix well, heat through and serve immediately.

Roasted pork with a layer of meat, a thin layer of fat and crisp, golden-brown skin contrasts beautifully in taste and texture with the vegetable. Although unconventional, thick slices of crisp fried bacon make an excellent substitute.

Gaeng Ped Moo
Red Pork Curry

Pork is the most popular meat in Thailand and is prepared in many different ways. This is a very simple, quickly prepared curry.

- 1/2 cup coconut cream
- 1 tablespoon red curry paste (page 139)
- 13 ounces pork fillet, cut into 1 1/2-inch slices
- 1/3 cup pea-sized eggplants (optional)
- 1 1/2 cups coconut milk
- 1 1/2 tablespoons fish sauce
- 1/4 teaspoon salt
- 1 1/2 teaspoons sugar
- 5 kaffir lime leaves, halved
- 1 fresh red chili, finely sliced lengthwise
- 1/2 cup basil leaves (*horapa*)

Bring coconut cream to a boil, stirring constantly. Add the red curry paste, pork and eggplant, stir well, and cook until done (about 5 minutes).

Add fish sauce, salt, sugar, kaffir lime leaves and chili. Stir and heat through, then remove from heat and garnish with the basil leaves.

Gaeng Mussaman
Mussaman Beef Curry

Spices such as cardamom and cinnamon were brought to Thailand by Indian Muslim traders. This curry uses the basic Mussaman curry paste and other spices.

- 3 tablespoons Mussaman Curry Paste (page 139)
- 1/2 cup coconut cream
- 1 pound beef sirloin or stewing beef
- 2 cups coconut milk
- 5 cardamom seeds, roasted until fragrant
- 1 stick cinnamon, about 3 inches in length
- 7 ounces potatoes, peeled and cut into large chunks
- 1 heaped tablespoon unsalted peanuts, chopped
- 10 shallots
- 3 bay leaves
- 3 tablespoons chopped palm sugar
- 2 tablespoons fish sauce
- 3 tablespoons tamarind juice

Cook curry paste and coconut cream together for 5 minutes, then add the beef and fry for 8–10 minutes. Add the coconut milk, bring to a boil and simmer gently for 10 minutes. Add all the remaining ingredients and cook until the potatoes and meat are tender.

Serve with sliced pickled ginger, pickled vegetables and rice.

HELPFUL HINT
If pork tenderloin is not available, use any other lean cut of pork and increase the cooking time accordingly.

Mussaman Beef Curry.

Red Chicken Curry with Bamboo Shoots.

Gaeng Kheow Wan Gai
Green Chicken Curry

A fragrant, creamy curry that is sure to wake up your tastebuds. Remove the skin from the chicken if you wish to reduce the oiliness. This dish can be prepared in advance—just add the basil and chilies when reheating the dish before serving.

1/2 cup coconut cream
3 tablespoons Green Curry Paste (page 139)
13 ounces chicken breast, sliced
1 1/2 cups coconut milk
2 kaffir lime leaves
1 1/2 tablespoons fish sauce
1 teaspoon sugar
1 1/3 cups eggplant, cut into bite-sized pieces
1/4 cup basil leaves (*horapa*)
2–3 red chilies, cut into length wise strips

Heat coconut cream until it begins to separate, then add the curry paste and stir well. Add chicken and cook until it changes color.

Add coconut milk, lime leaves, fish sauce and sugar. Bring to a boil, then add eggplant. Simmer until the chicken is cooked, then add the basil and chilies. Remove from the heat and serve.

Panaeng Nuea
Dry Beef Curry

This typically southern curry is hot and fragrant, and uses Indian spices. The use of palm sugar, peanuts and kaffir lime leaves, however, is distinctly Thai.

1 tablespoon coriander seeds, ground
2 teaspoons cumin seeds, ground
3 tablespoons Mussaman Curry Paste (page 139)
1/2 cup coconut cream
12 ounces beef, cut into thin strips
1 1/2 cups coconut milk
1/2 cup ground roasted peanuts
1 1/2–2 tablespoons fish sauce
3 tablespoons chopped palm sugar
6 kaffir lime leaves, torn in half
1 red chili, thinly sliced

Mix the ground coriander and cumin with the curry paste. Heat coconut cream until some of the oil surfaces, then add the curry paste and slowly bring to a boil, stirring the mixture constantly. Add beef strips and cook for 5 minutes, add remaining coconut milk and the rest of ingredients except the kaffir lime leaves and chili. Stir well and simmer until the meat is tender and the oil has come out of the coconut milk.

Add the kaffir lime leaves and chili, remove from the heat and serve with steamed rice.

Gaeng Ped Gai Naw Mai
Red Chicken Curry with Bamboo Shoots

Fresh bamboo shoots are available seasonally in Thailand, and have a sweetness and texture that cannot be matched by the canned variety. However, the latter makes an acceptable substitute.

1/2 cup coconut cream
1 tablespoon Red Curry Paste (page 139)
12 ounces boneless chicken, diced
1 1/2 cups coconut milk
10 ounces bamboo shoots, sliced lengthwise
2 tablespoons fish sauce
1/4 teaspoon salt
1 1/2 teaspoons sugar
5 kaffir lime leaves, halved
1 fresh red chili, finely sliced lengthwise
1/2 cup basil leaves (*horapa*)

Bring coconut cream to a boil in a pot. Simmer, stirring constantly, until the coconut cream separates. Put in the red curry paste and the diced chicken, stir well, and add coconut milk and bamboo shoots.

Cook until the chicken is tender, then add fish sauce, salt, sugar, kaffir lime leaves and chili. Remove from heat and garnish with basil.

Note: If using canned bamboo shoots, drain and boil in fresh water for about 5 minutes to get rid of any metallic taste. Fresh bamboo shoots should be sliced and simmered until tender before being added to the curry.

Gaeng Ped
Roast Duck Curry

Buy a red-roasted duck from an Asian barbecue shop or restaurant for this curry. Pea eggplants or snake beans, added at the last moment, add a slightly crunchy texture to the smooth curry and provide a nice foil to the richness of the roasted duck.

1 roasted duck
1/2 cup coconut cream
3 tablespoons Red Curry Paste (page 139)
1 1/2 cups coconut milk
2–3 large tomatoes, cut into wedges
1 cup pea-sized eggplants, whole, or green beans, cut into 1/2-inch slices
4 kaffir lime leaves
2 tablespoons fish sauce
1 teaspoon sugar
1/2 teaspoon salt
10 basil leaves (*horapa*)
4 red or green chilies, cut into fine lengthwise strips

Remove all bones from the duck and cut the meat into bite-sized pieces.

Heat coconut cream over medium heat and add the red curry paste, stirring well. Add the duck and stir well, then add the coconut milk, tomatoes, eggplants, kaffir lime leaves, fish sauce, sugar and salt. Bring to a boil, then remove from the heat.

Sprinkle with the basil leaves and red or green chilies. Serve with steamed rice.

Roast Duck Curry.

Kha Kob Phad Ped
Frogs' Legs with Chili and Basil

Frogs, found in the *klongs* or canals and rice paddies of Thailand, are sometimes euphemistically called "paddy chicken." Their flavor is delicate and similar to chicken.

$1/3$ cup oil
8 pairs of frogs' legs
1 tablespoon green peppercorns
3 red chilies, sliced lengthwise
3 inches galangal, cut into fine matchsticks
2 teaspoons fish sauce
$1/2$ teaspoon chopped palm sugar
Large handful basil leaves (*horapa*)

Heat the oil in a wok until very hot. Add frogs' legs and peppercorns and stir-fry over high heat for a couple of minutes.

Add chilies, galangal, fish sauce and sugar. Mix well and cook for another minute. Stir in the fresh basil, take off the heat and serve.

Serve with plain steamed jasmine rice.

Pla Nuea Orn
River Fish with Chili Sauce

Although freshwater fish are preferred for this dish in Thailand, any good white-fleshed sea fish can be used. A stunning dish that is also very easy to make.

1 (2 pound) whole freshwater fish or 2 smaller fish
5 ounces dried red chilies, soaked in water, seeded and chopped
$1/2$ cup garlic, peeled and chopped
$1/2$ cup shallots, peeled and chopped
$1/4$ tablespoon shrimp paste
Oil for deep-frying
Fish sauce to taste
1 teaspoon sugar
10 kaffir lime leaves, very finely shredded

Scale and clean the fish thoroughly. (The Thais and Chinese would leave the head on.) Make diagonal cuts about $1/2$ inch deep along the back of each fish to give them a decorative appearance and to allow them to cook faster.

Mix chopped ingredients with the shrimp paste. Fry in 3 tablespoons of oil until fragrant, then add fish sauce and sugar.

Dry the fish thoroughly, then deep-fry until cooked. Put on a serving plate and top with sauce. Sprinkle with kaffir lime leaves and serve immediately.

Pla Muk Tod
Fried Squid with Garlic and Black Pepper

A delicious way to cook squid. Be sure to use fresh and not frozen squid, as the latter exudes water when cooked, causing the squid to stew rather than fry.

Charcoal-Grilled Shrimp with Sweet Sauce.

Casseroled Crabs with Cellophane Noodles.

$1 1/4$ pounds fresh squid
2 tablespoons oil
$1/2$ cup garlic, chopped
1 teaspoon black peppercorns, crushed
2 tablespoons oyster sauce
2 tablespoons light soy sauce
1 teaspoon sugar
Cilantro leaves to garnish

Remove tentacles from the squid and cut out the hard beaky portion. Remove the skin from the body of the squid, clean inside and cut into bite-sized pieces. Dry thoroughly and set aside.

Put oil in a wok over medium heat. Fry the garlic until golden-brown, then add the squid and its tentacles, together with the seasonings. Cook for a couple of minutes until the squid turns white. Serve hot, sprinkled with cilantro leaves.

Poo Jaa
Deep-Fried Stuffed Crab Shell

Use either mud crabs or blue swimmer crabs for this. The filling can be prepared in advance and the crabs stuffed and deep-fried just before serving.

4 whole crabs
5 cups oil
3 eggs, well beaten

1 tablespoon cilantro leaves
2 red chilies, cut into lengthwise strips

Stuffing
6 ounces ground pork
$1/3$ cup minced shrimp
$1/2$ cup fresh crabmeat
2 tablespoons finely chopped onion
1 tablespoon finely sliced scallion
1 teaspoon ground white pepper
1 teaspoon sugar
$1/4$ teaspoon light soy sauce
$1/4$ teaspoon salt

If using cooked crabs, remove the backs carefully and discard any spongy matter. Wash shells and set aside. Remove crabmeat from body, legs and claws and measure out $1/2$ cup. Keep the rest aside for another dish. If using raw crabs, steam first, then prepare as directed above. Mix all the stuffing ingredients together and fill the crab shells.

Heat the oil in a pan, dip the stuffed crabs in the beaten egg to coat well all over and deep-fry for about 10–15 minutes until cooked. Remove and drain well on paper towels. Sprinkle with the fresh cilantro and chili before serving.

Poo Ob Woon Sen
Casseroled Crabs with Cellophane Noodles

Use either crab claws or whole crabs cut into serving pieces for this recipe. Although slices of pork fat are usually used in Thailand, bacon improves the flavor. Large shrimp can be substituted for the crabs.

Stock
2 cups Chicken Stock (page 139)
2 tablespoons oyster sauce
2 tablespoons black soy sauce
1/2 tablespoon sesame oil
1 teaspoon brandy or whisky
1/2 teaspoon sugar

2 slices bacon, cut into 1 inch-pieces
2 whole crabs, shelled, or 1 pound crab claws
2 cilantro roots, cut in half
2 inches ginger, pounded or chopped finely
3–4 cloves garlic, chopped
1 tablespoon white peppercorns, crushed
8 ounces cellophane noodles, soaked in cold water for 5 minutes
1 teaspoon butter
3 tablespoons black soy sauce
1/4 cup chopped cilantro leaves and stems
2 scallions, cut into 1 1/2 inch-lengths

Place all the stock ingredients in a pan, bring to a boil and simmer for 5 minutes. Leave to cool. Take a heatproof casserole dish and line the bottom with bacon.

Put in the crab, cilantro

Fried Clams in Roasted Chili Paste (below) and Steamed Mussels (above).

root, ginger, garlic and peppercorns. Place noodles over the top, then add the butter, soy sauce and stock.

Cover, bring to a boil and simmer for 5 minutes. Mix well with tongs and add the cilantro and scallions. Cover and simmer for about 5 minutes more until the crabs are cooked. Drain off excess liquid before serving.

Goong Pow
Charcoal-Grilled Shrimp with Sweet Sauce

The fragrance of seafood grilling over charcoal is irresistible. In Thailand, this dish is made with large freshwater shrimp.

3 large freshwater shrimp or small crayfish
Foil or banana leaf

Sauce
1/3 cup water
1 tablespoon sugar
1/2 teaspoon salt
1 1/2 tablespoons chopped garlic
1/2 tablespoon chopped chilies
1 teaspoon chopped fresh cilantro
2 tablespoons lime juice

To make the sauce, heat water and sugar in a pan over low heat, stirring until the sugar has dissolved. Turn off the heat, add the salt and stir well. Remove

from the heat and allow to cool, then add the remaining ingredients and mix thoroughly.

Clean the shrimp and wrap each securely in foil or banana leaf. Grill over a hot charcoal fire for about 12 minutes. Serve with the sauce.

Hoi Ma-laeng Poo Ob
Steamed Mussels

This simple dish lives and dies on the strength of its ingredients, so use the best mussels you can afford and add lots of fresh, sweet-smelling basil.

4 1/2 pounds mussels, cleaned well
a large handful of basil leaves (*horapa*)

Sauce
1/2 cup lime juice
2 tablespoons fish sauce
1 teaspoon sugar
2 cilantro roots, chopped
2 cloves garlic, crushed
1/2 cup water

Place mussels in a steamer over boiling water and sprinkle with basil leaves. Steam for 10 minutes. Remove from the heat and wait for 2 minutes before opening the steamer. (Leaving the mussels to sit covered for a couple of minutes after steaming helps the flavor of the basil

permeate the mussels.)

Meanwhile, mix the sauce ingredients together, bring to a boil, then leave to cool.

Serve the mussels with the sauce for dipping.

Hoy Lai Ped
Fried Clams in Roasted Chili Paste

1/3 cup oil
1 1/4 pounds clams in their shells, cleaned well
1 1/2 tablespoons chopped garlic
5 fresh red chilies, sliced lengthwise
2 tablespoons roasted chili paste (page 139)
2 teaspoons light soy sauce
1/2 cup Chicken Stock (page 139)
Large handful basil leaves (*horapa*)

Heat the oil in wok, add the clams and garlic and cook until the clams open slightly. Add the chilies, chili paste and soy sauce, mix well, then add chicken stock. Stir in the basil and serve immediately, accompanied by rice.

HELPFUL HINT
Soak the clams in several changes of water for an hour or so before cooking to ensure they are thoroughly clean.

Fresh fruit is the mainstay of Thai desserts—what Westerners may called desserts are usually eaten between meals as fillers. Rice flour and tapioca starch, sticky rice, coconut milk, a twist of pandan leaf, and palm sugar are indispensable ingredients.

Tab Tim Grob
Red Rubies

This rather poetic name is given to tiny diced water chestnuts colored bright red and served in sweetened coconut milk. Although troublesome to peel, fresh water chestnuts have a delicate sweetness and excellent texture. If these are unavailable, jicama can be used.

1 cup (about 8 ounces) finely diced water chestnuts
Red food coloring
1/2 cup tapioca starch
5 cups water
1/2 cup sugar
3/4 cup water
3/4 cup coconut milk
Crushed ice

Sprinkle water chestnuts with food coloring and stir until bright red. Put the flour in a plastic bag and add the water chestnuts; shake to coat the pieces. Put in a colander or sieve and shake to allow excess flour to fall away.

Red Rubies (top), Bananas in Coconut Milk (right) and Rice Balls in Coconut Milk.

Bring 5 cups water to a boil, add the water chestnuts and simmer for 3 minutes. Drain and plunge in cold water. Drain again and set aside on a cloth.

Boil the sugar and the water to make a syrup, cool, then add the coconut milk.

To serve, put a little of the water chestnuts into dessert bowls and add some of the syrup and ice.

Kloey Buad Chee
Bananas in Coconut Milk

There are more than a dozen different types of bananas in Thailand. This recipe uses the tiny sweet variety sometimes known as finger bananas or lady finger bananas. If using large bananas, cut on the diagonal into 3-inch lengths.

2 cups thin coconut milk
1/2 cup sugar
1/4 teaspoon salt
3 small bananas, cut diagonally in half

Pour coconut milk into a pot, add sugar and salt. Bring to a boil, stirring constantly to prevent the coconut milk from separating. Add the bananas and cook gently for 5 minutes, then remove from the heat. Serve hot or cold.

Sangkaya Fak Thong
Pumpkin Custard

A simple sweet that goes straight from the stove to the table, this rich coconut cream custard is a favorite in Thailand.

5 eggs (2 of them duck eggs if possible)
1 cup coconut cream
1 cup chopped palm sugar or 1/2–3/4 cup white sugar
1 whole small pumpkin, about 8 inches in diameter

Beat eggs with coconut cream and sugar until the mixture is frothy.

Cut the top off the pumpkin and carefully scoop out the seeds and fibers. Pour in the coconut cream mixture, cover with the top of the pumpkin and place in a steamer. Cover the steamer and place over boiling water. Cook for about 30 minutes or until the mixture has set.

Refrigerate or leave to cool and cut into wedges to serve.

Note: Duck eggs add richness and a firmer texture to the custard. If using palm sugar, strain the custard through a sieve before pouring into the pumpkin.

Bua Loi
Rice Balls in Coconut Milk

3 cups glutinous rice flour
4 cups coconut cream
2 cups sugar
1 teaspoon salt

Mix the rice flour with enough water to make a stiff paste. Knead well and form into pea-sized balls.

Bring a large pot of water to a boil, toss in the balls and remove when they float to the surface. Drain.

Bring half the coconut cream with the salt to a boil, stirring constantly to prevent it from separating, then add the flour balls. When the mixture returns to a boil, remove from the heat and stir in the remaining coconut cream. Serve in small bowls.

Note: Canned corn and cooked, colored diced water chestnut (prepared as for Red Rubies) can be added to the Rice Balls in Coconut Milk if you want a more colorful dessert.

Pumpkin Custard.

Khao Mao Tod
Deep-Fried Bananas

Bananas are rolled in a mixture of rice flakes, grated coconut and palm sugar before being dipped in batter and deep-fried.

1 1/4 pounds freshly grated coconut
1 cup palm sugar, chopped
12 ounces rice flakes (*khoa mao*)
10 small finger bananas
Oil for deep-frying

Batter
3 cups glutinous rice flour
1 cup coconut milk
1 cup water
1 egg, lightly beaten
1 tablespoon sesame seeds

Combine the coconut, palm sugar and rice flakes and sauté in a nonstick pan, stirring frequently, for 1/2 hour. Set aside.

Mix the batter ingredients and let it stand for 3 hours.

Just before serving, roll each banana in the sautéed mixture, dip in the batter and fry in hot oil until golden brown. Serve hot.

HELPFUL HINT
Flattened rice grains or rice flakes are found under a variety of names in most Asian countries, and are often known by the Filipino name, *pinipig*. Any type of rice flake or even wheat flake can be substituted.

Chicken Stock

Homemade chicken stock greatly improves the flavor of recipes in which it is used. The stock can be put in 1-quart containers and frozen for up to 3 months.

- 5–6¹/₂ pounds chicken bones
- 6 quarts water
- 1¹/₂ onion, roughly chopped
- 4 ounces celery, roughly chopped
- 1 tablespoon coriander seeds
- 1 teaspoon black peppercorns

Wash bones in cold water and put in a stockpot. Cover with cold water. Bring rapidly to a boil, then drain the bones and discard water.

Cover bones with 6 quarts of water and add all other ingredients. Simmer for 4 hours, removing the foam as it accumulates. Strain through cloth.

Nam Prik Gaeng Ped

Red Curry Paste

Basic curry pastes can be stored in a covered glass jar in a refrigerator for 1 month, or in the freezer for 3–4 months.

- 1 tablespoon coriander seeds
- 1 teaspoon cumin seed
- 13 dried bird's-eye chilies, cut, soaked in hot water for 15 minutes and seeded
- 3 tablespoons finely chopped shallots
- 4 tablespoons finely chopped garlic
- 1 tablespoon finely chopped galangal
- 2 tablespoons finely sliced lemongrass
- 2 teaspoons finely chopped kaffir lime rind
- 1 tablespoon finely chopped cilantro root
- 20 black peppercorns
- 1 teaspoon shrimp paste

Dry-fry the coriander and cumin seeds in a wok over low heat for about 5 minutes, then grind to a powder. Add the remaining ingredients, except the shrimp paste, and blend well. Add the ground spice mixture and shrimp paste and blend again to obtain about ³/₄ cup of fine-textured paste.

Nam Prik Gaeng Kheow Wan

Green Curry Paste

- 1 tablespoon coriander seeds
- 1 teaspoon cumin seeds
- 15 green bird's-eye chilies
- 3 tablespoons finely chopped shallots
- 1 tablespoon finely chopped garlic
- 1 teaspoon finely chopped galangal
- 1 tablespoon finely sliced lemongrass
- ¹/₂ teaspoon finely chopped kaffir lime rind
- 1 teaspoon finely chopped cilantro root
- 5 black peppercorns
- 1 teaspoon salt
- 1 teaspoon shrimp paste

Dry-fry the coriander and cumin seeds in a wok over low heat for about 5 minutes, then grind into a powder. Put the rest of the ingredients except the shrimp paste into a blender and blend to mix well. Add the spice seed mixture and shrimp paste and blend to obtain ¹/₂ cup of fine-textured paste.

Nam Prik Gaeng Mussaman

Mussaman Curry Paste

- 3 tablespoons finely chopped shallots
- 1 tablespoon finely chopped garlic
- 1 teaspoon finely chopped galangal
- 1 heaped tablespoon finely sliced lemongrass
- 2 cloves
- 1 tablespoon coriander seeds
- 1 teaspoon cumin seeds
- 5 black peppercorns
- 3 dried chilies, cut, soaked in hot water for 15 minutes and seeded
- 1 teaspoon salt
- 1 teaspoon shrimp paste

Dry-fry the shallots, garlic, galangal, lemongrass, cloves, coriander and cumin seeds in a wok over low heat for about 5 minutes, then grind into a powder.

Add the rest of the ingredients, except the shrimp paste, and blend to mix well. Combine the blended mixture and the shrimp paste and blend again to obtain ¹/₂ cup of fine-textured paste.

Nam Prik Thai Orn

Green Peppercorn Dip

- 2 tablespoons fresh or bottled green peppercorns
- 3 cloves garlic
- 1 teaspoon sugar
- ¹/₂ tablespoon dried shrimp
- 2–3 tablespoons lime juice
- 6 sour fruits such as green mango or green apple, sliced

If using bottled or canned green peppercorns, be sure to wash off brine thoroughly.

Pound or blend the garlic and 1 tablespoon of peppercorns in a mortar, then add sugar, dried shrimp and lime juice. Mix well and add the remaining tablespoon of peppercorns. Stir until well mixed. Serve with sour fruit, vegetables and fried or grilled fish.

Nam Prik Pow

Roasted Chili Paste

- 2 cups vegetable oil
- 8 shallots, sliced
- 6 cloves garlic, sliced
- 1 cup dried shrimp
- ¹/₂ cup small dried chilies
- 1 tablespoon palm sugar
- 3 tablespoons fish sauce
- 1¹/₂ tablespoons tamarind juice
- ¹/₄ teaspoon salt

Heat the oil in a wok and fry the shallots and garlic until golden brown. Remove from oil and drain. Add the dried shrimp and chilies and fry until golden brown. Remove from oil and drain.

In a mortar or blender, grind the shrimp, garlic, chilies, shallots and sugar until the mixture is well blended. Add the fish sauce, tamarind juice, salt and cooled oil from the wok and blend to obtain a finely textured paste.

> **HELPFUL HINT**
> Serve dips with a selection of raw baby vegetables, salted duck egg and crisp pork skin.

Kapi Kua

Shrimp Paste and Coconut Milk Dip

- 2 dried chilies, cut and soaked
- 5 shallots
- 5 stems lemongrass, finely sliced
- 3 slices galangal
- 3 tablespoons minced *krachai*
- 3 tablespoons shrimp paste, roasted
- 1 cup coarsely chopped smoked fish
- 4 cups coconut milk
- 1 tablespoon palm sugar
- 2 tablespoons fish sauce
- 5 red chilies

Pound dried chilies, shallots, lemongrass, galangal, *krachai* and shrimp paste with half the smoked fish until well mixed. Heat coconut milk and simmer until it separates and the quantity has reduced. Add the paste and continue cooking until fragrant. Add sugar, the rest of the fish, fish sauce and chilies and simmer until thick. Serve with grilled shrimp or fluffy crisp fish flakes in a pan and cook over low heat, stirring frequently, until the sauce has thickened and reduced. Cool to room temperature and garnish with cilantro leaves when serving.

Nam Prik Pla Yaang

Dip with Grilled Fish

- 3–4 red bird's-eye chilies
- 1 dried chili, cut and soaked
- 3 cloves garlic, grilled in skin until blackened
- 2 shallots, grilled in skin until blackened
- 1 cup grilled, flaked fish
- ¹/₂ teaspoon shrimp paste, roasted
- 2 tablespoons lime juice
- 1 tablespoon fish sauce
- 1 teaspoon sugar
- 1 teaspoon kaffir lime juice

Pound bird's-eye chilies, then add dried chili, peeled garlic and shallots and continue pounding until a fine paste is formed.

Add lime juice, fish sauce and sugar. Mix well and add kaffir lime juice.

Serve with vegetables and grilled or fried fish.

The land of the Perfume River has been blessed with an astonishing variety of foods from the earth and from the water.

VIETNAM

Not only is Vietnam the site of an economic revival but a great culinary tradition is re-emerging too.

Left: The quiet journey home from market.

Right: Fresh carrots being readied for market in the central highlands. Vietnamese food is characterized by its lavish use of fresh vegetables and herbs.

With lengths of unspoiled dramatic coastline, sheltered harbors, well-irrigated lowlands and vast forests, Vietnam is a remarkably beautiful and fertile land, rich in agricultural resources.

It is also a country on the cusp of change; after years of war, an almost palpable sense of optimism hangs in the air. The effects of *doi moi*, the economic reform policy allowing small-scale private enterprise, introduced by the communist government in 1986, are becoming more and more evident. The accumulation of personal wealth is even encouraged.

The food markets are a hive of activity: these days produce is trucked in from nearby villages, coastal waters and the central highlands. Throughout the day, crowds of people fill their baskets from the rows of fresh vegetables and tropical fruits, live fish and game, pickled meats and vegetables, candied fruit, dried and packaged goods, rice and bottles of pungent *nuoc mam* fish sauce.

The Land and its People

Vietnam is fortunate in being able to grow a diverse variety of vegetables and fruits throughout the country and little food is imported. Rice and seafood are in abundant supply, due in part to its location on the eastern coast of the southeast Asian Indochinese peninsula and a 1,600-mile coastline. It boasts countless dykes, canals and waterways, which include the Red River, the Perfume River and the Mekong River, one of the longest rivers in Southeast Asia.

Vietnam shares its border with China, Laos and Cambodia. In the cooler northern region, where undulating limestone hills recall southwest China and where many of Vietnam's ethnic groups have their homes, the cuisine shares distinct similarities with Chinese food.

The center of the country is less agriculturally rich, and in the temperate south, the cuisine more closely resembles that of neighboring Southeast Asian countries, such as Thailand and Malaysia.

The food of the south is more varied and rich than that of Hué or Hanoi, and generously spiced.

The Red River Delta in the north and the Mekong Delta in the south are the two main rice-growing areas, although lush green rice paddies dotted with water buffalo and rows of women with their distinctive conical hats can be seen throughout the country. Sixty percent of arable land in Vietnam is given over to rice production, leaving little pasture for cattle farming. Hence beef, in particular, is a luxury for most Vietnamese, and the famous series of dishes, *bo bay mon* (literally, beef done seven ways), is highly regarded.

In spite of urbanization and increasingly populated cities, roughly 80 percent of the population relies on rice for its livelihood. Rice is used in a diverse range of dishes and in the production of wine and vinegar. The grains are also converted into flour and used to make rice noodles and transformed into rice paper sheets for *goi cuon*, the Vietnamese fresh spring rolls. Glutinous rice cooked overnight, then wrapped into attractive banana leaf parcels, becomes breakfast-time *xoi* or the traditional *banh tay* and *banh chung* eaten during Tet, the Vietnamese Lunar New Year holiday.

The Making of a Cuisine

The Vietnamese people have a history of foreign influences, from neighbors, sojourners and settlers, all of whom have left their mark: Malay, Chinese, Indian, Thai, French and American. The Chinese offered their use of bean curd, soybeans and spices such as the star anise. The use of dill in *cha ca*, Hanoi's famous fish dish served at the popular Cha Ca La Vong restaurant, and also in fish congee, could have been a French influence. The Indians left their ground rice pancakes.

At the heart of Vietnamese cuisine is the salty, pale brown fermented fish sauce known as *nuoc mam*. The cuisines of Cambodia, Thailand and Burma use a similar sauce, however, the Vietnamese variety seems to have a particularly pungent flavor. *Nuoc mam* is made by layering fresh anchovies with salt in huge wooden barrels, a process that takes about six months and involves pouring the liquid which drips from the barrel back over the anchovies. Arguably, the best *nuoc mam* comes from the island of Phu Quoc near the Cambodian border.

Nuoc mam cham, the ubiquitous dip made of *nuoc mam* diluted with lime juice, vinegar, water, crushed garlic and fresh red chilies is used as a dipping sauce at the table, served with dishes like *cha gio* (spring rolls) and *chao tom* (sugar cane shrimp), or simply as a dip for pieces of fish or meat.

What sets Vietnamese cuisine apart from that of other Southeast Asian countries is the pervasive use of fresh leaves and herbs, making it lighter and more refreshing than, say, Thai food. Its use of crisp, uncooked vegetables, subtle seasonings, raw herbs and unique flavor combinations—sharp, sweet and fresh and fragrant at the same time—is unforgettable.

While Vietnamese restaurants in other regions of the world rarely manage to offer more than one kind of mint, basil or cilantro, markets throughout Vietnam sell a remarkable array of such herbs, as well as leaves such as the deep-red, spicy perilla leaf, *tia to*, and the pungent saw-leaf herb (long coriander).

Fresh herbs turn up in all sorts of dishes. Soup kitchens serving the glorious noodle soup *pho* also offer a huge plate of raw herbs to be stirred into the steaming soup. The herbs are also served with *ban xeo*, a kind of crêpe enclosing shrimp, pork, mung beans and bean sprouts, and with spring rolls or grilled meats, and in salads.

Other factors that contribute to the subtlety and uniqueness of Vietnamese food are the refined cooking techniques, the often unusual serving of varying dishes and the combination of flavors.

A simple but refined meal in Hué, once the political centre and today still an important culinary city.

Imperial Cuisine

Hué, situated on the banks of the tranquil Perfume River, was once an important seat of learning and culture, as well as the imperial seat for nearly 150 years.

To satisfy jaded imperial palates, but lacking in the agricultural diversity of either the north or the south, the imperial kitchens at Hué had to show an enormous amount of ingenuity by refining ordinary dishes until they became something truly special, so that eating could be viewed as art, ritual and sensory pleasure at the same time.

A typical imperial banquet today would include up to a dozen dishes, such as a beautifully fragrant, peppery chicken soup with lotus seeds (*sup ga*), crisp, golden brown spring rolls (*nem ran*), delicate rice flour patties stuffed with minced shrimp (*banh* Hué), grilled pork in rice paper (*thit nuong*) served with a tasty peanut sauce, delicious crab claws stuffed with pork (*cua phich bot*), and the famous minced shrimp wrapped around sugar cane (*cha tom lui mia* or *chao tom*). Main dishes might include fish grilled in banana leaf (*ca nuong la chuoi*), pungent beef in wild betel leaves (*bo la lot*), rice with vegetables (*com* Hué), gently sautéed shrimp with mushrooms (*tom xao hanh nam*), and finally the glutinous rice dessert husband-and-wife cake (*phu the*), which comes in a perfectly formed little box made from pandan leaf.

These dishes are actually variations of those served in other parts of Vietnam, and the ingredients may be vegetables, eggs or fish, rather than exotic sea delicacies or the best cuts of meat. What sets these dishes apart is the sophisticated cooking techniques and the careful presentation.

For example, the favorite *chao tom lui mia* seems so simple—if only! Tiny shrimp are carefully shelled, then marinated in *nuoc mam*. They are then pounded until they form a thick paste, and egg white, onion, garlic, sugar and pepper added. The mixture is pounded again with a touch of pork fat, and finally wrapped around sugar cane sticks and grilled.

The presentation of food was—and is—very important, not only in the use of color and the arrangement of food on the plate, but also in the manner of serving. Rice, for example, might be draped with an omelet coat, or cooked inside a lotus leaf and further enhanced with the addition of delicate lotus seeds.

Portions are delicate, since perhaps dozens of dishes are served in the course of a meal. All these naturally increased the length of preparation time, with the result that the number of cooks and kitchen staff reached unprecedented heights—a luxury which perfectly befitted the privileged life of an emperor.

The most talented proponents of imperial cuisine today are virtually all women, each of them descended by some route or other from imperial households. Due to its size and relatively small population, Hué today is not a culinary mecca compared with Ho Chi Minh City or Hanoi. There is, however, a renewed interest in the cuisine of Hué, and a number of modern Vietnamese chefs have made it their mission to turn the simple art of cooking into something extraordinary.

The Food of the People

Through the more than four troubled decades of constant struggle and fighting in Vietnam, there was barely enough rice to go around, let alone interest in what to buy at the market and how to perfect a particular recipe. But since the mid-1980s, a combination of economic upturn and the return of many overseas Vietnamese (encouraged by the government to start new businesses) has resulted in, among other things, the rebirth of a thriving restaurant scene.

Culinary skills are being relearned, courses for the training of professional chefs are being launched and the Vietnamese are once again discovering the joys of cooking. Top-quality, fresh ingredients are widely available.

All over Ho Chi Minh City and, to a slightly lesser extent, in Hanoi, restaurants are built around courtyards in French colonial buildings or designed to resemble old Vietnamese family homes. French restaurants are once again establishing themselves and fashionable Italian restaurants are making an appearance.

Vietnamese cuisine is based on rice, fish, and fresh vegetables. Little oil is used in cooking, except for deep-frying, and salads are lightly dressed. Healthy, invigorating soups such as the tasty *canh chua thom ca loc* are featured on menus, fresh fruit and delicious home-made yogurts are often served for dessert, and drinks like freshly squeezed sugar cane juice are widely available.

Modern Vietnamese cuisine is a marriage of the old and the new. Recipes from past generations are coupled with new dishes created for the increasingly sophisticated and well-traveled local consumer. A good example is *thit kho to*, pork cooked slowly in a claypot, a dish of peasant origins that now appears on restaurant menus alongside *cua rang me*, a fried crab dish richly perfumed with tamarind.

Baguettes at a food stall are a reminder of Vietnam's colonial past.

The sometimes lengthy preparation times and cooking processes required by Vietnamese cuisine can render it something of a luxury for people with busy lives, so many chefs and teachers within Vietnam have begun experimenting with new and innovative methods that preserve the spirit of the cuisine, but allow it to be prepared quickly and simply at home.

As this move towards quicker cooking has been evolving, there has also been a resurgence of interest in the traditional dishes of the Hué court. While more attention is being paid to the presentation of food, very few changes, if any, are made to cater to the tourist trade. What changes are occurring in the recipes are subtle and often imperceptible: *ga bop*, a chicken salad flavored with onion, *rau ram* (*laksa* leaf or polygonum) and a simple seasoning of salt, pepper and lime juice, has traditionally been made with chicken skin and bones, but new restaurants are preparing it with lean chicken meat.

The Vietnamese Table and Kitchen

Eating in Vietnam is a shared experience, an informal ritual. On the small table that the family has gathered around is a large bowl of steaming rice, a cauldron of aromatic soup, a meat dish, a vegetable dish and a generous plate of leaves for each diner to wrap around a delicious hand roll and dip into the *nuoc mam cham*. Tea is drunk throughout the meal.

The adage "the fresher the ingredients, the better the food," is especially true of Vietnamese cooking. The various herbs and lettuces are almost always served raw, and salads are never over-dressed, so that the full flavors are present. Vegetables and fish in particular, which make up a large part of the Vietnamese diet, are gently cooked and lightly seasoned, allowing the true flavors of the food to come through.

The home and its kitchen is central to Vietnamese culture. A week before Tet, the god of the hearth (Tao Quan) must be supplicated with a ceremony performed in the kitchen, where offerings of fruit, paper models of luxury consumer goods and a ceremonial costume are placed on the altar.

Traditional Vietnamese cooks generally squat, feet tucked beneath them, preparing much of their food on the floor around the stove on a wet, tiled area, where all utensils, pots, pans and food items are cleaned before use. Even as incomes gradually increase and some of the modern conveniences (refrigerators, plumbed sinks, built-in work surfaces and electric rice cookers) are making their way into a number of Vietnamese kitchens, much of the preparation and cooking is still done in the traditional manner.

Most of the cooking is done over an open hearth (ovens are not used), with one member of the family on duty to fan the flames. A wok is still the most versatile implement in any Vietnamese kitchen, usually set over a wood fire. Grilling is another common cooking method. A large pot is standard for soups and stocks, and since rice is the staple, a simple rice cooker with its lid is usually steaming away on a low fire.

As in other countries, food stalls are a popular haunt, both for local gossip and a quick meal, and usually appear on the sidewalks in front of old shophouses. Clusters of tiny chairs and tables surround a steaming hot cauldron of soup set on an open flame, with people huddled over their morning bowl of restorative *pho*. At another streetside restaurant, a team of busy female chefs is busy making open-faced omelets in blackened pans over small charcoal grills. Or it may be vendors with carts filled with baguettes, cheese, sliced pâté and sausages making sandwiches. It's all in a day's work.

The result of time-consuming preparation is a memorable dining experience.

SUGGESTED MENUS

Family meals

- Stuffed Steamed Rice Wrapper Rolls (page 146);
- Stuffed Squid (page 152), Stir-Fried Vegetables with Fish Sauce (page 150) and Pork Stew with Coconut Juice (page 154) served with rice;
- Husband and Wife Cakes (page 156).

Or, lead off with the
- Preserved Salted Fish Stew (page 151); followed by
- Prawn and Green Mango Salad (page149), Fried Bean Curd with Lemongrass (page 155) and Grilled Beef in Wild Betel Leaves (page 155) served with rice;
- Banana Cake (page 156) is a popular way to finish.

A dinner party

Most of the recipes in the appetizers section lend themselves readily to dinner-party nibbles, so try serving
- a selection of fried and steamed rice paper rolls (pages 146–48) with a few dipping sauces;
- Banana Blossom Salad with Duck and Ginger (page 149), served either from a platter in the middle or in individual portions;
- Braised Mushrooms with Soy Sauce (page 150), Spicy River Prawns (page 152) and a Spicy Beef Stew (page 155) served with rice;
- Pineapple Tartlets (page 156) and vanilla icecream.

One-pot meals

The noodle soups of Vietnam deserve honorable mention, so for breakfast, lunch or dinner, do as the locals do and try one of the following:
- Hanoi Chicken Soup (page 148);
- Beef Noodle Soup (page 148);
- Grilled Pork with Rice Noodles (page 155). Very satisfying!

A melting pot menu

- Simmered Winter Squash (page 95) from Japan;
- Squid with Bamboo Shoots from China (page 38) and from Vietnam, Fried Grouper with Ginger Sauce (page 153), served with rice and a simple salad or stir-fried vegetables;
- freshly sliced seasonal fruits, such as mangoes or pineapple.

THE ESSENTIAL FLAVORS OF VIETNAMESE COOKING

The key to Vietnamese cuisine is freshness, so choose the best of available herbs and leaves for the table salad: **laksa leaf** (*daun kesum*), **lettuces**, **bean sprouts**, **basil** and **cilantro**. These also accompany rice paper rolls. **Chilies** are sliced into **nuoc mam** for dipping sauces. Flavorings widely used include **garlic**, **lemongrass**, **shallots** and **scallions**. **Rice** is a must.

The freshness and exuberance of Vietnamese food is no more evident than in the range of hand rolls they make, which make use of fragrant, crispy leaves and a little meat or seafood. The rolls are filling and substantial without heaviness.

Goi Cuon
Shrimp Rolls

- 1/2 cup water
- 2 tablespoons white vinegar
- 1 tablespoon rice wine
- 1/2 teaspoon salt
- 1 pound shrimp, shells on
- 2 tablespoons vegetable oil
- 8 ounces pork loin
- 20 pieces rice paper
- 1 medium head butter lettuce
- 1 cup fresh basil leaves
- 1 cup fresh mint leaves
- 2 small red chilies, thinly sliced
- 1 cup bean sprouts
- 1 bunch chives, cut 3–4 inch lengths

In a frying pan, combine water, vinegar, rice wine and salt. Bring to a boil. Add shrimp and simmer until just done. Cool and peel.

Heat oil in a separate pan, and sear pork for about 2 minutes or until lightly browned all over. Add liquid from shrimp to the pan, simmer pork for 15 minutes or until tender. Remove from heat, drain and slice thinly. Rub rice paper with a moist towel until soft and flexible. Place a little of the pork, shrimp, lettuce, basil, mint, chilies, bean sprouts and chives on the paper and roll up firmly. Cut into finger-length pieces and serve with Peanut Sauce (see page 157).

HELPFUL HINT
If you find that the dried wrappers do not soften sufficiently when you wipe them, soak them in tepid water until flexible. Place on a tea towel to soak up any excess moisture and proceed with the recipe. Work in small batches.

Banh Cuon
Stuffed Steamed Rice Wrapper Rolls

This is a variation on the spring rolls that use freshly steamed wrappers. The steaming of the fresh rice flour wrappers is actually quite easy and fun once you get the hang of it.

Stuffing
- 1/2 cup dried wood ear mushrooms
- Water to cover
- 2 tablespoons vegetable oil
- 8 shallots, chopped
- 1 clove garlic, crushed
- 1 cup finely diced preserved white radish
- 10 ounces ground pork or minced shrimp

Fresh Rice Flour Wrappers
- 1 cup rice flour
- 3 cups water
- Salt

Garnish
- 1/4 cup cilantro leaves
- 1/2 cup fried shallots
- 1 red chili, shredded

Sauce
- 1 tablespoon sugar
- 1/4 cup water
- 2 tablespoons fish sauce
- 1 tablespoon rice wine vinegar
- 1 tablespoon fresh lime juice
- 1 medium red chili, shredded
- 2 cloves garlic, finely chopped

To make the stuffing, soak the mushrooms in water for 1 hour, drain and dice. Heat oil in a wok and sauté the shallots, garlic, radish, pork and mushrooms until tender. Set aside.

To make the wrappers, mix flour, water and salt to form a batter. Fill a steamer two-thirds full of water and bring to a boil. Double and stretch a piece of cheesecloth tightly over the top and secure with string.

Shrimp Mousse on Sugar Cane.

Brush the surface of the cheese-cloth with oil, pour on a small ladle of rice flour batter and spread it around in a circular motion. If possible, cover with an inverted bowl or lid, and leave for a few moments.

Once set, remove the steamed rice flour wrapper with a spatula, carefully lifting up at the corners. Repeat until all the batter is used up.

To make the sauce, dissolve sugar in water, add fish sauce, vinegar and lime juice. Add chili and garlic just before serving.

Place the wrapper on a smooth surface. Place roughly 1 tablespoon of filling on the wrapper and roll up gently. Garnish with fresh cilantro, shallots and chili and serve with the sauce.

Banh Uot Thit Nuong
Grilled Beef Roll

- 1 stem lemongrass, finely chopped
- 1 tablespoon soft brown sugar
- 1/4 cup fish sauce
- 12 ounces beef, thinly sliced
- 1/2 cup fresh mint leaves
- 1/2 cup fresh basil leaves
- 1/2 head butter lettuce
- 5 fresh steamed Rice Flour Wrappers (see previous recipe)
- 1 tablespoon sesame seeds, toasted
- 1/2 cup fresh cilantro leaves
- Dipping Sauce

Grilled Beef Roll with fish sauce dip (left) and Hué Spring Roll with shrimp paste dip (right).

1 cup Yellow Bean Sauce
(page 157)
4 tablespoons sweet chili sauce
1 tablespoon roasted peanuts,
finely chopped

Combine lemongrass, sugar and fish sauce. Marinate beef in mixture for 30 minutes, then briefly grill over a medium heat until lightly browned but still rare inside. Remove from grill and cut into small pieces.

To make the dipping sauce, combine the yellow bean sauce, chili sauce and peanuts. Mix together well.

Place some of the beef, a little of the mint, basil and lettuce leaves on a rice flour wrapper, then sprinkle with sesame seeds and add a cilantro leaf. Fold the edges to the inside, leaving the top end open with the cilantro leaf extended. Serve with the dipping sauce.

Cuon Hué
Hué Spring Roll

5 fresh steamed Rice Flour
Wrappers (page 146)
1 large rice paper, sprinkled with
water
8 sprigs water spinach
1/2 cup fragrant leaves (a mixture
of basil, mint and cilantro)
1 medium sweet potato, peeled,
cooked and thinly sliced
1/4 cup steamed rice vermicelli
4 ounces lean pork, boiled and
thinly sliced
4 ounces preserved sour shrimp

Shrimp Paste Dip
2 cloves garlic, finely chopped
2 tablespoons vegetable oil
1 tablespoon shrimp paste
1 sweet potato, boiled and mashed
1 tablespoon sugar

To make the shrimp paste dip, sauté garlic in oil until fragrant. Add shrimp paste, potato and sugar. Stir well and cook for a few minutes.

Spread steamed rice flour wrappers over softened rice paper (which makes it easier to roll but is discarded). Place water spinach, fragrant leaves, sweet potato and noodles in a line along the paper. Roll tightly.

Cut into 1-inch segments and display on a plate, topping each segment with a slice of pork and a shrimp. Serve with shrimp paste dip.

Ha Gio
Vietnamese Spring Rolls

These are the classic, deep-fried Vietnamese spring rolls, also referred to as Imperial Rolls.

Stuffing
1 pound lean, ground pork
8 ounces shrimp, minced
4 ounces crabmeat
5 shallots, finely chopped
2 cloves garlic, crushed
2 or 3 wood ear mushrooms,
soaked in water
1 1/2 ounces cellophane noodles,
soaked in water
1/2 medium carrot, cut into juli-
enne shreds
1 egg white (optional)
A pinch of pepper
1 teaspoon sugar
A pinch of salt
1 tablespoon fish sauce
25 pieces dried rice paper
Water
Vegetable oil for deep-frying
1 cup fragrant leaves (basil,
cilantro and mint)
1 small head iceberg lettuce
1/4 cup bean sprouts
2 tablespoons Fish Sauce Dip
(page 157)
2 tablespoons Carrot and Radish
Pickles (page 157)
1/2 cup rice noodles, softened

To make the stuffing, combine all ingredients in a large bowl and mix thoroughly.

Sprinkle rice paper with water until flexible. Put a heaped teaspoon of stuffing on the rice paper. Fold the left and right sides of the rice paper into the center, then roll up from the bottom edge away to the far end. Do not roll too tightly or the rolls will split when you deep-fry.

Deep-fry the rolls over medium heat until golden brown.

Serve with fragrant leaves, lettuce, bean sprouts, fish sauce dip, carrot and radish pickles and rice noodles. Wrap the leaves and lettuce around the rolls and dip into the sauce. Note: Chicken and duck also work well in this dish if you want some alternatives.

Chao Tom
Shrimp Mousse on Sugar Cane

This dish from the imperial city of Hué uses fresh sticks of sugar cane as skewers. The heated cane releases a burst of sweet cane juice when bitten into.

10 ounces shrimp, minced
1/2 teaspoon salt
1 teaspoon sugar
A pinch of pepper
2 tablespoons vegetable oil
8 x 4-inch pieces sugar cane
1 red chili, seeded and sliced
1 cup Sweet and Sour Sauce
(page 157)
1/2 cup cilantro leaves

Grind or pound shrimp with salt, sugar and pepper in a blender or food processor.

Using the oil, mold the shrimp paste around the sugar cane. Grill over medium charcoal heat until the outside is crisp and slightly brown. Alternatively oven-bake the skewers at 375 °F for about 20 minutes.

Serve with chili, sweet and sour sauce and cilantro.

HELPFUL HINT
Crab is a good substitute for shrimp if you want a variation.

Nem Nuong
Minced Pork Balls on a Skewer

1 pound lean pork neck
1/2 teaspoon salt
8 ounces pork fatback
2 tablespoons sugar
2 cloves garlic, diced
2 red chilies, finely chopped
Salt
1 tablespoon pepper
1/8 cup roasted peanuts, ground
1/4 cup Fish Sauce Dip (page 157)

Garnish
1 cup bean sprouts
2 medium starfruits, peeled and
sliced
2 medium unripe bananas, thinly
sliced
1 medium cucumber, peeled and
sliced
1 head butter lettuce
1 cup mint leaves
20 pieces rice paper

Pound the pork with 1/2 teaspoon salt to tenderize and set aside. Fry the pork fatback in its own fat for 10 minutes, then cut into very small strips. Marinate with sugar, garlic, chili, salt and pepper for 5 minutes. Combine both types of pork and shape into small balls. Place 3–4 on bamboo skewers and cook on the charcoal grill, turning frequently to avoid burning. Sprinkle with peanuts, fish sauce dip and and serve with garnish ingredients for diners to combine to taste.

(See page 154 for the picture of this dish.)

Vietnamese Spring Rolls.

Thin but flavorful, soups are drunk throughout a meal in Vietnam rather than at the beginning as in the West. The soups can be served in individual bowls or, as is often the case, set in one large bowl from which everyone helps themselves.

Bun Thang
Hanoi Chicken Soup

This is one of the many warming winter soups that has been popularized in Hanoi, and is now commonplace throughout the country.

| 1 medium chicken
| ¹/₂ cup dried shrimp
| 12 ounces pork spare ribs, cut into large pieces
| 12 cups lightly salted water
| Pepper
| Sugar
| ¹/₄ cup fish sauce
| ¹/₂ cup diced shallots
| 4 baby leeks, finely cut
| 1 medium onion, sliced
| 4 cups fine rice noodles, blanched
| 1 egg, beaten, fried and cut into strips
| 10 ounces Vietnamese sausage, cut into thin strips
| 2 baby leek greens, chopped
| 3 tablespoons finely chopped cilantro leaf
| ¹/₄ cup fried shallots (page 121)
| Freshly ground pepper
| 1 lime, cut into wedges
| 2 small red chilies, sliced
| 1 cup bean sprouts
| 1 medium head butter lettuce
| 1 cup banana blossom, shaved
| 2 tablespoons shrimp paste

Boil chicken, dried shrimp and pork ribs in lightly salted water for about 20 minutes. Skim fat and season with pepper, sugar and fish sauce. Simmer for another 45 minutes until the chicken is cooked. Remove both the chicken and shrimp. Cool, then shred the chicken. Set aside. Add shallots, baby leeks and onion to the stock. Simmer for 20 minutes and season to taste.

Place a handful of rice noodles in each soup bowl, and cover with a portion of the egg, the shredded chicken, spare ribs, sausage, greens, cilantro and some of the fried shallots. Add boiling stock to cover.

Sprinkle with freshly ground pepper, the remaining fried shallots and lime juice. Serve with chilies, bean sprouts, lettuce, banana blossom and shrimp paste.

HELPFUL HINT
In Vietnam, pork ribs are often steamed before cooking, for health purposes and to tenderize the meat.

Pho Bo
Beef Noodle Soup

You'll find this soup everywhere in Vietnam, from street stalls to fancy restaurants. It is the classic breakfast meal, but it is just as delicious served any time of day or night.

| 1 medium piece fresh ginger
| 1 large onion
| 12 cups water
| 2 pounds beef bones
| 12 ounces beef brisket
| A pinch of salt
| 3 star anise
| 1 stick cinnamon
| Salt and pepper
| 1 cup bean sprouts
| 8 ounces flat rice noodles
| 8 ounces raw beef striploin, thinly sliced
| 1 medium onion, sliced
| ¹/₄ cup baby leeks, finely cut
| ¹/₂ cup ngo gai (saw-leaf herb) leaves, chopped
| ¹/₂ cup chopped cilantro leaves
| 1 tablespoon chili sauce

| 3 tablespoons Yellow Bean Sauce (page 157)
| 2 small red chilies, sliced
| 2 limes, cut into wedges
| Mint leaves
| *Ngo ga*i leaves
| Cilantro leaves

Grill ginger and onion until the skins are burned.

In a deep pan, combine water, bones and beef brisket. Bring to a boil, skimming frequently, to remove residue. Add

Beef Noodle Soup.

salt, ginger and onion, star anise and cinnamon.

After 45 minutes, remove the beef and slice very finely. Drain the soup into a separate container, adding salt and pepper to taste.

Wash and drain bean sprouts. Quickly blanch rice noodles and bean sprouts in boiling water to soften, but do not overcook. Arrange in soup bowls. Top with sliced beef brisket, raw beef striploin, sliced onion, chopped baby leeks, *ngo gai* and cilantro. Pour the boiling soup into the bowl and sprinkle with freshly ground pepper. The boiling stock will cook the raw beef.

Serve with chili and yellow bean sauces, sliced chili, lime, mint, *ngo gai* and cilantro leaves.

HELPFUL HINT
Grill the ginger and onion over an open flame or in a pan. Chicken noodle soup is a delicious alternative to beef, and most Vietnamese restaurants offer both versions.

Clam Soup.

Pungent with fish sauce, Vietnamese salads are a little like the Thai—the bite of chili is soothed by crunchy leaves, tempered with sweet palm sugar and finished with little crispy bits of shallots and peanuts . . . the explosion of flavors in the mouth is quite a sensation! Most salads are quickly and easily assembled once the preparation is done, often requiring nothing more than a light toss with a small amount of dressing just before serving.

In a large bowl combine lotus stems, *rau ram*, salt, sugar and lime juice. Toss gently. Place on a serving plate.

Cut shrimp in half lengthwise and arrange on the salad. Garnish with peanuts, cilantro and shallots. Serve with fish sauce dip and shrimp crackers.

Lotus Stem Salad with Shrimp.

Goi Ngo Sen
Lotus Stem Salad with Shrimp

The lotus flower is the symbol of purity. The stems have a crisp, crunchy texture that is similar to celery, which can be used as a substitute.

- 8 ounces cleaned lotus stems, cut into 2-inch lengths
- 1 tablespoon *rau ram* (polygonum) leaves, finely chopped
- 1 teaspoon salt
- 1 1/2 tablespoons sugar
- 1 tablespoon lime juice
- 6 medium shrimp, cooked, peeled and deveined
- 1 tablespoon peanuts, coarsely ground
- 3 tablespoons cilantro leaves
- 2 tablespoons fried shallots (page 121)
- 1/3 cup Fish Sauce Dip (page 157)
- 6 shrimp crackers

Squid Salad.

Goi Muc
Squid Salad

Piquant, sweet and hot, the flavors of this salad really get the tastebuds working. Squid is easy to work with but becomes rubbery if overcooked, so barely cook the squid and quickly plunge it into iced water to keep its texture.

- 1 pound cleaned squid
- 4 cups water
- 2 tablespoons lime juice
- 1/4 cup rice wine
- 3 cloves garlic, crushed
- 1 teaspoon sesame seed oil
- 1 teaspoon sugar
- 1 teaspoon cracked black pepper
- 1/2 cup baby celery stems, thinly sliced
- 1/2 cup cilantro leaves
- 1 small red chili, finely chopped
- 1/3 cup baby leek pickles or shallots (optional)
- 2 tablespoons peanuts, crushed
- 1/2 cup Fish Sauce Dip (page 157)
- Rice crackers, to garnish

Cut squid crosswise into narrow 2-inch pieces. Bring a large pan of water to a boil and blanch squid quickly (1–2 minutes). Cool in iced water.

In a large bowl, combine remaining ingredients with the squid and mix well.

Arrange salad on a platter and serve with rice crackers.

HELPFUL HINT

In Vietnam, as elsewhere in Asia, the squid is crisscrossed with tiny cuts before cooking for a decorative finish and to speed up the cooking process. Squid can also be tenderized by soaking it in milk for a day before cooking.

Goi Xoai Xanh Tom Hap
Shrimp and Green Mango Salad

This is essentially a variation on the traditional Vietnamese shrimp salad, using tart, unripe mango instead of lotus root. Green papaya may also be used.

- 12 medium shrimp
- 1 cup finely sliced green mango
- 1 tablespoon chopped *rau ram* (polygonum) leaves
- 1/4 cup Fish Sauce Dip (page 157)
- 1 small red chili, finely sliced
- 2 tablespoons fried shallots (page 121)
- 2 tablespoons chives

Clean and devein the shrimp. Quickly steam in a pan with very little water until bright pink and tender. Remove from pan and cool.

In a large bowl, combine the shrimp, mango, *rau ram* and fish sauce dip. Toss well. Arrange on a platter and garnish with chili, shallots and chives.

Goi Vit Bap Chuoi
Banana Blossom Salad with Duck and Ginger

The richness of duck is combined with ginger in this unusual salad.

- 1 young banana blossom, finely sliced
- 2 cups ice water
- 1 tablespoon lemon juice
- 2 duck breasts
- 1/2 cup Fish Sauce Dip (page 157)
- 1 teaspoon finely cut *rau ram* (polygonum leaves)
- 1 tablespoon finely chopped ginger
- 1 tablespoon coarsely ground peanuts
- 1 tablespoon fried shallots
- 1/4 cup cilantro leaves

Place banana blossom in ice water with lemon juice, and soak for 1 hour.

Boil (or steam) the duck in a shallow saucepan with a little water until tender. Cool, remove skin and slice thinly.

Drain the banana blossom and toss in a bowl with fish sauce dip, *rau ram*, ginger, peanuts and duck. Arrange on a platter and sprinkle with fried shallots. Garnish with cilantro.

HELPFUL HINT

If you can't find banana blossom, use shaved celery. The duck can be baked, fried or grilled if you like.

These dishes are meant to be served as part of a shared meal with steamed jasmine rice. Seafood and fish are very popular in Vietnam, and cooked in many styles.

Nam Xao Nuoc Tuong
Braised Mushrooms with Soy Sauce

The sweet, soy sauce gravy really lifts the bland flavor of the mushrooms. Any variety of large mushrooms will do and different types can be mixed together for variety.

| 8 ounces straw mushrooms |
| 2 cloves garlic, crushed |
| 1 tablespoon vegetable oil |
| A pinch of pepper |
| A pinch of salt |
| 1 teaspoon sugar |
| 2 tablespoons soy sauce |
| 1/4 cup water |
| Freshly cracked pepper |
| Cilantro leaves |

Rinse the mushrooms, pat dry on absorbent paper.

Sauté garlic in oil until lightly browned and fragrant, add mushrooms, stirring quickly, then season with pepper, salt, sugar and soy sauce. Add water and simmer for 3 minutes.

Spoon onto a serving dish and sprinkle with pepper and cilantro leaves.

Canh Bi Ro Ham Dua
Braised Pumpkin with Coconut Milk

This is a traditional Buddhist vegetarian dish finished with raw peanuts.

| 2 cups pumpkin, peeled and cut into 3/4-inch cubes |
| 2 cups thin coconut milk |
| 2 cups sweet potato or taro root, cut into 3/4-inch cubes |
| 1/2 cup wood ear mushrooms |
| 1/4 cup thick coconut cream |
| 1/2 cup raw peanuts, soaked in warm water |
| 1/2 cup loofah or green zucchini, thinly sliced |
| Salt |
| 1 teaspoon sugar |
| Cilantro leaves |
| 2 tablespoon *rau ram* (polygonum) leaves, sliced |

Stir-Fried Vegetables with Fish Sauce.

Place pumpkin and thin coconut milk in a deep sauté pan. Bring to a boil. Cook until pumpkin is half done.

Add the sweet potatoes and wood ear mushrooms to the pumpkin mixture. Reduce heat and simmer until nearly done. Add thick coconut cream, peanuts, loofah and bring to a boil again. Remove from the heat. Season to taste with salt and sugar. Serve in a bowl and sprinkle with fresh cilantro and *rau ram* leaves.

Ca Tim Nuong
Grilled Eggplant with Crab

This recipe is common to Cambodia and southern Vietnam and makes surprising use of eggplant, one of the many vegetables grown in central Vietnam.

| 6 long (Japanese) eggplant |
| 1/4 cup cooking oil |
| 2 tablespoons fried shallots (page 121) |
| 1 1/2 cups fresh crabmeat |
| 1 tablespoon scallions, finely sliced |
| Cilantro leaves |

| Sauce |
| 1 medium red chili, minced |
| 1 1/2 tablespoons peanuts, crushed |
| 1/4 cup fish sauce |
| 1/2 teaspoon sugar or honey |
| 3 tablespoons water |

Cut eggplants in half and brush with some of the oil. Grill over an open flame or under a broiler, turning regularly, until the skin turns a darkish brown and the flesh is soft. Peel off the skin and discard.

Fry the shallots in the remaining oil.

Place eggplants on a serving plate and sprinkle with crabmeat. Combine the ingredients for the sauce and pour over the eggplants. Serve garnished with the fried shallots, scallions and cilantro leaves.

Rau Xao
Stir-Fried Vegetables with Fish Sauce

| 12 cups salted water |
| 1 cup sliced carrots |
| 1 cup cauliflower pieces |
| 1 cup baby corn |
| 1 cup black mushrooms |
| 1 cup tender kale or broccoli stems |
| 2 tablespoons vegetable oil |
| 1 tablespoon rice wine |
| 2 tablespoons fish sauce |
| 2 cloves garlic, crushed |
| Salt and pepper |

Blanch the vegetables in lightly salted boiling water, remove and place in a large bowl of cold or iced water.

Heat oil in a wok or large sauté pan and stir-fry the drained vegetables. Add the rice wine, then the fish sauce and garlic. Season with salt and pepper to taste. Serve with plenty of steamed rice.

HELPFUL HINT

When blanching vegetables, they should remain in the water just long enough to slightly soften. Place them in cold (or iced) water immediately after cooking to ensure a crisp texture.

Preserved Salted Fish Stew.

place on a lotus leaf. Sprinkle with chopped baby leek. Fold into a neat package and serve. Note: A large grape or fig leaf can be used in place of the lotus leaf.

Mam Kho
Preserved Salted Fish Stew

This hearty stew calls for *mam sac* (salted fish), considered a delicacy in Vietnam. Any firm-fleshed fish can replace the snake-headed mullet.

- 2 tablespoons vegetable oil
- 2 cloves garlic, finely chopped
- 1/2 cup finely chopped shallots
- 1/4 cup sliced fresh pork belly or pancetta
- 1/3 cup finely chopped lemongrass
- 1/2 cup peeled and washed shrimp
- 1/2 teaspoon cracked black pepper
- 2 1/2 cups water
- 10 ounces salted fish (mam sac)
- 10 ounces snake-head mullet
- 2 small red chilies, seeded and sliced
- 1 1/2 cups (about 1 medium) cubed eggplant
- 2 teaspoons sugar
- 1 tablespoon scallions, finely sliced
- 1 tablespoon Fried Garlic (optional) (page 121)

Heat oil in a large pan, add garlic, shallots, pork belly, eggplant, lemongrass and pepper. Sauté until soft.

In a large saucepan, add water and both types of fish and bring to a boil. Simmer for 10 minutes or until the fish completely breaks apart. Remove fish and set aside. Remove bones and discard. Strain the stock, then boil again with the sliced chili, sugar, and the pork and eggplant mixture.

Simmer for 5 minutes or until reduced by one-third. Add shrimp and cook for another 3 minutes. Set a portion of the fish in individual bowls. Add stock.

Serve garnished with scallions and fried garlic.

Note: There are many different grades of *mam sac*, however, any dried or salted fish will work well with this recipe—cod is a good choice. Soak the salted fish in water for 10–15 minutes and brush clean to remove any dirt or impurities.

Rau Muong Xao Tuong
Pan-Fried Water Spinach with Yellow Bean Sauce

Water spinach, which is available in many Asian grocery shops, has hollow, crunchy stems. The best substitute is mature spinach.

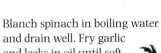

Grilled Eggplant with Crab.

- 1 pound water spinach, washed
- 2 cloves garlic, crushed
- 2 baby leeks, finely sliced, white part only
- 2 tablespoons vegetable oil
- 2 tablespoons Yellow Bean Sauce (page 157)
- Salt and pepper

Blanch spinach in boiling water and drain well. Fry garlic and leeks in oil until soft, then add spinach and yellow bean sauce. Fry over high heat. Season with salt and pepper.

Com Hoang Bao
Imperial Rice

A recipe to tempt jaded imperial appetites! The dried lotus leaf used to wrap the rice imparts a slight smokiness to the rice.

- 4 shallots, chopped
- 2 tablespoons cooking oil
- 3 ounces pork or chicken, diced
- 4 ounces small shrimp
- 4 ounces dried lotus seeds, boiled and drained
- 1/4 teaspoon salt
- A pinch of pepper
- 2 cups steamed rice
- 1 egg, fried and chopped (optional)
- 1 large lotus leaf
- 2 baby leeks, chopped

Quickly sauté shallots in oil. Add pork, shrimp, lotus seeds, salt and pepper and cook until pork is done. Mix with steamed rice and stir well. If egg is used, add to the fried mixture at the same time as the rice.

Remove from the heat and

Muc Nhoi Thit
Stuffed Squid

Use squid tentacles in the stuffing mixture and save the sacs for stuffing.

Stuffing
1 tablespoon peanut oil
3 tablespoons finely sliced shallots
1 clove garlic, finely sliced
1 pound lean pork neck, minced
1/4 cup cellophane noodles
6 wood ear mushrooms, finely chopped
1 teaspoon five-spice powder
1 tablespoon soy sauce
10 sets squid tentacles, finely chopped
A pinch of salt
A pinch of pepper
1 teaspoon sugar
10 medium squid, washed and cleaned

Sauce and Garnish
1/4 cup diced shallots
3 cloves garlic, crushed
1/4 cup butter or oil
3 large tomatoes, peeled, seeded and chopped
Salt and pepper
Cilantro leaves
Freshly ground pepper

To make the stuffing, heat oil in pan, add shallots and garlic, and cook, stirring until soft. Combine shallot mixture with the other stuffing ingredients in a bowl and mix well. Stuff the sacs with the mixture and secure with a small toothpick.

To make the sauce, sauté shallots and garlic in oil until they are soft.

Add stuffed squid and sauté on both sides for about 10 minutes or until slightly browned and cooked through. Remove from pan, set aside and keep warm.

Add tomatoes, salt and pepper to taste to the pan, and simmer until reduced to a thick sauce. Place squid on a large platter and remove toothpicks. You can leave the squid whole or cut into more manageable pieces. Pour the sauce over the squid, garnish with cilantro and freshly ground pepper. For a variation, try grilling the squid.

Muc Nuong
Grilled Squid

Grilled meats and seafood are very popular in Vietnam and many recipes, like this, rely upon the specific flavors imparted from the open wood-burning grill.

1 pound cleaned squid
1 tablespoon salt
1/2 cup cilantro leaves

Marinade
A pinch of pepper
2 cloves garlic, crushed
2 tablespoons peanut oil
1 teaspoon five-spice powder
1 teaspoon curry powder
1 tablespoon finely chopped lemongrass
1 tablespoon thick soy sauce
1 teaspoon sesame oil
1 tablespoon lime juice
1 teaspoon sugar

Crab with Tamarind Sauce.

Rub the squid with salt and rinse. Slit and flatten the squid sac and make diagonal cuts on the inside surface. Cut into bite-sized pieces.

Combine all the marinade ingredients, then marinate the squid for 1 hour.

Grill the squid over a charcoal grill until just tender, about 2 minutes each side. Arrange on a serving platter and garnish with cilantro. Serve with fish sauce dip (page 157).

HELPFUL HINT
This is a versatile marinade, suitable for other types of fish or poultry.

Tom Cang Kho
Spicy River Prawns

This is a southern recipe that calls for giant, freshwater prawns, which are often as big as lobsters.

3 cloves garlic, finely diced
1 small red chili, finely chopped
2 tablespoons cooking oil
1 teaspoon cracked black peppercorns
2 tablespoons sugar
1/4 cup fish sauce
1/2 cup water
6 giant prawns or crayfish, unpeeled
1/2 cup cilantro leaves

In a deep pan, sauté garlic and chili in oil until soft. Add peppercorns, sugar, fish sauce, water and prawns. Cook uncovered for 10 minutes, or until the prawns turn bright pink. Remove prawns and arrange on a platter.

Reduce the stock until slightly sticky. Pour over the prawns and garnish with fresh cilantro.

Cua Rang Voi Sot Me
Crab with Tamarind Sauce

4 whole medium crabs
Peanut oil for deep-frying
1 tablespoon tamarind pulp
1/4 cup Chinese rice wine

Fried Grouper with Ginger Sauce.

4 cloves garlic, chopped
2 tablespoons vegetable oil
3 tablespoons fish sauce
1 teaspoon crushed white pepper
1/4 cup white part baby leeks, cut into 1 inch pieces

Clean the crabs, take off the tops, rinse thoroughly, cut in half and break the claws. Heat peanut oil in wok until very hot, deep-fry crabs for 30 seconds, or until the color changes. Set the crabs on paper towels to absorb excess oil. Dissolve tamarind pulp in rice wine.

In a large pan or wok, sauté garlic in vegetable oil until soft, add crab and continue cooking for 2–3 minutes on a high heat. Add tamarind mixture, fish sauce and pepper. Reduce for another 2 minutes, then add baby leeks. Remove from the heat.

Place crabs on a platter and pour tamarind sauce over. Serve with steamed rice.

Note: Although this dish is traditionally prepared in a wok, a deep-fryer may make the cooking easier. You can also substitute freshly ground black pepper, although white pepper is preferred by Vietnamese cooks.

delightful sesame rice crackers—the mixture is perfect for dipping into.

- 1 tablespoon diced garlic
- 2 tablespoons diced shallots
- 2 tablespoons finely chopped lemongrass
- 1 tablespoon finely chopped red chili
- 3 tablespoons finely chopped wood ear mushrooms
- 2 tablespoons vegetable oil
- 1 tablespoon five-spice powder
- 1 tablespoon Vietnamese curry powder
- 3/4 pound baby eel, finely chopped
- 2 tablespoons coarsely chopped peanuts
- 1/2 cup cilantro leaves
- 1 red chili, thinly sliced
- Sesame seed rice crackers

Sauté garlic, shallots, lemongrass, chilli and mushrooms in the oil. Add five-spice powder, curry powder and eel. Sauté for 5 minutes, or until eel is cooked. Place on a platter and garnish with peanuts, cilantro and chili. Serve with crackers.

HELPFUL HINT

Wood ear mushrooms are used primarily for texture. However, any fresh mushroom that adds texture and flavor is a good substitute.

Crab in Beer Broth.

Ca Mu Chien Voi Gung
Fried Grouper with Ginger Sauce

Vietnam boasts an abundance of ocean and freshwater fish. Ginger and galangal have been used to impart their unique flavors to this dish.

Sauce
- 1 tablespoon oil
- 2 tablespoons finely sliced ginger
- 1 tablespoon finely sliced lemongrass
- 2 red chilies, finely sliced
- 3 fresh *shiitake* mushrooms, finely sliced
- 1 teaspoon soy sauce
- 1/4 cup fish sauce
- 1/2 cup water (or fish or chicken stock)

- 1 teaspoon salt
- 1 teaspoon ground white pepper
- 1 fish, grouper or sea bass, 2 pounds, slit on both sides
- 2 tablespoons oil
- 2 tablespoons scallions finely chopped

Combine the sauce ingredients, simmer on low heat for 5 minutes and set aside.

Salt and pepper the fish, brush with oil and broil slowly on both sides until the fish is cooked.

Place on a large platter, pour the sauce over the fish and garnish with scallions.

Cua Hap Bia
Crab in Beer Broth

This innovative dish, which uses beer in its broth, is said to have been developed by a French colonial administrator.

- 4 whole large crabs (3 1/2 pounds), rinsed and cleaned
- 2 tablespoons vegetable oil
- 1/2 teaspoon salt
- 1/2 teaspoon pepper
- 1 teaspoon sesame oil
- 1 tablespoon oyster sauce
- 1 clove garlic, crushed
- 1 large onion, cut into wedges
- 2 tablespoons vegetable oil
- 1 red chili, sliced
- 3/4 cup beer
- 1 large tomato, cut into wedges
- 1 tablespoon Fried Garlic (optional) (page 121)
- 1 cup watercress

Fry crabs in vegetable oil with salt, pepper, sesame oil, oyster sauce and garlic over a very high heat for 5 minutes. Add onion, tomato and chili. Stir-fry quickly and add beer. Cover and simmer for 10 minutes or until crabs are cooked. Serve in bowls, adding a little of the broth. Garnish with fried garlic and watercress.

Ca Chep Kho Rieng
Braised Carp with Galangal Sauce

This recipe can be used with a variety of whole fish, steaks or fillets.

- 6 carp or halibut steaks, cut into 4 ounce steaks
- 3 tablespoons vegetable oil
- 2 tablespoons galangal, finely sliced
- 3 tablespoons fish sauce
- 1/2 tablespoon Caramel Syrup (page 157)
- 1/2 cup of water

Sauté fish steaks in oil with *galangal*. Add fish sauce, caramel syrup and water. Braise slowly on both sides until fish is done.

Arrange on a platter and serve with steamed rice.

Luon Xao Lan Xuc Banh Trang Me
Minced Eel with Sesame Seed Rice Crackers

This recipe must have been created to make use of those

Pork Stew with Coconut Juice.

1 hour. Preheat the oven to 375 ° F. Set chicken in a baking pan. Combine marinade 2 ingredients and pour over the chicken. Place chicken in oven and roast.

Mix the marinade 3 ingredients. Baste the chicken with this marinade every 10–15 minutes. Bake until the skin is a golden brown color and chicken is well cooked.

Cut up the chicken and assemble on a serving platter. Serve with deep-fried sweet buns or steamed sticky rice.

Thit Heo Kho Nuoc Dua
Pork Stew with Coconut Juice

Marinade
4 cloves garlic, finely chopped
Salt to taste
1 tablespoon palm sugar
4 tablespoons fish sauce

2-pound pork leg, cut into
  3-ounce pieces
3 tablespoons vegetable oil
4 cups young coconut juice
5 eggs, hard-boiled and peeled

Combine marinade ingredients and marinate pork for 1 hour.

In either a wok or a frying pan, sear pork in heated oil. Add coconut juice. Skim the top, reduce heat and simmer until pork is tender, 30–45 minutes. Add the eggs and simmer for another 15 minutes.

Serve with preserved bean

sprouts, pickled or preserved mustard greens and steamed rice.

Cha Lua
Pork Sausage

1 pound pork loin
8 ounces meat from small pig's
  head
2 cups salted water
1/4 cup cooking oil
5 shallots, diced
2 cloves garlic, crushed
1/2 cup finely chopped wood ear
  mushrooms
2 tablespoons cracked black
  pepper
1/4 cup sesame seeds, toasted
2 eggs, beaten
1 large banana leaf
3 tablespoons fish sauce
2 limes, cut into wedges

Boil pork and pig's head in salted water for 20 minutes. Drain and debone, cut meat into small cubes. Heat oil in a large frying pan, cook shallots and garlic until soft. Add pork, mushrooms and peppercorns. Cook, stirring, until mushrooms are soft. Finish with sesame seeds. Remove from the heat, stir eggs through pork mixture.

Place mixture on the banana leaf, wrap and tie with a string. Steam banana leaf package for 2 hours over boiling water.

When done, unwrap and slice thinly. Serve with fish sauce and lime wedges.

Ca Nau Ngot
River Fish with Dill and Tomato

6 cups light chicken stock (page
  157)
1 1/4 pounds freshwater fish fillets,
  cut into large chunks
2 medium tomatoes, cut into wedges
Salt and pepper
1 tablespoon chopped dill
Fresh dill (garnish)

Bring stock to a boil, add fish and simmer for 5 minutes. Skim the foam off the surface, add the tomatoes and season with salt, pepper and dill. Cook for another few minutes. Garnish with fresh dill before serving.

Ga Quay Mat Ong
Honey-Roasted Chicken

This recipe works well with any type of fowl or game. Since considerable time is involved with the marinades and cooking, it is probably best suited for a large bird and special occasion.

1 large chicken, left whole

Marinade 1
1 teaspoon pepper
1 teaspoon salt
1 tablespoon sugar
1 teaspoon sesame oil

Marinade 2
3 tablespoons honey
2 tablespoons sweet soy sauce
1 tablespoon lime juice
1 tablespoon annatto seed oil
1 teaspoon sesame oil

Marinade 3
1 teaspoon pepper
1 teaspoon salt
1 tablespoon sugar
1 teaspoon sesame oil

Combine all marinade 1 ingredients. Rub on the inside of the chicken and close with a needle or a bamboo stick. Marinate for

Minced Pork Balls on a Skewer (left) recipe on page 147 and Grilled Pork with Rice Noodles (right).

Spicy Beef Stew.

Dau Hu Chien Sa
*Fried Bean Curd
with Lemongrass*

1 cup peanut oil
1¼ pound bean curd, cut into 1-
    inch x 2-inch pieces
3 tablespoons finely chopped
    lemongrass
1 red chili, finely chopped
2 cloves garlic, chopped
1 tablespoon vegetable oil
1 teaspoon five-spice powder
Salt and pepper

Heat oil in deep pan, fry bean
curd in hot oil and drain on
paper towels. Set aside.

In a separate sauté pan or
wok, sauté the lemongrass, chili
and garlic in hot vegetable oil
until soft. Add the bean curd
and mix well. Season with five-
spice powder, salt and pepper.
Set on a serving platter.

Bun Thit Nuong
Grilled Pork with Rice Noodles

1 pound pork loin,
    cut into medium cubes

Marinade
1 teaspoon finely chopped garlic
⅓ cup sliced baby leeks
3 tablespoons fish sauce
Pepper and sugar

Garnish
12 ounces rice noodles, blanched
2 cups Carrot and Radish pickles
    (page 157)
1 cup bean sprouts
2 medium cucumbers, finely sliced
½ cup basil leaves
⅓ cup chopped baby leeks
¼ cup peanut sauce (see page
    157)

Combine the marinade ingredients and marinate the pork for
20 minutes.

Skewer the pork and grill
over charcoal. Turn the skewers
frequently so that the pork is
evenly cooked, and continue
basting with the marinade.
Place on a plate and serve with
garnish ingredients.

Bo La Lot
Grilled Beef in Wild Betel Leaves

The Vietnamese are
famous for their
hand rolls and almost
every dinner features
at least two or three different versions at the start
of the meal.

Marinade
1 tablespoon five-spice
    powder
1 tablespoon curry powder
1 teaspoon turmeric powder
1 tablespoon sugar

1 tablespoon soy sauce
1 tablespoon finely chopped
    lemongrass
2 cloves garlic, finely chopped
1 teaspoon pepper
1¼ pounds ground beef
10 ounces pork fatback
Salt and sugar
21 wild betel leaves
Vegetable oil
7 wooden skewers

Garnish
2 starfruits, thinly sliced
3 unripe bananas, thinly sliced
1 cucumber, peeled and thinly
    sliced
1 cup fish sauce dip (page 157)
Lettuce leaves for wrapping

Combine the marinade ingredients and marinate the beef for
30 minutes.

Fry pork fatback, allow to
cool, then cut into matchstick
pieces (vermicelli size). Marinate
with salt and sugar and set aside
for 15 minutes. Soak wild betel
leaves and drain.

Combine beef and pork fat,
mix thoroughly, then wrap portions in wild betel leaf (the rolls
should be roughly 2 inches
long). Place 3 rolls on each
skewer. Brush with oil and grill
on both sides for 5 minutes,
until the leaves are slightly
charred. Serve with garnish and
fish sauce dip.

HELPFUL HINT
You can also try adding fresh
rice noodles into the roll. Grape
leaves may be substituted for
the betel leaves.

Bo Kho
Spicy Beef Stew

6 tablespoons cooking oil
2 tablespoons annatto seeds
2 pounds top round beef,
    cut into large cubes
1 large onion, finely chopped
5 cloves garlic, finely chopped
1 tablespoon salt
2 tablespoons sugar
1 tablespoon curry powder
1 cup beer
1 stem lemongrass, bruised
3 star anise
1 stick cinnamon
1 cup thickly chopped carrots

Garnish
1 cup mint leaves
2 red chilies, sliced
Salt, Pepper and Lime Mix
    (page157)

Heat half of the oil with annatto
seeds and stir quickly until the
oil takes on the reddish-brown
color of the seeds. Set aside,
strain and remove the seeds.

Marinate the beef cubes
with onion, half the garlic, salt,
sugar and half of the annatto
seed oil mixture for 45 minutes.

Heat the remaining annatto
seed oil and cook the remaining
garlic until soft. Add curry powder, beer and marinade. Add the
beef and braise, adding a little
water, the lemon grass, star
anise and cinnamon. Add the
carrots in the last 5 minutes of
cooking, when the beef is tender, and simmer until done.

Serve with garnish.

*Grilled Beef in
Wild Betel Leaves.*

As in other countries, these "desserts" are not eaten at the end of a meal as a sweet but rather, throughout the day as fillers or snacks. In any case they make good finales, and despite the strangeness of some of the ingredients, all are delicious!

Banh Goi
Wrapped Rice Cakes

1 3/4 cups rice flour
1 1/3 sugar
1 1/3 cups pandan leaf juice
5 ounces yellow mung beans, soaked in water for 5 hours or overnight
1 tablespoon vanilla extract
2 tablespoons cooking oil
6 blanched banana leaf squares, 8 inches x 8 inches
1 1/2 cups coconut milk
3 tablespoons sugar
1 pinch salt
1/2 tablespoon cornstarch
2 tablespoons sesame seeds, toasted

Mix rice flour with 2/3 cup of the sugar and 2 cups of the pandan leaf juice. Cook over a low heat until the mixture thickens to a paste-like consistency. In a separate pot, cook mung beans with remaining sugar and vanilla extract to a similar consistency. Cool and roll into small balls.

Brush cooking oil on banana leaves, then place the rice flour paste in the middle. Top with mung bean "ball" and cover with rice flour paste. Wrap into small square packages and

steam for 10 minutes.

To make the sauce, bring coconut milk to a boil, add sugar, a pinch of salt, remaining pandan leaf juice and cornstarch. Serve the wrapped rice cakes with coconut sauce and sesame seeds.

Banh Phu
The Husband and Wife Cakes

The name of this traditional dessert comes from the two parts that are traditionally tied together with a string of coconut and encased in a delicate box made of pandan leaves.

4 cups water
1 pound tapioca starch
1 1/2 cups sugar
1/2 cup shredded coconut
5 ounces yellow mung beans, soaked in water
2/3 cup sugar syrup
1 tablespoon cooking oil
1 tablespoon pomelo blossom essence or 1 1/2 teaspoons lemon extract and 1 1/2 teaspoons of orange juice
20 pandan leaves (optional)

To make the dough, mix water, flour, sugar and shredded coconut. Heat over a low flame and stir for 10 minutes. Set aside. To make the stuffing, steam mung beans until they are tender. Mash to a paste. Stir in the sugar syrup and cooking oil. Cook over low heat until thick, then add the pomelo blossom essence. Remove from the heat. Pour a thin layer of dough into individual cupcake tins or other

small mold, add a portion of the stuffing and top with another layer of dough. Place tins in a steamer and cook for 20 minutes. They are ready when the dough is transparent.

To make the boxes, cut a pandan leaf into 8-inch x 3-inch pieces, leaving the rib running down the middle. Divide one side into five 1/2-inch segments. Make corresponding creases on the uncut side. Overlap both ends and use the creases to help you form a box. Fold in the cut segments and secure with a toothpick. Place a square of pandan leaf in the bottom of the box, then brush inside and out with cooking oil. To make the lids, cut out 8 1/2-inch x 4-inch pieces of leaf and proceed as for the bases.

Banh Chuoi Nuong
Banana Cake

This cake is also delicious served with a scoop of vanilla icecream.

1 1/4 pounds ripe bananas
1 cup sugar
1 cup coconut milk
1/2 teaspoon vanilla extract
7 slices sandwich bread
2 tablespoons melted butter

Slice bananas diagonally and sprinkle with half the sugar.

Cook the remaining sugar in coconut milk until dissolved, then add the vanilla. Remove crusts from the bread. Soak the bread in the sweetened coconut milk. Butter a 12-inch nonstick pan. Arrange a layer of banana on the bottom of the pan. Cover with a layer of bread, then another layer of bananas, another of bread,

Banana Cake (left) and Pineapple Tartlets (right).

and finish with a layer of bananas. Drizzle the remaining butter over the top, then cover with foil and bake in a preheated oven at 350° F for 1 hour.

Leave the cake to rest for 12 hours before cutting.

Banh Nuong Nhan Thom
Pineapple Tartlets

Dough
1 cup soft butter
1/4 cup sugar
1/2 cup milk
4 cups flour

Filling
1 pineapple, peeled, cored and chopped
1/2 cup sugar
1 drop vanilla extract
1 egg, beaten

To make the dough, blend butter, sugar and milk with a whisk in a mixing bowl. Add flour and continue whisking until the texture is smooth. Place the dough on a lightly floured surface and roll it out to a thickness of 1/8 inch with a rolling pin. Press dough into a small mold to make shells. Cut remaining dough into small strips.

To make the filling, place pineapple and sugar in a saucepan over a low heat and stir continuously until the mixture thickens. Add vanilla extract. Fill shells with the mixture, then lay dough strips in a crisscross over the top. Brush the top with egg, and bake in a preheated oven at 300° F until golden brown.

Wrapped Rice Cakes (left) and The Husband and Wife Cakes (right).

Ca Rot
Carrot and Radish Pickles

- 1 cup julienned carrot
- 1 cup julienned giant white radish
- 1 tablespoon salt
- 2 tablespoons sugar
- $^1/_4$ cup white vinegar

Sprinkle carrot and radish with salt, allow to stand for 10 minutes. Press vegetables gently with a dry towel to remove excess moisture. Rinse and drain. In a mixing bowl, combine sugar and vinegar with vegetables, then marinate for at least 2 hours before serving. Best served chilled.

Nuoc Mam Cham
Fish Sauce Dip

- $^1/_4$ cup water or fresh coconut juice
- 1 teaspoon rice vinegar
- 1 teaspoon sugar
- 1 red chili, seeded and finely chopped
- 2 cloves garlic, crushed
- 1 tablespoon lime juice
- 2 tablespoons fish sauce

Boil water or coconut juice with vinegar and sugar. Cool.

Combine chili, garlic, and lime juice and add to the coconut mixture. Lastly, stir in the fish sauce.

For a variation, add shredded radish and carrot pickles (see previous recipe).

Mam Nem
Fermented Anchovy Dip

- 2 tablespoons fermented anchovy sauce
- $^1/_2$ cup water
- 2 teaspoons vinegar
- 2 tablespoons crushed pineapple
- $^1/_2$ stem lemongrass, finely chopped
- 1 red chili, finely chopped
- 1 clove garlic, crushed
- A pinch of pepper
- 1 teaspoon sugar

Combine all the ingredients and stir well. Season to taste with pepper and sugar.

Nuoc Tuong
Yellow Bean Sauce

- 1 cup yellow beans, boiled and drained
- 2 tablespoons coconut milk
- 2 tablespoons ground peanuts
- 2 teaspoons sugar
- 3 cloves garlic
- 1 medium red chili
- 1 stem lemongrass
- 2 tablespoons vegetable oil

Combine all ingredients, except oil, in a food processor. Blend until finely chopped and well combined. Heat oil in pan and stir-fry all ingredients for 2 minutes. Cool before serving.

Sot Dau Phong
Peanut Sauce

- 1 clove garlic, finely sliced
- 2 teaspoons vegetable oil
- 4 ounces pork or chicken liver
- 1 tablespoon red chili, finely chopped
- $^1/_2$ cup Yellow Bean Sauce (see above)
- 1 stem lemongrass, finely chopped
- $^1/_4$ cup coconut milk
- 1 teaspoon sugar
- 1 teaspoon salt
- 2 tablespoons tamarind juice
- 1 cup peanuts, finely ground

Sauté garlic in oil until soft, add liver, chili, yellow bean sauce, lemongrass, half the coconut milk, sugar, salt, tamarind juice and peanuts. Bring to a boil. Remove from heat. Blend in a food processor and add remaining coconut milk.

Nuoc Mau
Caramel Syrup

- 1 cup water
- 1 cup brown sugar

Bring water and sugar to a boil. Stir and reduce until liquid is a dark brown color. Remove from heat, add a few tablespoons of water and stir. Pour into a heatproof container. Cover with a lid.

Muoi Tieu Chanh
Salt, Pepper and Lime Mix

- 1 teaspoon salt
- 1 teaspoon pepper
- Juice of $^1/_2$ lime

Combine salt and pepper, squeeze lime juice into the mixture and stir well.

Sot Chua Ngot
Sweet and Sour Sauce

- 3 cloves garlic, finely chopped
- 1 tablespoon oil
- 2 tablespoons sliced shallots
- 2 pickled shallots, sliced
- 1 small carrot, diced
- 1 small bell pepper, diced
- 1 medium red chili, diced
- 1 tablespoon sugar
- Salt and pepper
- 1 teaspoon tomato sauce
- 2 tablespoons vinegar
- 1 tablespoon cornstarch mixed with 1 teaspoon water

Sauté garlic in oil until slightly colored. Add shallots, pickled shallots, carrot, bell pepper, chili, sugar, and salt and pepper to taste. Keep frying, add tomato sauce and vinegar. Bring to a boil, then add cornstarch mixture. Reduce heat, stir and simmer for 1 minute.

Peanut Sauce (top) and fish sauce with garlic and chilies (bottom).

Nuoc Leo Ga
Chicken Stock

- 12 cup water
- 1 medium chicken
- 1 tablespoon whole white peppercorns
- 1 cup sliced onions
- 1 medium carrot, chopped
- 1 stalk celery, chopped
- A pinch of salt
- A pinch of pepper

Combine the ingredients in a stockpot; bring to a boil. Simmer for 2–3 hours, until stock is reduced by half. Strain and set aside. Once cool, skim layer of fat from the top.

Nuoc Leo Bo
Beef Stock

- 16 cups water
- 4 pounds beef bones
- 2 tablespoons sliced ginger
- 2 star anise
- A pinch of salt and pepper

Combine ingredients, bring to a boil and simmer for 3 hours. Strain and set aside. Once cool, skim layer of fat from the top.

HELPFUL HINT

Place stock in sealed containers and refrigerate or freeze if they are to be stored for a longer time. Refrigerated stock will last for a week.

MEASUREMENTS AND CONVERSION TABLES

Measurements in this book are given in volume as far as possible. Teaspoon, tablespoon and cup measurements should be level, not heaped, unless otherwise indicated. Australian readers please note that the standard Australian measuring spoon is larger than the UK or American spoon by 5 ml, so use only $^3/_4$ tablespoon when following the recipes.

LIQUID CONVERSIONS

Imperial	Metric	US cups
$^1/_2$ fl oz	15 ml	1 tablespoon
1 fl oz	30 ml	$^1/_8$ cup
2 fl oz	60 ml	$^1/_4$ cup
4 fl oz	125 ml	$^1/_2$ cup
5 fl oz ($^1/_4$ pint)	150 ml	$^2/_3$ cup
6 fl oz	175 ml	$^3/_4$ cup
8 fl oz	250 ml	1 cup
12 fl oz	375 ml	$1^1/_2$ cups
16 fl oz	500 ml	2 cups

Note:
  1 UK pint = 20 fl oz
  1 US pint = 16 fl oz

SOLID WEIGHT CONVERSIONS

Imperial	Metric
$^1/_2$ oz	15 g
1 oz	30g
$1^1/_2$ oz	50 g
2 oz	60 g
3 oz	90 g
$3^1/_2$ oz	100 g
4 oz ($^1/_4$ lb)	125 g
5 oz	150 g
6 oz	185 g
7 oz	250 g
8 oz ($^1/_2$ lb)	280 g
9 oz	300 g
10 oz	500 g (0.5 kg)
16 oz (1 lb)	1 kg
32 oz (2 lb)	

OVEN TEMPERATURES

Heat	Fahrenheit	Centigrade/Celsius	British Gas Mark
Very cool	225	110	1/4
Cool or slow	275–300	135–150	1–2
Moderate	350	175	4
Hot	425	220	7
Very hot	450	230	8

INDEX